Cambodia's Foreign Policy

Cambodia's Foreign Policy

By ROGER M. SMITH

University of Washington

PREPARED UNDER THE AUSPICES

OF THE SOUTHEAST ASIA PROGRAM

CORNELL UNIVERSITY

Cornell University Press

ITHACA, NEW YORK

CORNELL UNIVERSITY PRESS

First published 1965

Second printing 1966

Library of Congress Catalog Card Number: 65-15375

PRINTED IN THE UNITED STATES OF AMERICA
BY VALLEY OFFSET, INC.
BOUND BY VAIL-BALLOU PRESS, INC.

TO MYRA

Acknowledgments

I WOULD like to express my sincere appreciation and gratitude to Professors George McT. Kahin, D. G. E. Hall, Clinton Rossiter, Lauriston Sharp, Mario Einaudi, and O. W. Wolters for their guidance and encouragement both in the writing of this book and during my graduate years at Cornell University.

I am especially indebted to Professor Kahin, who has sustained and encouraged my work to a degree only I can fully appreciate.

This study could not have been carried out without the assistance of numerous Cambodians, Frenchmen, and Americans, many of whom are now or were previously in the service of their governments. My debt to them is, I hope, adequately demonstrated in the text. I would like to accord my special thanks to H.R.H. Prince Norodom Sihanouk, Chief of State of Cambodia, for taking the time to answer many of my questions and for providing me with access to members of his government. I am also grateful for the manifold assistance granted me by H.E. Mr. Nong Kimny, former Ambassador of Cambodia to the United States. It was through his good offices that I was able to gain much valuable information about Cambodia's foreign policy. The many other Cambodians, Americans, and Frenchmen who gave freely of their time in countless hours of conversation will know that my failure to mention their names here does not signify my lack of gratitude.

This work is dedicated to my wife, Myra, who has shared with me the trials and joys of research in Cambodia. Her interest and encouragement have been constant and her assistance immeasurable in seeing this study through to its completion.

I am also grateful to the Ford Foundation's Foreign Area Training Program, whose support I enjoyed as a Fellow during 1960–1962, when the research upon which much of this study is based was carried out. I am, of course, solely responsible for the contents and conclusions of this study.

ROGER M. SMITH

University of Washington
January, 1965

Contents

Contents

Cambodia's Foreign Policy

CHAPTER I

Introduction

THE concept of nonalignment in international affairs is a relatively recent phenomenon which is rooted in the cold war. It embodies the attempts of less powerful states to resist the pressures of mightier nations to draw them into their ideological camp. Unlike the neutral nation during World War II and before, the nonaligned nation does not relinquish its right to participate actively in international affairs. It is neutral only insofar as it asserts its right to refrain from entering into an alliance with any existing bloc; for this reason proponents of nonalignment have sometimes referred to their position as "active neutrality." Nonaligned nations emphatically defend their right to pass judgment on each international development, unhampered by cold-war considerations, and to cast their weight accordingly. That they are able to do so is a peculiar outcome of the manner in which the cold war is being conducted. Each camp endeavors to woo the militarily weak, nonaligned nations, offering them economic and political favors and promising to defend them against the aggression of the opposing bloc. Courtship instead of threats of reprisals is the means by which the two blocs compete for the commitment of these nations to their side.

In commanding the attention of the two competing major blocs, the nonaligned nation has acquired influence in international affairs which is disproportionate to its size and military strength. And now that France has virtually withdrawn from the Western bloc and promises to develop a nuclear power and following of her own, and the rift between China and the rest of the Communist bloc has reached a stage where *rapprochement* appears to be improbable, the thoughts and actions of the leaders of the currently uncommitted nations may all the more significantly affect the course of future international relations.

Cambodia shares with other nonaligned nations of Southeast Asia certain prominent characteristics: they are all recent subjects of Western European powers; all of them emerged from their colonial experience with pressing economic and social problems and limited means to meet them, with the result that they have had to rely upon foreign assistance; and all have had to face political instability, a problem which in some cases continues to absorb much of the government's attention. Cambodia is worthy of study for other reasons as well: of all the nonaligned Southeast Asian nations, she appears to have dealt most effectively with internal opposition to the government; in the Laotian crisis of 1960–1961 she demonstrated the ability of a nonaligned nation to help to mediate a dispute between the big powers; her policy of nonalignment has least often been subjected to questioning by either of the two cold-war blocs; and last, of all Southeast Asian nations Cambodia has received the least attention of American scholars and journalists, and as a result little is known about her in the United States today.

In the pages that follow, an attempt has been made to reveal the major considerations which have led Cambodia to elect a policy of nonalignment in the cold war. To accomplish this purpose, it has been felt necessary to begin with an extensive treatment of her history, in particular those aspects which deal with the decline of the once magnificent Khmer Empire, its dismemberment by the Thai and Vietnamese, and the absorption of what remained by the French empire, with the consequent virtual obliteration of its identity for almost a century. The main body of the study is devoted to Cambodia's successful struggle for independence, her relations with the major powers, and her relations with her immediate neighbors, Thailand and Vietnam. The study is concluded with an analysis of how well Cambodia in attempting to achieve her objectives has been served by her policy of nonalignment.

CHAPTER II

Historical Sketch

THE kingdom of Cambodia is what remains of the once splendid Khmer Empire. At the zenith of their power, during the eleventh, twelfth, and thirteenth centuries, the Khmer kings, from their capital at Angkor on the plain of Siem Reap, ruled vast areas of Southeast Asia which today are occupied by parts of Vietnam, Laos, Thailand, and the northern portion of the Malay peninsula.

Cambodia's roots have been traced back to Funan, the Kingdom of the Mountain, which is believed to have been founded in the first century A.D.[1] From its center of power in the present-day province of Takéo, Funan exercised dominion over the lower valleys of the Mekong River, the area round the Tonlé Sap (Great Lake), and a part of the

[1] Much of this section is based upon Georges Coedès, *Les états hindouisés d'Indochine et d'Indonésie* (2d ed.; Paris: E. de Boccard, 1964). See also Etienne F. Aymonier, *Le Cambodge*, 3 vols. (Paris: E. Leroux, 1900–1904); Lawrence Palmer Briggs, *The Ancient Khmer Empire* (Philadelphia: American Philosophical Society, 1951); D. G. E. Hall, *A History of Southeast Asia* (2d ed.; London: Macmillan, 1964); Adhémar Leclère, *Histoire du Cambodge* (Paris: P. Guethner, 1914); G. Maspero, *L'Empire khmer* (Phnom Penh: Imprimerie du Protectorat, 1904) ; and J. Moura, *Le royaume du Cambodge*, 2 vols. (Paris: Leroux, 1883).

Funan and, later. Chenla are the names given to these kingdoms by the Chinese. Their real names are unknown. See D. G. E. Hall. *op. cit.,* p. 24.

Mekong delta region, and probably also commanded vassal-age from smaller states in northern Cambodia, southern Thailand and Laos, and the northern portion of the Malay peninsula. Asian merchants and adventurers, traveling along the international trade route in the South China Sea, were aware of Funanese society, which engaged in wet-rice cultivation and had a well-developed system of authority based on the controlled distribution of water and a religious mythology in which water spirits and sacred mountains figured prominently.

Rise and Fall of the Khmer Empire

In the sixth century, weakened by civil strife and dynastic quarrels, Funan was overcome by a vassal state, Chenla, situated in the Bassac region of present-day southern Laos. During the next three hundred years the people of Chenla, who were also Khmers, succeeded in bringing under their dominion central and upper Laos, western Cambodia, and southern Thailand.

Like its predecessor, Chenla was afflicted with dissension within the monarchy, and in the eighth century it split into rival northern and southern centers of power, named Chenla-of-the-land and Chenla-of-the-sea respectively, with capitals in the present Cambodian provinces of Kompong Thom and Takéo. During the next century Chenla-of-the-sea was further riven by dynastic rivalries, a condition which rendered it defenseless in the face of Javanese attempts to establish suzerainty. It was not until 802, with the ascension of Jayavarman II (802–850) to the throne of Chenla-of-the-sea, that Javanese suzerainty was cast off and reunification of the Khmers undertaken. This accomplished, Jayavarman moved his capital from Kompong Cham to the plain of Siem Reap, and from there, during the next three hundred and fifty years, he and his successors extended the borders of the Khmer Empire into northern Laos, to the South China Sea in the east and southeast, and to the Bay of Bengal in the west. According to Yaśovarman I (889–900), founder of the first city on the Angkor site, "the earth which he protected was bounded by the frontier of China and the sea." [2] It was also during this period that the Empire's cultural and technical endeavors attained their fullest development. The magnitude of its accomplishments is evident today in the remains of the Angkor complex of magnificent temple-palaces and of an extensive hydraulic network, which controlled the distribution and conservation of water for the mainstay of the economy, rice.

During the first millennium A.D., Khmer culture was subjected to an almost continuous inflow of Indian ideas and practices relating to royalty, law, and religious mythology. Perhaps the most influential of these among the Khmer kings were notions on the organization of the state and the religious justification of kingly rule. As they were assimilated and modified, they reached their apogee in the politico-religious concept of the *devaraja,* or god-king, which was adopted by Jayavarman II, the founder of the Empire.

The cult of the *devaraja* sprang from the belief that the state was a manifestation of the universe, and its capital the earthly symbol of the city of heaven. [3] As it was prac-

---

[2] From the stele of Lolei, quoted in Briggs, *op. cit.,* p. 113.

[3] See Georges Coedès, *Pour mieux comprendre Angkor* (2d ed.; Paris: Adrien-Maisonneuve, Librairie d'Amérique et d'Orient, 1948), Chap. V, and Bernard P. Groslier, with the collaboration of C. R. Boxer, *Angkor et le Cambodge au XVIᵉ siècle d'après les sources portugaises et espagnoles* [Annales du Musée Guimet, Tome 63] (Paris: Presses Universitaires de France, 1958), Chap. IV.

ticed in the Khmer Empire, a divine king served as intermediary between the gods, especially those controlling
water and the fertility of the soil, and the social order, the
economy of which was based on irrigated rice. The sacred
personality of the king himself was believed to be embodied in a royal *linga* and to be transmitted to him by the
gods through the medium of Brahman priests. The prosperity of the Empire was thought to be closely linked with
worship of the *linga,* and thus the great temples, which
were the glory of the Empire, were erected by each king
as sanctuaries for it.

For the peasantry, however, the court was a distant
structure with which they could scarcely identify.[4] If the
world of the monarchy and the aristocracy had any meaning for the people, it was probably in its role as the ultimate source of authority and as the preserver of peace,
order, and economic well-being. Unfortunately massive
temple-building programs and expansionist wars, undertaken in the name of the *devaraja,* necessitated the organization of *corvées* and the imposition of heavy taxes upon
the peasantry.[5] With the consequent neglect of the hydraulic system and the diversion of manpower from agriculture
to construction programs and military campaigns, the economic strength of the nation declined. Beginning in the
mid-twelfth century, the peasantry began to express its
discontent in a prolonged series of revolts.

During the reign of Suryavarman II (1112–*ca.* 1150),

[4] Groslier, *op. cit.,* pp. 155–164. On the later introduction of
Theravada Buddhism and its role among the monarchy and people,
see Paul Mus, "Le sourire d'Angkor: art, foi et politique boud-
dhiques sous Jayavarman VII," in A. B. Griswold and Jean Bois-
selier, eds., *Artibus Asiae,* XXIV, 3/4 (special number, 1961), pp.
363–381.

[5] Groslier, *op. cit.,* pp. 118–121; and Briggs, *op. cit,* pp. 258–261.

the Empire's domain was extended by a series of successful wars against the neighboring Kingdom of Champa, which controlled the area now known as Cochinchina (almost all of present-day South Vietnam), against the Vietnamese, and against peoples living along the present Thailand–Burma frontier. It was also under his direction that Angkor Wat, the largest religious building in the world and the greatest single work of architecture in Southeast Asia, was erected. His death was followed by thirty years of civil strife waged by rival aspirants to the throne. During this period, marauding Chams, bent upon avenging their recent defeat, attacked, captured, and sacked the Khmer capital. The invaders were finally pushed back and Champa was again defeated, this time by the armies of Jayavarman VII (1181–*ca.* 1218). The campaigns against the Chams have been immortalized in the finely sculptured bas-reliefs of the many-towered Bayon, whose erection was believed to have been ordered by Jayavarman himself. Under his reign, the Empire attained its greatest extent and experienced its last years of glory. Jayavarman's feats in war and temple construction were possible only at a tremendous expenditure of money, energy, and labor by the people. The result was that the people's morale, the Empire's economy, and eventually the Empire itself declined.

This decline was catalyzed by the Thai people, who had been slowly migrating from China into the Indochina peninsula for several hundred years. In the late thirteenth century, following the establishment of Sukhothai, the Thai began to replace Khmer authority in the Menam Basin and along the upper Mekong River.[6] Before the end

[6] See Coedès, *Les états hindouisés d'Indochine et d'Indonésie*, pp. 30, 346–350.

of the century, they extended their rule over almost all of what is now Thailand and substantial parts of northern Malaya. This took place at the expense of Khmer frontier provinces, though Cambodia proper remained intact.

A series of forays by the Thai in the fourteenth and early fifteenth centuries, culminating in the sack of Angkor in 1431, brought about the subsequent collapse of the Empire. Cambodia itself, however, was never vanquished by the Thai. The Khmers recaptured Angkor the next year, but it was abandoned by them as their capital, for it was too close to Ayutthaya, the new center of Thai power. A new Cambodian capital was established south of Angkor, nearer the confluence of the Mekong and Basaac rivers.

Simultaneously with these events, a new force was making itself felt in the eastern portion of the peninsula. Having recently thrown off Chinese domination, the Vietnamese in the mid-fifteenth century turned their attention to the conquest of Champa, which stood in the way of their southward expansion. In the politics of the period, the Khmer kings probably did not realize that Champa provided Cambodia with an effective buffer against Vietnam. When in 1471 the Vietnamese overpowered Champa, the Cambodian king was too preoccupied with grave dissensions in the royal family and with persistent Thai pressures from the northwest to be concerned with the fate of the Chams. Thus, with Champa reduced to a mere principality, Vietnam gained easy access to the underpopulated southeastern Cambodian provinces. The effects of this presence, however, were not to be seriously felt until early in the seventeenth century.

From the fall of Angkor (1431) to the establishment of the French protectorate (1864), the history of Cambodia is largely an account of internal strife and of the efforts of Cambodian kings to stave off subjugation by Siam and Vietnam. The Thai claimed suzerainty over Cambodia after 1431, and by interfering in disputes over succession and supporting political factions favorable to themselves, hoped to substantiate their claim. In these maneuvers they achieved little. King Ang Chan (1516–1566) and his son, Barom Reachea I (1566–1576), succeeded in repelling Thai attacks and inflicting heavy losses on the invaders.[7] During the sixteenth century, the Thai were distracted from their designs on Cambodia by three different invasions by Burma; in 1569, the Thai capital was captured by the Burmese, who occupied it for the next fifteen years. The Cambodians took advantage of Thai efforts against the Burmese to recapture the provinces of the northwest. In 1593–1594, after having recovered Ayutthaya, the Thai again took the Cambodian capital, Lovek, on the shores of the Tonlé Sap, but once more they were forced to retreat. During the succeeding ten years, however, civil strife in Cambodia gave the Thai the opportunity to invade, and this time to seat a king on the throne who was wholly under their domination.

By the early seventeenth century, the Vietnamese, under the Nguyen dynasty, had moved into the Mekong delta region of Cambodia and secured the right to establish settlements and a trading center at Saigon. They were aided in this endeavor by the Cambodian kings, who saw in the Vietnamese a means to offset Thai influence and control. In return, Cambodia yielded to Vietnam control of the delta and granted Vietnamese settlers the rights of nationals.[8] By the end of the 1600's, Vietnam had absorbed

[7] See Groslier, *op. cit.*, pp. 14–15.
[8] Moura, II, *op. cit.*, pp. 61–62.

all of the lower delta region and organized it along Vietnamese administrative lines, and by the second half of the eighteenth century, the area which is now known as Cochinchina had been occupied and fortified.[9] To ensure their title to and control over the delta region, Vietnam attempted to exercise influence over Cambodia's rulers. The Vietnamese claims to suzerainty, however, apparently never materialized. Although by the middle of the eighteenth century Vietnam had annexed and settled Cochinchina, Siam had little difficulty in establishing the primacy of its influence over that of Vietnam, which, during the last decades of the century, was torn by dynastic struggles among the Nguyen kings, the Tayson pretenders, and the Trinh of Tonkin.

Succession to the Cambodian throne continued to be controlled by Siam. Not only were the kings compelled to seek Siamese investiture, but they were also required to pay regular tribute to the Thai monarch and to send military contingents to assist Thailand in her battles with Burma. Moreover, beginning in the 1790's, the northwestern Cambodian provinces of Battambang and Siem Reap were ruled directly by Siam, a situation which prevailed without interruption until the establishment of the French protectorate in 1864. The governors of these provinces were appointed by the Thai king and paid allegiance to him rather than to the Cambodian monarch.

The great clash between Thai and Vietnamese interests in Cambodia took place during the first half of the nineteenth century. With the aid of French adventurers recruited by the Bishop of Adran, Pigneau de Behaine, the

---

[9] *Ibid.*, pp. 81–85, and Lê Thánh Khôi, *Le Viet-Nam, histoire et civilisation, le milieu et l'histoire* (Paris: Editions de Minuit, 1955), pp. 268–272.

Nguyen prince, Phuc Anh, had triumphed over his opponents and had himself crowned emperor of a unified Vietnam under the name of Gia Long. Thus, in the nineteenth century the Vietnamese were again able to confront Siam in Cambodia.

To retain their country's independence and as much territory as remained after more than three hundred years of foreign encroachment, Cambodia's kings adopted the strategy of playing one rival against the other. Ang Chan II (1806–1834) had been crowned by Siam. This demonstration of Siamese influence prompted Vietnam to demand his recognition of its suzerainty as well. Ang Chan complied with the demand, probably because he felt that the Vietnamese would exercise a countervailing influence.[10] His homage to Vietnam, however, encountered Siam's disapproval, and when he refused to aid the Thai in their war with Burma, they attacked. Ang Chan appealed for succor from Gia Long, who provided him with an army which, in 1813, drove out the Thai army. In subsequent negotiations with Gia Long, Siam, which did not want to become involved in another conflict while still engaged in a war with Burma, recognized his dominant position in Cambodia.[11] As they withdrew from Cambodia, however, the Thai occupied the Cambodian provinces of Melou Prey, Tonlé Repou (in present-day Kompong Thom), and Stung Treng.

During the next two decades, growing discontent among the people, fanned by a severe economic depression and harsh Annamese controls, erupted in several revolts.[12]

[10] It was consistent with common practice in Southeast Asia for weak states to pay "tribute" to both sides in such a situation.

[11] Moura, II, *op. cit.* pp. 100–104; and Leclère, *op. cit.*, pp. 407–412.

[12] Leclère, *op. cit.*, pp. 413–416.

Knowledge of this discontent, together with the British defeat of Burma in 1825–1826 which removed a threat from their western frontier, led the Thai in 1833 to attempt to recover their dominant position in Cambodia. Taking advantage of Vietnamese preoccupation with a revolt in Cochinchina, Siam launched a three-pronged attack which swept across all of Cambodia and into Cochinchina. The main Thai thrust easily overcame a Cambodian army led by Ang Chan at Kompong Chhnang and forced him to abandon Phnom Penh and seek refuge in Vietnam. His brothers, Ang Im and Ang Duong, were left behind in Phnom Penh by the Thai to win over Cambodian support for Siam, while the Thai advanced southeastward toward Chaudoc and Hatien. The Thai, however, failed to accomplish their ends; heavy Vietnamese resistance compelled them to retreat, and Ang Chan's brothers retired with them. Shortly thereafter, Vietnam sent an occupying force of 15,000 troops into Cambodia, and when Ang Chan died in 1834, it seized effective control of the government. They then secured the election of Ang Chan's daughter, Ang Mey, as queen [13] and undertook intensive efforts to "Vietnamize" the country: the capital's name was changed to Nam Viang; Cambodia was reorganized along Vietnamese administrative lines; Vietnamese

[13] According to Cambodian chronicles, the appointment of Ang Mey as queen angered the Cambodian nobility, who looked upon it as a move by Annam to annex all of Cambodia as a province. In a meeting of the nobles, it was bitterly remarked that "if the election [of a ruler] does not find a prince, it is nullified; if a prince is not accepted by the people and the King of Siam, there will be a war; if a princess is elected and the King of Siam does not intervene, it is the end of Kampuchea, and its occupation by Annam is definite." A religious dignitary summed up their feelings: "We need to go to Siam," he declared. Quoted in *ibid.*, pp. 420–421.

résidents were installed in each province to manage the Cambodian governors; officials were compelled to adopt Vietnamese names, customs, and dress; and Buddhism, the strongest institution in the country, came under attack as priests were driven from their *wats* (temples), and the *wats* destroyed.[14] As continued Thai support of Ang Im and Ang Duong posed a serious threat to their plans, the Vietnamese devised a scheme to rid themselves of this menace. In a message to Ang Im, who had been installed as governor of Battambang by the Thai, they intimated that efforts to make him king were being hampered by his brother, Ang Duong. Im allowed himself to be persuaded by this tale and denounced his brother to the Thai. When Ang Duong was arrested by the Thai, Im fled to Phnom Penh, but once he arrived the Vietnamese escorted him not to the throne but to a jail in Hué.[15]

Only a few additional measures seemed necessary to complete the conversion of Cambodia into a Vietnamese province. In 1840, the Cambodian government was forcibly moved to Saigon, and the compilation of a census and registration of land-holdings were begun. These traditionally unpopular measures—the census was identified with the *corvée,* and land registration with taxation—when executed by foreigners incited apparently spontaneous revolts all over Cambodia. Innumerable bands of guerrillas attacked and massacred Vietnamese wherever they found them. Communications between towns were cut; isolated Vietnamese garrisons were overwhelmed, and

[14] *Ibid.,* pp. 421–424; Moura, II, *op. cit.,* p. 111. See also Lê Thánh Khôi, *op. cit.,* pp. 333–336. Vietnamese action in Cambodia is to be contrasted with that of the Thai who, in the northern provinces of Cambodia, respected Cambodian institutions. On this subject, see Georges Coedès, "Les premières capitales du Siam," *Arts Asiatique,* 3, 1956, pp. 243–267.

[15] Leclère, *op. cit.,* pp. 426–427.

cities, where the Vietnamese remained in control, were besieged. Some of the Cambodians were led by Buddhist monks, but the revolution had no organization and no central direction. Representatives of the nobility petitioned Siam for assistance in expelling the Vietnamese and establishing Ang Duong as the rightful king of Cambodia. Siam did not long hesitate; two armies, composed mainly of Cambodians conscripted from the provinces ruled by Siam, attacked along both sides of the Tonlé Sap; and for the next six years Thai and Vietnamese armies fought each other on Cambodian soil. Their conflict resulted in a stalemate, however, and a peace settlement between Siam and Vietnam was finally reached in 1846. In the following year, Ang Duong was crowned by the representatives of both countries and he agreed to send tribute to both governments.

French Protectorate

Seven years of warfare fought on Cambodia's territory left her economy prostrate. Commerce was at a standstill; the fields had not been worked regularly for several years and poverty was widespread; cholera epidemics had decimated the populations of several large towns. To the extent that it was possible with an empty treasury, Ang Duong tried to rehabilitate his country: He established a seaport at Kampot and entered into trade relations with Singapore and Bangkok; he instituted a limited public-works program in order to repair the main transportation routes in the country; a public-welfare program was established to distribute rice, and he issued orders that the gifts which the governors traditionally presented to the king each year should be used to benefit the people.[16]

[16] See *ibid.*, pp. 434–441. For contemporary accounts of the situation in Cambodia, see C. E. Bouillevaux, *Voyage dans l'Indo-Chine,*

Ang Duong, realizing that the stalemate between Annam and Siam was but a temporary relief for Cambodia,
decided to seek the protection of a still greater power. His
choice fell on France, which had already succeeded in
making its influence felt on the Indochinese peninsula. In
1853, he wrote to Napoleon III, asking for his protection
and assistance in regaining the provinces lost to Vietnam
in the Mekong delta region.[17] Napoleon's ambassador,
Charles de Montigny, not understanding the nature of
Cambodia's association with Siam, imprudently exposed
to the Siamese during a stopover in 1856 in Bangkok the
French plan to enter into negotiations with Cambodia.
Thus forewarned, the Thai threatened Ang Duong with
war if he signed a treaty with France. Consequently, when
de Montigny arrived in Cambodia he found the king unwilling to receive him.[18]

In 1857, in retaliation against persecution of French
Jesuit missionaries and revocation of economic privileges,
France launched its first attack against Vietnam. When
an uprising among the Chams in Cambodia ended in their
flight to Cochinchina, Ang Duong decided to pursue them,
hoping thereby to provoke Vietnam into war with Cam-

1848–1856 (Paris, 1856), and Henri Mouhot, *Travels in the Central
Parts of Indo-China* (London, 1864).

[17] For the text of his letter see Rois de Kampuchea, *Ang Duong,
Norodom, N. Sihanouk* (Phnom Penh: Imprimerie du Palais Royal,
n.d. ([1957?])), pp. 3–5.

[18] Leclère, *op. cit.*, pp. 443–444, and Moura, II, *op. cit.*, pp. 128–
132. In any case, the commercial treaty which the French were at
this time prepared to offer Ang Duong did not provide Cambodia
with the kind of protection or assistance he desired. See Charles
Meyniard, *Le Second Empire en Indochine* (Paris, 1891), pp. 403–
406, and R. Stanley Thomson, "The Establishment of the French
Protectorate over Cambodia," *Far Eastern Quarterly*, IV, no. 4
(Aug., 1945), pp. 316–317.

bodia and thus open the way to requesting aid from both Siam and France in obtaining the retrocession of the delta provinces. Ang Duong died in 1859 without realizing his aspiration to regain the provinces for Cambodia.

In accordance with Ang Duong's wishes, his eldest son, Ang Vodey, who was then studying in Bangkok under the sponsorship of King Mongkut, was proclaimed King Norodom by the Royal Council of Ministers. Mongkut voiced his assent (Vietnam, still at war with France, was not consulted), and Norodom returned to Cambodia in 1860. His appointment, however, evoked resentment among members of his own family, and a revolt led by his youngest brother, Sivotha, caused him to flee to Bangkok in 1861.[19] The rebellion was poorly organized and was easily quashed by Ang Sôr, a second brother of the king. In 1862, with the backing of Siam, Norodom was reinstated as king. Meanwhile, France had defeated Annam and had established a colony in Cochinchina; moreover, having acquired by conquest Vietnam's rights of suzerainty, the French colonial officers began to look upon Cambodia from the points of view of strategy—i.e., protection of Cochinchina's western flank—and economic privilege. French officers traveling in Cambodia in 1863 reportedly suggested to Norodom that France could offer him protection against Siam and against internal dissension as well.[20] Finally on August 11, 1863, following brief negotiations, Norodom accepted the French offer to transform into a protectorate their rights of suzerainty.[21] Before ratifications of a protectorate treaty could be exchanged, how-

[19] See Hall, *op. cit.*, pp. 613–614.   [20] *Ibid.*, p. 615.
[21] For the text of the treaty see L. de Reinach, *Recueil des traités conclus par la France en Extrême-Orient, 1684–1902* (Paris, 1902), pp. 98–103.

ever, Siam intervened, with the intent of securing her dominant position in Cambodia. By reminding Norodom that the royal insignia were still in her possession,[22] she succeeded in persuading him to go to Bangkok for his coronation. As he set out on his journey, French troops captured his palace, and he was induced to turn back to the Cambodian capital. Norodom was coerced into accepting Napoleon III's ratification of the treaty establishing the French protectorate. On June 3, 1864, Norodom was crowned by the representatives of Siam and France.

Disclosure, in 1864, of a secret agreement in which Siam confirmed her suzerainty over Cambodia caused great consternation among the French.[23] The accord had been signed the year before and had represented a condition for the return of the crown and other regalia to Norodom by the Siamese. In addition to gaining Cambodia's official acknowledgment of her tributary status to her, Siam, in the treaty, relegated Norodom to the position of "Viceroy of Cambodia" and obtained Cambodia's recognition of Siam's claim to Battambang and Siem Reap.[24]

The exposure of this secret document constrained France to come to terms with Siam. The French purchased Siam's agreement to abrogate this accord with another treaty in which France recognized Siam's claims to Battambang and Siem Reap, thus giving her control of rice-rich

[22] Norodom had left them in Bangkok for safekeeping before returning to Cambodia the year before. See Hall, *op. cit.*, p. 615.

[23] See Leclère, *op. cit.*, p. 454, and Paulin Vial, *Les premières années de la Cochinchine, colonie française* (Paris, 1878), I, 260–261.

[24] For the text of this treaty see A. de Villemereuil, *Explorations et missions de Doudart de Lagrée: extraits de ses manuscrits* (Paris, 1883), pp. 95–101. See also Fernan Bernard, *A l'école des diplomates: la perte et le retour d'Angkor* (Paris, 1933), pp. 44–45.

lands and access to the bounty of the Tonlé Sap's waters. The new treaty was signed in Paris on July 15, 1867, over the bitter protests of Norodom.[25]

In successfully persuading Siam to relinquish suzerainty rights over Cambodia, France emerged as the sole foreign power in Cambodia. The French protectorate, however, was not uncontested within Cambodia. Revolts, led by a self-proclaimed prince named Pukoumbo, broke out in 1866–1867. French-Cambodian troops, some of whom were under the command of the king's brother, Ang Sôr (later called Sisowath), were able to quell the rebellions. Following Pukoumbo's defeat in 1867, France attempted to introduce much-needed reforms in the poorly organized and corrupt Cambodian administration. These attempts further alienated Norodom, who continued to rue the loss of the northern provinces. The French were able to overcome the king's opposition to their modifications only by threatening in 1877 to withdraw and leave Norodom to the mercy of Sivotha, who was then organizing still another rebellion. But after Sivotha's defeat, France became preoccupied with events in Tonkin, and the reforms fell into disuse. Norodom began to resume full control over Cambodia. When, in 1884, he refused to participate in a customs union with French–controlled Vietnam, the Governor-General of Cochinchina, Charles Thomson, reasserted France's dominance. On July 17, 1884, Thomson arrived in Phnom Penh from Saigon with a contingent of French troops and several gunboats. With these placed in strategic postions around the royal palace, Thomson co-

[25] For further details surrounding this matter see Lawrence Palmer Briggs, "Aubaret and the Treaty of July 15, 1867 between France and Siam," *Far Eastern Quarterly*, VI, no. 2 (Feb., 1947), pp. 122–138.

erced Norodom into signing the convention which made Cambodia a *de facto* colony of France.[26] The king was left with only the right to "enact . . . the administrative, judicial, financial and commercial reforms which the French government judges necessary in the interests of the protectorate." After 1884, all that distinguished the protectorate from a colony was the monarchy, which was still nominally the highest authority. The king's power was further diminished when in 1897 France decreed that "the government of the country will be exercised by a Council of Ministers. This Council, composed of six Cambodian ministers, will function under the presidency of the representative of France, the Résident-Supérieur." [27]

Further to assure themselves of their authority in Cambodia, the French controlled succession to the throne. Traditionally the Cambodian kings designated their own successors, usually their eldest sons, and in instances when they died before having announced their choices the king's High Council undertook the selection of the new king.

[26] According to one account of Thomson's meeting with Norodom, Kol de Monteiro, a descendant of a Portuguese adventurer who was the king's interpreter, told the king, "Sire, this is not a convention which is proposed to Your Majesty; it is an abdication." See Paul Collard, *Cambodge et cambodgiennes* (Paris, 1925), p. 111. See Protectorat du Cambodge, *Recueil des actes du gouvernement cambodgien* (Saigon: Imprimerie Albert Portail, 1920), I, pp. 63–65, for the text of the convention.

[27] Ordonnance of July 11, 1897, quoted in Jean Imbert, *Histoire des institutions khmères, Annales* de la Faculté de Droit de Phnom Penh, II, 1961, p. 57. It was alleged at the time that the French installed political enemies of the king on the Council, the better to control him and Cambodia. See the letters written by Norodom's son, Prince Yukanthor, as quoted in Norodom Sihanouk, *La monarchie cambodgienne et la croisade royale pour l'indépendance* (Phnom Penh: Imprimerie Rasmey, 1961), pp. 45–46, and *Rois de Kampuchea*, pp. 6–8.

But when Norodom died in 1904, the French ignored the wishes of the late king and instead appointed as monarch his brother, Sisowath, as a tribute to his loyalty and assistance in crushing several revolts. Sisowath was succeeded by his son, Monivong, in 1927. When the latter died in 1941, the French administrators passed over Monivong's son, Monireth, who appeared to be too independent and independence-minded at a time when France was beset with defeat in Europe and Japanese encroachments upon Indochina. They elevated young Norodom Sihanouk, a great-grandson of King Norodom and a nephew of Prince Monireth, to the throne. At the time he was a high school student in Saigon and because of his youth was believed to be weak and tractable.[28]

France's primary interest in Cambodia was defensive. Because of its geographical situation it could serve the French as a buffer against any future attempts of the Thai and the British to extend their influence into the rich coastal areas of the peninsula, which is today known as Vietnam. The principal activity of the French in Cambodia, therefore, was directed toward the maintenance of law and order. Only secondarily did France concern herself with the development of natural or human resources in Cambodia. Much of the revenue from Cambodia was

[28] The French justified their decision by pointing to a quarrel between the Norodom and Sisowath branches of the royal family over the throne and noting that Sihanouk, an offspring of both sides, would help to reconcile the dispute. See Jean Decoux, *A la Barre de l'Indochine, Histoire de mon Gouvernement Général, 1940–1945* (Paris Plon: 1949), pp. 285–286. It must have been well known to the French, however, that Monireth was also the offspring of both branches. See Princess Yukanthor, "Personalité de S.M. Norodom Suramarit," *France-Asie* (Saigon), XII (Oct., 1955), 113, 242–247.

channeled into Cochinchina for the support of public services there. All foreign trade was trans-shipped at Saigon and financed and controlled from there. The extensive road and rail network built by the French was designed to bring the protectorate closer to Cochinchina, especially for the purpose of shipping rice, rubber, and other agricultural products to Saigon. The result was, in effect, that the development of Cochinchina proceeded at the expense of stunting Cambodia's own economic growth.[29]

Although Cambodia's economic development suffered as a consequence of France's preoccupations in Cochinchina, many Cambodians today express gratitude for what they feel was an important feature of French rule: the preservation of Cambodia's identity and territorial integrity. The French intervened in time to forestall the total assimilation of Cambodia by Siam and Vietnam. It is true that in order to secure her position in Cambodia, France ceded to Siam the vital provinces of Siem Reap and Battambang. But this deed was rectified forty years later when Siamese violations of other treaties led the French to re-open the issue. In return for French concessions along the Mekong River border with Laos, Siam temporarily abandoned her claims to these Cambodian provinces in conventions signed in 1902, 1904, and 1907.[30] We have seen that before the arrival of the French the Cambodians

[29] See F. Baudoin, *Le Cambodge pendant et après la Grande Guerre, 1914–1926* (Phnom Penh, 1927), p. 25; and A. Pannetier, *Notes cambodgiennes: Au coeur du pays Khmer* (Paris, 1921), Chaps. IV and VII.

[30] See Protectorat du Cambodge, *Recueil des actes,* pp. 57, 145–149. See also L. Palmer Briggs, "The Treaty of March 23, 1907 between France and Siam and the Return of Battambang and Siem Reap to Cambodia," *Far Eastern Quarterly,* V, no. 4 (Aug., 1946), pp. 439–454.

themselves had been unable to wrest these provinces from the direct control of Siam.

That France was instrumental in preventing the Thai from reclaiming the provinces became evident in 1940, three months after they signed a nonaggression pact with France. In an *aide-mémoire* addressed to the Vichy government on September 9, Thailand requested: "His Majesty's government would appreciate it if the French government would have the kindness to give its assurance that in the event of an interruption of French sovereignty, France would return to Thailand the Cambodian and Laotian territories." [31] This and other Thai demands were rejected by France; a series of incidents along the Mekong River resulted by December, 1940, in a state of undeclared war between them.

On January 9, 1941, a Thai force invaded Cambodia. The ensuing engagement on land with French forces was light, but on January 17 the French administered a decisive defeat to Thailand in a naval battle near the island of Kôh Chang. At this point, the Japanese, who were already asserting their dominance in Southeast Asia, intervened, and under their supervision a treaty was signed in Tokyo on March 11, 1941, by which France surrendered the provinces of Battambang, Siem Reap, and parts of Kompong Thom and Stung Treng to Thailand.[32]

[31] Quoted by Norodom Sihanouk in his "Une politique de neutralité dans l'Asie troublée," *Le Monde Diplomatique* (Paris), Oct., 1963, p. 14.

[32] For the text of the treaty see *Contemporary Japan* (June, 1941), pp. 840–842. Brief commentaries on this affair are to be found in Bernard B. Fall, *The Two Viet-Nams* (New York: Praeger, 1963), p. 44, and D. Lancaster, *The Emancipation of French Indochina* (London: Oxford University Press, 1961), pp. 94–95. A contemporary Thai view is given by Luang Vichitr Vadakarn, *Thailand's Case* (Bangkok: Thai Commercial Press, 1941).

At the conclusion of World War II and with the subsequent reinstatement of French influence in Cambodia, France, acting through the good offices of the United States, was able to regain these provinces for Cambodia.[33]

Struggle for Independence

Until its last years, before World War II, the period of French rule in Cambodia was relatively tranquil. To be sure, the peace was disturbed from time to time by revolts master-minded by disgruntled members of the royalty, but these insurrections never commanded significant popular support and were intended not so much to oust the French as to dethrone a particular Cambodian king. The imposition of the colonial administration probably did not introduce any perceptible changes into the daily lives of the peasantry. Its impact appears to have been restricted to the small aristocracy, whose position in many respects was made even more secure. Members of the Cambodian elite were absorbed into the colonial administration where, if their talents and energies were not given free rein, they were at least assured of a comfortable existence.[34] Because of the administration's neglect of public education,[35] a class of intellectuals, independent of the

[33] For the text of the Washington Treaty of 1946, by which the provinces were returned to Cambodia, see Roger Lévy, *L'Indochine et ses traités, 1946* (Paris: Centre d'Etudes de Politique Etrangère. Publ. No. 19, 1947), pp. 82–87.

[34] For details of the colonial administration, see René Morizon, *Monographie du Cambodge* (Hanoi, 1931), pp. 51–55; and A. Silvestre, *Le Cambodge administratif* (Phnom Penh, 1924), pp. 42–54. See also M. de Lens, *Le Mékhum dans l'Administration Cambodgienne* (Phnom Penh, 1939), and André Homont, "La commune cambodgienne," *Annales* de la Faculté de Droit et des Sciences Economiques de Phnom Penh, III (1961), 7–123.

[35] For details of the pre-World War II education system, see

aristocracy, was slow in evolving—a class which might have inspired among the populace a spirit of nationalism and carried the burden of organizing and leading a revolt against foreign domination.

It was 1937 before the first dedicated effort to sow the seeds of nationalism among the people was made. In that year, Son Ngoc Thanh, the editor of the first Cambodian-language newspaper, launched his campaign to rouse the people from their indifference and to persuade them to support a movement for greater autonomy under the French protectorate. Born in Cochinchina, Son is reported to be of Cambodian–Vietnamese descent and to have received his early education in Saigon. Later a job on board a French ship took him to France, where he received some university training. Upon his return to Cochinchina he tried, without success, to enter the colonial civil service. At about this time he became friendly with a small group of young French liberals who occupied minor positions in the colonial administration. At their invitation, Son went to Cambodia, where he found employment in the national library. Once in Cambodia he was introduced to Pach Chhoeun, a teacher of Pali at the Buddhist Institute, and together, with the encouragement of their French friends, they founded *Nagaravatta,* the journal which was to be the spokesman of the nationalist movement.

When the Japanese occupation forces arrived in Cambodia in 1941, they established contacts with Son Ngoc Thanh and Pach Chhoeun, and, beginning in 1942, the Buddhist Institute became a center for nationalist ele-

---

Morizon, *op. cit.,* pp. 180–182, and Charles Bilodeau, "Compulsory Education in Cambodia," in *Compulsory Education in Cambodia, Laos, Viet-Nam,* UNESCO, Studies on Compulsory Education, XIV (Paris, 1955).

ments. In mid-1942 two Buddhist monks were arrested for circulating anti-French tracts. When news of their imprisonment reached Pach Chhoeun, he organized, with the encouragement of Japanese officials, a demonstration by the Buddhist clergy. The French authorities retaliated by arresting him and banishing him to the concentration camp on the island of Poulo Condore. A directive for the arrest of Son Ngoc Thanh was also issued, although available evidence indicates that he had had no part in any phase of the demonstration. He sought refuge with the Japanese military command in Phnom Penh, whence he was sent to Japan.[36]

In March, 1945, attempts to get a nationalist movement off the ground received impetus from an unexpected direction. The Japanese military command based in Cambodia suddenly took over the colonial administration, imprisoned French officials, and directed King Sihanouk to proclaim the independence of his country. There is no evidence that, until then, the Japanese had actively interfered with French authority in Cambodia. Throughout the Japanese occupation only a small garrison was maintained

[36] The foregoing discussion of Son Ngoc Thanh is based on private communications to the author from Cambodian and French sources he regards as reliable.

Pach Chhoeun was released soon thereafter at King Sihanouk's behest. His continued opposition to the French, however, again brought about his arrest in 1943; this time he was charged with violating freedom of expression (in his capacity as a teacher). When the Japanese took over from the French in 1945, the king again had Pach Chhoeun released from custody. During Son Ngoc Thanh's government, Aug.–Sept., 1945, Pach Chhoeun was Minister of National Economy. Following the arrest and exile of Son, he went to France for a "rest cure," and remained there until 1950. After his return to Cambodia, he served for a brief time as Minister of Information in the Huy Kanthoul cabinet (1951–1952) before retiring from politics.

there. The sudden change in Japanese policy was part of a general attempt by the Japanese to bolster their declining position in the war and to counteract the French underground movement in Indochina.

With the political reins now apparently returned to their hands, interest in the national destiny was rekindled among the small group of Cambodians who had been in the French administration or close to the king. There emerged two divergent views on the course which Cambodia should follow. Those who headed the new government permitted by the Japanese (and ultimately under Japanese authority) favored the return of France and a slow evolution toward independence. The king and his uncle, Prince Monireth, were among the adherents of this view. They believed Cambodia to be ill prepared to cope with the numerous political and economic problems which would face a newly independent nation and were thus unwilling completely to sever ties with France.

In contrast a group of young radicals, among whom anticolonial sentiments ran high, opposed the return of the French. It was believed that this group received its major direction from Son Ngoc Thanh, who had reappeared in Cambodia with the dismissal of the French and who by June, 1945, was serving as foreign minister in the new cabinet.

On August 9, 1945, members of the Yuvan Kampuchearat (Cambodian Youth Corps),[37] with Japanese support,

[37] One of several paramilitary "youth and sports" movements organized by the French throughout Indochina. Its ostensible purpose was to nurture irredentist sentiments in favor of the return of Battambang and Siem Reap from Thailand. In reality its purpose was the development of anti-Japanese sentiments. In practice many of its members became anti-French as well as anti-Japanese. For a statement of its aims in Cambodia see *Mouvement Yuvan Kampu-*

arrested several members of the cabinet, apparently with the intention of installing men who were more nationalistic in their outlook. Son Ngoc Thanh and Prince Monireth, however, freed the jailed ministers; on August 14, on the eve of Japan's capitulation to the allies, King Sihanouk, who had been serving as his own prime minister, resigned from the cabinet and named Son to that position.[38] Son was reported to have been supported by a corps of two thousand armed volunteers, and under the circumstances Sihanouk did not dare oppose him for fear of being deposed. In a government-sponsored plebiscite held in early October, in which some 500,000 votes were cast, the people expressed their approval of Son Ngoc Thanh.[39] His victory, however, was short-lived.

As tension in the capital increased following the August coup, King Sihanouk expressed his desire to abdicate in favor of Prince Monireth. Another uncle, Prince Montana, however, persuaded Sihanouk to remain on the throne. Son Ngoc Thanh also urged Sihanouk to retain the crown. Monireth, who had been passed over by the French in 1941 in their search for a successor to his father, King Monivong, then took steps to subvert Son's position. He persuaded one of Son's lieutenants, Khim Tit, to steal away to British occupation forces in Saigon and request the immediate occupation of Cambodia and Son's arrest as a traitor. In mid-October, British and French officers, escorted by Indian troops, flew to Phnom Penh and on October 16 arrested Son on grounds that his activities

---

chearat, Statutes (Phnom Penh, 1944). See also Jean Decoux, *op. cit.*, pp. 407–408, and Norodom Sihanouk, *Jeunesse cambodgienne* (Phnom Penh: Editions de l'Association Aymonier, 1944), pp. 3–4.

[38] See *Le Cambodge* (Phnom Penh), Aug. 15, 1945.

[39] See *Le Cambodge*, Oct. 8, 1945.

threatened the security of allied forces and were detrimental to Cambodian interests. Son was subsequently tried for treason in Saigon by the French, but because he enjoyed widespread popularity within the government and among the people and because the issue was a controversial one, he was exiled to France instead of being executed.

French administrators returned to Cambodia in late 1945, but the protectorate was not re-established. Having now to contend with an awakened political consciousness —especially in the person of Prince Sisowath Youtévong, a cousin of the king, who returned from France at about the same time to assume the leadership of the agitators for independence—the French proposed a period of dyarchy leading to eventual independence. This idea was accepted, and a joint Franco–Cambodian commission, the Commission d'Etudes Franco–Khmères (CEFK), was formed to seek an accord between French and Cambodian interests and to draft a constitution which would prepare the way for self-rule.

On January 7, 1946, a *modus vivendi* was signed which made Cambodia an "autonomous state within the French Union." [40] The provisions of the agreement conceded Cambodia's right to self-government, but also restricted its autonomy by granting to the French commissioners the power of veto over "legislative and regulatory texts and acts . . . proclamations and circulars or instructions of general application as well as decisions reserved, because of their importance, for the signature of His Majesty, the King."

In fact, France continued to rule Cambodia more or

---

[40] See the text in *Journal Officiel de la Fédération Indochinoise* (Saigon), Mar. 21, 1946, pp. 78–81. See also, Roger Lévy, *L'Indochine et ses traités* (Paris, 1947), pp. 41–46.

less as it had before the war. A Cambodian army was created, but France remained responsible for public order. Cambodia's foreign relations were conducted by the French government. Most important public services, including the treasury, secondary and higher education, customs, mines, railways, immigration, some judicial matters, and certain public works, were transferred to the newly established Indochinese Federation. Over every official position transferred to Cambodians there hovered the shadow of a French "advisory" counterpart. It was only in the administration of purely local affairs that Cambodians enjoyed complete independence.

The period of tutelage was left vague. The belief of many Cambodians that they were the victims of French chicanery augmented their impatience with the colonial regime. Some even suspected King Sihanouk of treason against his people. But France succeeded in maintaining its control until 1953, for its largest organized opposition was the Democrat party, which was riven by petty jealousies and the desire of its members to improve their financial positions—a desire that the French were not above trying to satisfy. As a result, the initial efforts made by a minority of Cambodians to win significant concessions from the French failed.

During this period King Sihanouk never publicly wavered from his view that patient negotiations were essential to progress toward independence. He tried to make the people understand that the economic and political conditions of the country would not permit it to retain, for long, independence won at the cost of permanent alienation from France. Until Cambodia could become self-sufficient, a friendly France would be amenable to lending economic and technological assistance. Moreover, the very real possibility had to be considered that the sudden withdrawal of French troops would invite Thai and Vietnamese incursions. Thus, Sihanouk argued, while independence from France was the ultimate goal, the weaning process had to be gradual and carefully planned.[41] It was in this mood that negotiations, which were to continue for eight years, were begun.

Other Cambodians were convinced that only force of arms would win independence. Following Son Ngoc Thanh's arrest, many of his followers fled to Thai-held Cambodian territory in the north, where they formed themselves into armed bands called Khmer Issarak, or Free Cambodians.[42] Some went to Bangkok, where they gained the support of Thai Prime Minister Pridi Phanomyong. The Thai, realizing that the re-establishment of French influence in Cambodia would mean that they would have to return Cambodian territory obtained by the 1941 treaty, may have viewed the Khmer Issarak's activities as working in their favor. A government-in-exile was formed by the Khmer Issarak, but its armed forces never seriously threatened the French. The subsequent return of Battambang, Siem Reap, and other territory to Cambodia by the Washington Conference of 1946 was fol-

---

[41] For an expression of the king's views at this time, see *New York Times*, Feb. 13, 1947. See also Sihanouk's message to the first Democrat government as reported in *La Liberté* (Phnom Penh), Feb. 21, 1948, and French views concerning Sihanouk's position in *Le Siam et l'Indochine française,* Notes documentaires et études, no. 607, Apr. 24, 1947 (Paris: Services français d'information, Ministère de la Jeunesse, des Arts, et des Lettres, 1947), p. 6.

[42] According to Virginia Thompson and Richard Adloff, the Khmer Issarak was formed in Bangkok in 1940, but no evidence is adduced to support this assertion. See *Minority Problems in Southeast Asia* (Stanford: Stanford University Press, 1955), p. 173.

lowed by a waning of Thai interest in the Khmer Issarak.[43] When general amnesties were granted in 1947, many Issarak members surrendered to the government. Subsequently most of them joined the Democrat party. Those who remained in armed opposition maintained close contacts with the Democrats, mainly through the Comité Khmer de Libération Nationale, led by an Issarak chief from Siem Reap—Dap Chhuon.[44]

Still another group opposed the French in Cambodia: the Viet Minh. While the Khmer Issarak was gaining control along the western and northern borders, the Viet Minh infiltrated the southern provinces, where they organized a Khmer People's Liberation Army which received its orders from the South Vietnam Resistance Executive Committee.[45] In addition, they established contact with certain Khmer Issarak elements, whom they tried to entice into cooperation with material aid and guidance. In this they were never wholly successful, for by late 1946 the Issarak had already begun to splinter, with each faction maintaining its own private army and controlling its own territory. Some elements did accept Viet Minh aid,[46]

[43] For further details of Khmer Issarak activities and of Thailand's role in them see *Le Cambodge*, Dec. 14, 1946; *La Liberté*, Mar. 20 and May 15, 1947; *Indochine Française*, Oct., 1947; *Bulletin de la France d'Outre-Mer*, May, 1948; "Evolution du Mouvement Khmer Issarak," *Indochine—Sud-Est Asiatique*, Oct.–Nov., 1950; and B. Rajan, "Le train de la contrebande," *Indochine—Sud-Est Asiatique*, July, 1952.

[44] For a statement of Khmer Issarak policies, see *La Liberté*, Mar. 9, 1949.

[45] See Bernard B. Fall, *The Viet Minh Regime, Government and Administration in the Democratic Republic of Vietnam*, Cornell University, Southeast Asia Program, Data Paper No. 14 (Ithaca, N.Y.; Apr., 1954), pp. 54–57.

[46] See Pierre Christian, "Le Viet Minh au Cambodge," *Indochine Sud-est Asiatique*, Feb.–Mar., 1952.

but only for short periods of time, and then turned against the Viet Minh and actively fought them. The lack of receptivity among the Khmer Issarak to Viet Minh overtures was probably in great part due to the antipathy and distrust with which Cambodians have traditionally regarded the Vietnamese.

In 1950–1951, the Viet Minh set up a "resistance government" in southern Cambodia with the cooperation of a handful of Cambodians who served as frontmen. Little is known about the political orientation of these men, but evidence is lacking that they belonged to the Khmer Issarak movement.[47]

In the meantime, the clash between the conservative views held by the king, Prince Monireth, and other members of the royalty who wished to maintain the full power of the monarchy and those being promoted by the group of young elite which looked forward to the creation of a parliamentary democracy, necessitated an immediate compromise. In this, King Sihanouk took the initiative by proposing a series of reforms which were designed to reconcile these competing interests.[48] Most important of these were provisions which granted freedom of association, thus permitting the establishment of political parties; freedom of the press, which gave both sides the opportunity to propa-

[47] See Sam Sary and Mau Say, *Bilan de l'oeuvre de Norodom Sihanouk pendant le mandat royal de 1952 à 1955* (Phnom Penh: Imprimerie Portail, 1955) pp. 20–27. Hereafter cited as *Bilan.* See also, Southeast Asia Treaty Organization, Research Services Office, *Background Brief: Communism and Cambodia* (Bangkok, RSO/BB/25, Dec. 31, 1959).

[48] See "Proclamation Royale, 13 avril 1946," in Sam Sary, *La grande figure de Norodom Sihanouk, telle qu'elle est dépeinte par les documents de valeur historique découverts dans les archives du palais royal* (Phnom Penh: Imprimerie du Palais Royal, 1955), pp. 8–10. Hereafter cited as *La Grande Figure.*

gandize their views; and the promise that the people would be consulted, through their elected representatives, on a constitution.

Three parties were immediately formed.[49] The Democratic Progressive party, organized by Prince Norodom Montana, Sihanouk's uncle, advocated gradual evolution toward a constitutional monarchy. Another uncle of the king, Prince Norodom Norindeth, formed the Liberal party, which also advocated the progressive evolution of Cambodia's institutions, but stated explicitly that this should be accomplished under the aegis of France.[50] The group demanding the most radical changes was the Democrat party, founded by Prince Sisowath Youtévong and a small group of young Cambodians who returned from university study in France in late 1945; they were quickly joined by many of Son Ngoc Thanh's followers, who formed the party's so-called "left wing." The Democrats sought the immediate establishment of a liberal democracy in which a popular assembly elected by universal suffrage would be fully responsible for the conduct of the government.

This political activity was confined almost entirely to Phnom Penh. The people continued in their traditional acquiescence to government and remained sublimely indifferent to the game of politics being played in the capital. Only a small group of Cambodians interested themselves in the possibilities attendant on autonomy and the birth of a constitutional monarchy. This group was re-

[49] See *Le Cambodge*, Aug. 31, 1946, and *La Démocrate* (Phnom Penh), July 8 and 22, and Aug. 5, 1946.

[50] See *Discours prononcé par le chef du Parti Libéral le 2 juin 1946 à l'occasion de la création de ce groupement* (Phnom Penh, 1946).

cruited from the ranks of the educated and the small corps
of civil servants who saw in the reforms a means of increasing their social prestige and material wealth. Their
attitude became increasingly evident during 1947–1952 as
the parties' façades of organization and program broke
down under the weight of personal interests.

Sixty per cent of the registered voters turned out for the
election of delegates to the Consultative Assembly on September 1, 1946. The Democrats won 50 seats, while the
Liberals obtained 16 and independents, 3. The Democratic Progressive party failed to place any of its candidates.

The Consultative Assembly met on September 25 and
immediately took it upon itself to designate Prince Youtévong as the chief of government. King Sihanouk accepted
the argument that Youtévong, as the majority party's
choice, should replace Prince Monireth, his own ap-
pointee, as premier.[51] Furthermore, in spite of the intentions of the CEFK, the Democrat-controlled Consultative
Assembly transformed itself *de facto* into a Constituent Assembly with rights equal to those of the commission. The
commission was interested in creating a strong executive
and, at first, rejected Youtévong's demands for full civil
liberties and for a strong National Assembly. But the
young prince's persistence won for Cambodia the full extent of constitutionalism as then practiced in France, the
only difference being that in Cambodia sovereignty was
vested in a semihereditary king rather than in the people.
The king's power to dissolve the National Assembly,
which was to be employed so dramatically in 1953, was

[51] Actually, Monireth, who had been appointed in 1945 to succeed Son Ngoc Thanh, had already resigned in exasperation over
the action taken by the Assembly.

made a provision of the constitution with the support of Prince Montana, who also forced the creation of an upper house further to reduce the authority of the Assembly.[52]

The elections for the first National Assembly were held in December, 1947. Two new parties joined the Democrats and Liberals in this contest. The Democrat party,[53] which in its campaign had advocated the transfer of more powers to Cambodia and the withdrawal of Cambodian troops supporting French forces confronting the Viet Minh, achieved a resounding victory. Fifty-five of seventy-five seats were won by them; the Liberal party took all the rest. In the next few months two successive governments led by Chheam Van and Penn Nouth were overthrown, the latter as a result of disagreement upon the question of which branch of government would determine Cambodia's relations with France and upon the issue of the Khmer Issarak and the increasing strength of the Viet Minh. A minority government led by Yem Sambaur followed.

Meanwhile, in the months following the promulgation of the constitution in May, 1947, France became increasingly preoccupied with its campaign against the Viet Minh. As more and more reinforcements were necessitated, French Union troops, including Cambodian units, were withdrawn from Cambodia and transferred to Vietnam. Unpoliced, dissident elements in Cambodia flour-

[52] The struggle between Youtévong and the CEFK was reported in *Le Cambodge*, Apr. 27, 1947, and *La Démocrate*, Sept. 21, 1947. Sihanouk has since claimed credit for the establishment of the constitutional monarchy. See *Réalités Cambodgiennes* (Phnom Penh), Feb. 8, 1958, and Aug. 29, 1959.

[53] A serious setback was suffered by the Democrats in July, 1947, when they were suddenly deprived of the leadership of Prince Youtévong. Youtévong, who died of tuberculosis, was succeeded by Chheam Van.

ished. The Khmer Issarak reached the height of its influence during this period, and the Khmer People's Liberation army, directed by the Viet Minh, stepped up its activity in the southeastern provinces. France was blamed for the country's plight, and Sihanouk, submitting to public pressure as well as to the realities of the situation, appealed to the French for a redefinition of Franco-Khmer relations.

In a note to the French government on November 27, 1947, Sihanouk expressed his concern over military arrangements which left his regime defenseless against threats from rebel and foreign elements. He demanded greater control of Cambodian troops in the French Union army and more autonomy in affairs pertaining to internal security.[54] Nearly a year later, November 9, 1948, on the occasion of his birthday, in a public exchange of pleasantries with the French High Commissioner, Sihanouk broached the subject of independence: "I spoke of independence because I am fully convinced that this word and all that it implies constitutes the key to our problem." [55] Sihanouk's correspondence of 1949 further reveals the extent to which internal pressures were forcing him into a new position. In his letter of October 25 he tried to convince the French that the concessions granted to Bao Dai by the Elysée Agreement should also be made applicable to Cambodia.[56]

The government headed by Yem Sambaur employed a

[54] See France, Présidence du Conseil, Secrétariat Général du Gouvernement, *Actes définissant les rapports des Etats associés du Viet Nam, du Cambodge, et du Laos avec la France,* Notes et Etudes Documentaires, no. 1, 295 (Mar. 14, 1950) (Paris, 1950), pp. 18–19. See also, *La lettre et l'esprit des accords Franco-Khmers* (Phnom Penh: Imprimerie Albert Portail, 1953).

[55] *La Grand Figure,* p. 17.   [56] See *ibid.,* pp. 26–30.

new tactic to hamper rebel operations. Warning that dissidence would leave the country prey to Viet Minh imperialism, Sambaur offered amnesty to those rebels who immediately laid down their arms. This gesture, seconded by a plea from Sihanouk, evidently produced the desired results, for within the year many Khmer Issarak turned in their arms. The most dramatic of these surrenders was that of Dap Chhuon, who, with his army of several thousand men, had effectively controlled Siem Reap province. Following his surrender, he and many of his men joined the royal army in a public ceremony.

The Cambodian constitution, meanwhile, had been approved by the president of the French Union in December 1948, and later was ratified by the French government on November 8, 1949, together with a treaty which recognized the *de jure* independence of the Kingdom.[57] By this treaty Cambodia regained the right to establish diplomatic relations with other nations, subject to French approval. It received control over its army and police, but in time of war, a condition then prevailing, these were to be placed under French command. Frenchmen would continue to enjoy extraterritorial privileges. But in almost all other internal matters Cambodia obtained complete control.

King Sihanouk and Yem Sambaur tried to present the treaty to the National Assembly as a Cambodian victory.[58] Opposition to the government by the Democrats and by the French colonial administration aggravated the discordance existing between the executive and the legislature.

[57] For the text of the treaty, see *Bulletin Officiel de Haut-Commissariat de France en Indochine* (Saigon), Mar. 26, 1953, pp. 262–267.

[58] See *La Liberté*, Nov. 23, 1949.

Partly out of jealousy of the minority government's success in dealing with France and partly because the treaty failed to grant full independence to Cambodia, the Democrats ignored Yem Sambaur's request for ratification. Moreover, on the issue of whether or not the executive was an instrument of the legislature, the deputies censured Sambaur's government. Charging them with obstructing the treaty negotiations, Sambaur threatened to dissolve the Assembly unless the deputies withdrew their motion. The deputies remained recalcitrant. Sambaur then persuaded the king to sign a dissolution decree, and he himself resigned with his ministers. Under the provisions of the constitution elections for a new Assembly should have been held within two months. The president of the Assembly, Ieu Koeus, and the minister of interior, Sonn Voeunsai, now heading a caretaker government, however, decided that free elections could not be guaranteed because of widespread insecurity. Instead, they placed full power in King Sihanouk's hands. The king, anxious about the treaty negotiations which Yem Sambaur had so far been conducting successfully, reappointed him as premier. At the same time Sihanouk criticized the Democrats for lacking respect for the constitution. This served only further to alienate the Democrats and, thereafter, their opposition to Sambaur increased, as did the activity of the dissident Issarak, with whom the Democrats maintained close connections.

Unable to obtain ratification of the treaty from the National Assembly, Sambaur then tried to secure activation of its major provisions by negotiating protocols of application with the French. The French, at this time, revealed their true position by retracting some of the concessions they had made, notably those concerning the military and judiciary. Furthermore, they refused to grant arms to the

Cambodian army with which it could attempt to bring the Khmer Issarak and Viet Minh under control. Together with their refusal to grant meaningful concessions to Cambodia, this policy played into the hands of the rebels.[59]

While these negotiations were being conducted, Viet Minh subversive activities in Cambodia reached their peak. A certain Son Ngoc Minh, alleged to be related to Son Ngoc Thanh, was brought in to direct the Khmer People's Liberation army.[60] In March, 1950, Son Ngoc Minh consulted with the South Vietnam Resistance Executive Committee to draft a unified policy to pave the way for the formation of a "free, provisional government of Cambodia." The increase in guerrilla activities of the Khmer People's Liberation army forced the royal government to employ armed convoys on the highways. Yem Sambaur pressed France for an increase in the size of the five-thousand-man royal army so that the government might restore its control over the south and southeast. Despite these government moves, the Viet Minh were able to establish administrative control over many small villages; through the imposition of local taxes a Khmer People's Liberation Committee financed its organization and fed the Liberation army. In May, 1950, some three thousand Viet Minh troops invaded Cambodia, and the South Vietnam Resistance Executive Committee trans-

[59] See Sihanouk's remarks on this subject in *La Liberté*, Aug. 20, 1949.

[60] Prince Sihanouk, writing in *Réalités Cambodgiennes*, Mar. 1, 1958, had this to say about the Viet Minh and Son Ngoc Minh: "From the information I have been able to obtain, it appears that the Vietminh came to Cambodia with a very small force of Khmer auxiliaries, most of Cochinchina origin, formed in cells in South Vietnam and, for their superior cadres, from Tonkin. The head of this so-called "Government" was a certain Son Ngoc Minh about whom I have been able to obtain only contradictory reports."

ferred its headquarters to Prey Veng province in Cambodia.[61]

When, in mid-1950, Yem Sambaur refused to sign a provisional military accord, which would have confirmed French control of the army, the king was prevailed upon by the French to dismiss him and his government. In order to eliminate the petty bickering among parties, which was interfering with the efficient direction of the nation, Sihanouk then tried to persuade the parties to join in a national union government under Sambaur's leadership. Failing in this, he formed his own government, but in the face of continued Democrat opposition, he resigned in favor of his uncle, Prince Monipong.[62] During the life of two governments, directed by Monipong and Sonn Mam (1950–1951), the king met frequently with the heads of the several parties in a vain attempt to resolve the question of executive-legislative relations and to try to convince them of the necessity of continued negotiations with France. Instead, the heads of the parties convinced Sihanouk that new elections were in order.

The elections of September, 1951, were again dominated by the Democrats. Following the elections Son Ngoc Thanh was released from exile upon the intervention of King Sihanouk, who hoped that Son would be able to rally the rest of the Khmer Issarak against the Viet Minh.[63] In

[61] See *New York Times,* Mar. 26 and May 22, 1950.

[62] Sihanouk was so exasperated by Democrat opposition and by mounting French pressure to rid the government of anti-French elements that he considered abdicating in favor of Monipong. See *Samleng Khmer* (Phnom Penh), Nov. 3, 1950. He was dissuaded from this course by his close advisers. On the subject of French pressures, see his letter in *Rassemblement Nationale* (Phnom Penh), Sept. 20, 1950.

[63] See the letters exchanged between Sihanouk, Son Ngoc Thanh, the French High Commissioner at Saigon, the Minister for As-

being granted permission to return to Cambodia, Son promised both the king and the French to refrain from other political activity. He had hardly returned, however, when he began to call upon the people to defy French rule and, if necessary, to take up arms for nothing less than complete independence.[64] In January, 1952, he founded another nationalist newspaper, *Khmer Krauk* (Cambodians Awake!), through which he sought to rouse the people against France.[65] Son thus set himself against both the French and the policies of the king, but he enjoyed considerable support from among government officials, the Buddhist clergy, and the Khmer Issarak and the Democrats. He remained active in Phnom Penh for barely three months before the French moved to suppress *Khmer Krauk* and to place him under arrest. He escaped to Cambodia's northern forests, where, with a few close associates, he sought to unite the several Issarak bands into another Comité Khmer de Libération Nationale. In this he met with only limited success.[66]

It was at this point, mid-1952, that the king began to take matters into his own hands. Faced with increased Issa-

---

sociated States Relations, and the President of France, in *La Grande Figure,* pp. 122–141.

[64] See Pierre Christian, "Son Ngoc Thanh," *Indochine Sud-est Asiatique,* Oct., 1952, pp. 48–49.

[65] See especially the issues of *Khmer Krauk* dated Jan. 11, 22, and Feb. 22, 1952.

[66] See *New York Times,* Apr. 21, 1952; and *Le Monde,* Mar. 20, 1952. Christian, in "Son Ngoc Thanh," p. 49, claims that Son concluded an alliance with Son Ngoc Minh. King Sihanouk has charged Thanh with collaboration with the Viet Minh. See his letter to President Auriol, Mar. 5, 1953, in Gouvernement Royal du Cambodge, *Livre jaune sur les revendications de l'indépendance du Cambodge,* I (Paris: Imprimerie Centrale Commerciale, 1953), p. 17. Hereafter cited as *Livre Jaune, I.*

rak activity, with the prospect that Son Ngoc Thanh might soon win over the youth and, perhaps, the Buddhist clergy, among whom his views were thought to be already popular, and with the continued intransigence of the Democrat party,[67] Sihanouk demanded that the government take stronger action against the rebels. Instead, the Democrat cabinet of Huy Kanthoul arrested Yem Sambaur, a friend of the king and an enemy of the Democrats. At this, Sihanouk dismissed the government, charging that the ministers had not respected the policies set forth by him, but only those laid down by the central committee of the party:

The Ministers confuse matters of state with party matters [he declared] as though the interests of their party were ipso facto the interests of the state. . . . The King, himself, may have no more security than the others. You do not concede him any real authority over the conduct of the nation's affairs on the grounds that you possess that authority by vote of the people.[68]

He then issued a proclamation calling for emergency powers from the National Assembly for three years, during which time he promised to obtain complete independence for Cambodia. At the end of this period, he declared, he would submit his actions to the judgment of a popularly elected court, which would be supervised by six foreign nations.[69] His action met with the opposition of the Demo-

---

[67] See Sihanouk's letter to the French High Commissioner, May 26, 1949, in *La Grande Figure*, pp. 31–35; and his speech to the Council of the Kingdom, June 4, 1952, in *Bilan*, pp. 125–136.

[68] Royaume du Cambodge, *Proclamations et messages royaux à l'occasion de la constitution d'un gouvernement d'union nationale, présidé par S.M. Norodom Sihanouk, Roi du Cambodge* (Phnom Penh, 1952), pp. 16–18, 19–27.

[69] See the royal proclamations of June 15 and 21, 1952, and Sihanouk's message to the National Assembly and to the people,

crats, who viewed the king as reigning but not ruling in a constitutional monarchy. They refused to sanction his actions, noting only that he interpreted literally the constitutional provision that all power emanates from the king.

Sihanouk's first act as premier of the new government was to ban all public meetings. He then drafted an austerity budget which called for an increase in taxes and the allotment of 30 per cent of all revenues for military expenditures. Concluding that he could negotiate successfully for Cambodia's independence with France only if he could provide evidence that he was capable of controlling the country, in September he took personal charge of the royal army in Siem Reap and, with Dap Chhoun directing operations, staged an attack against Son Ngoc Thanh's men, during which "700 Red guerrillas" were dispersed along the Thai border. Upon his return to Phnom Penh late in the year, he was confronted with continued legislative opposition to his austerity budget and a report of a Khmer Issarak plot against the government. Having in vain asked the Assembly to pass his budget, to ratify the 1949 treaty and to vote approval of the emergency powers he had demanded in June, Sihanouk dissolved the Assembly on January 13, 1953, and declared martial law.[70] Then, leaving the country's affairs in the hands of trusted advisors, Sihanouk set out for France on the first phase of

---

of June 15 and 16, in *Bilan*, pp. 10 and 145 ff., and 141–144, respectively.

[70] See *Le Cambodge*, Jan. 14 and 15, 1953. See also, royal proclamation of Jan. 13, 1953; Decree 15–NS, Jan. 13, 1953 ("Pourtant dissolution de l'Assemblée nationale et du Conseil du Royaume"); Decree 760–NS, Jan. 13, 1953 ("Loi d'exception"); and Decree 765–NS, Jan. 27, 1953 ("Pourtant création du Conseil consultatif national"), in *Bilan*, pp. 151–155, 157, 159, and 161–162, respectively.

what has since been called in Cambodia the "Crusade for Independence."

In France, Sihanouk tried to convince President Vincent Auriol that the colonial authorities denied him the means to protect his people and that the Khmer Issarak, Democrats, and others appeared to believe that he, the king, was the principal obstacle to independence. In negotiations in March, he demanded full juridical sovereignty for Cambodia and control over the royal army and police.[71] But France was still preoccupied with what it considered to be more important problems in Vietnam. Auriol referred Sihanouk's letters to the government, invited him to Paris for lunch, and issued a communiqué which merely underscored France's unwillingness to hand over Cambodia's future to Cambodians. Thus snubbed, Sihanouk returned to Cambodia.

En route, he stopped in Washington, where he attempted to persuade Secretary of State John Foster Dulles that only with the granting of independence to the people of all Indochina could the Viet Minh be defeated. He told Dulles:

If a political solution is not found, the military effort, even though considerably augmented by American aid, will fail. . . . No success is possible if the interested people do not participate in the fight with the conviction that the fight is for their benefit. . . . To give real independence to the Indochinese state will oblige them to become fully conscious of their responsibilities in this fight, the issue of which is in the interest of the entire democratic world.[72]

---

[71] See *Le Monde,* Mar. 28, 1953. See also Sihanouk's letters of Mar. 5 and 18, 1953, in *Livre Jaune, I,* pp. 3–18, 28–30.

[72] Norodom Sihanouk, *La monarchie cambodgienne,* p. 70.

Secretary Dulles, however, remained convinced that only under French leadership could the fight be won.

Rest assured [he told Sihanouk] that we fully understand and appreciate your legitimate aspirations. I can promise you that once the menace of Communism is dispelled in your country, we will do everything in our power to induce France to recognize your complete and total independence and sovereignty. But, as long as our common enemies, the Viet Minh, are not defeated—and you know how they are capable of sweeping away the Khmer monarchy and your beautiful traditions, your ancient civilization and your young democracy—as long as this grave danger, which may be mortal for you, is not rolled back, we cannot discourage the French, who have suffered such heavy sacrifices in Indochina in order to defend our common liberties.

We are now at the most crucial moment of the war. It is necessary to win it. That is why, more than ever, we must unite, unite our forces, our means, and not dispute and divide ourselves. Your difference with France will only serve the cause of our common enemy.[73]

For Sihanouk, this was "putting the cart before the horse." [74] Profoundly disappointed by the results of his interview, he decided to alert American public opinion, through the medium of the *New York Times*, to the grave danger in Indochina and to the misappraisal by American and French policy-makers of the situation. In the event of a Communist attack on Cambodia, he warned, the possibility existed that any attempt to mobilize the people against the invaders would meet with failure, for there was a growing conviction among the people that the Viet Minh were fighting against France for Cambodia's inde-

[73] *Ibid.*, p. 71. See also, *Washington Post,* Apr. 19, 1953.
[74] *Ibid.*

pendence.[75] According to Sihanouk, his action in New York had the effect of persuading the French to reopen discussions with Cambodia.

A few weeks later, Sihanouk's prime minister, Penn Nouth, who had remained behind in Paris, procured the following concessions from the French: the king was recognized as commander-in-chief of the royal army, with full responsibility for the maintenance of internal security, and full control of the judicial system was returned to Cambodia.[76] An economic agreement was also signed which required the approval of the other associated states.[77] The French retained the right to try in a special court all non-Cambodian citizens of the French Union who were placed under arrest by local and national Cambodian police.[78] The French concessions fell short of Sihanouk's and Penn Nouth's expectations, and the latter departed from Paris soon after, hinting that further negotiations would become mandatory in the very near future.[79]

Meanwhile, King Sihanouk had arrived in Phnom Penh. But he remained there only long enough to relate his experience to the people. Then he dramatized his position by voluntarily exiling himself to Bangkok.[80] Penn

---

[75] *New York Times,* Apr. 19, 1953.   [76] *Livre Jaune, I,* p. 96.
[77] *Ibid.,* pp. 84–89.   [78] *Ibid.,* pp. 73–83.
[79] *Le Monde,* May 10–11, 1953.
[80] See "Royale Note (Personnelle), communiqué aux milieux politiques et diplomatiques de Bangkok," June 16, 1953, in *Livre Jaune, I,* pp. 123–125. In it, Sihanouk complained of French "tergiversations," and said France had given the impression that it neither wanted, nor would ever want, to accord real independence; he had left Cambodia hoping to avoid the revolt against France to which a growing number of Cambodians were looking forward. See also, "Message royal aux français," June 12, 1953, in *Livre Jaune, I,* pp. 120–121.

Nouth, to whom the king delegated full powers, remained in Phnom Penh to direct the government.

The shrewdness of Sihanouk's move is readily apparent upon an examination of the effects which he intended to produce. As the symbol of Cambodian authority, the king himself had held in rein the spreading anticolonial sentiments; now, without his mediating presence in the capital, the French had to face the possibility of a major revolt. Second, in demonstrating to his people the sincerity of his past attempts to obtain independence, he stole the thunder from the Communists and extreme nationalists who had accused him of subservience to the French. And finally, he attracted world attention to the plight of his country.

As anticipated, the news of the king's exile was received with great consternation in Paris.[81] Its impact upon the French was enhanced by the almost simultaneous occurrence of another significant event. Just about this time word was received of increased Chinese aid to the Viet Minh, but the French government, already under fire of critics of the war in Indochina, was unable to effect immediate popular support for an increase in defense spending.

Meanwhile, in Bangkok, King Sihanouk and his retinue were given a cool reception. The Thai government dissuaded Sihanouk from forming a government-in-exile and imposed a censorship on comment by its citizens on Cambodian affairs.[82] In the United Nations, Thailand failed to carry out Sihanouk's request that it bring the Cambodian case up for consideration.[83] The United States likewise remained silent on the issue. Sihanouk thereupon

[81] *Le Monde,* June 16, 1953.
[82] *New York Times,* June 19, 1953.
[83] *Ibid.,* June 22, 1953.

returned to Cambodia, where he stopped in Battambang, vowing to remain there until Cambodia was free.

In the meantime, tension mounted between French and Cambodians in Phnom Penh. French reinforcements were shipped to the capital to protect French lives and property, and a campaign of intimidation was begun. The French trained their artillery on the city, armed French citizens, and stationed Algerian, Moroccan, and Vietnamese soldiers at strategic points. On the Cambodian side, elements of the royal army, led by a former Khmer Issarak commander, Put Chhay, occupied all government buildings. In Battambang, Sihanouk made preparations for a nationwide revolution.[84]

Fortunately the French began to waver before plans for a revolution were put into effect. As they continued to suffer heavy losses in the fighting against the Viet Minh, they were forced into assuming a conciliatory attitude.[85] At first they offered "to complete the sovereignty and independence" of Cambodia, but on the basis of further negotiations. Sihanouk replied by demanding the complete transfer of control of the army, police, and judicial system.[86]

Eventually the French yielded on all points at issue.[87]

[84] See "Secret—Note Royale: Processus à suivre à partir de ce jour dans nos rapports avec la France," June 27, 1953, and "Extrait de la lettre royale addressée à S.E. Penn Nouth," July 18, 1953, in *La Grande Figure*, pp. 45–47 and 54, respectively.

[85] See *Livre Jaune, I*, pp. 133-134. See also *Le Monde*, July 3, 1953, and *New York Times*, July 4, 1953.

[86] See "Contre-proposition du Gouvernement Royal du Cambodge à la proposition Française contenue dans la déclaration du Gouvernement de la République en date du 3 juillet 1953," *Livre Jaune, I*, pp. 136-139. See also *Le Monde*, Aug. 29, 1953, and *New York Times*, Aug. 30, 1953.

[87] For the texts of the agreements reached between Cambodia and France, see Royaume du Cambodge, Ministère des Affaires Etrangères

Upon the transfer of military control, on October 17, 1953, Sihanouk, satisfied that his crusade had succeeded, began his triumphant tour through the countryside, arriving on November 8 in Phnom Penh, where he received a rousing welcome and was proclaimed a "national hero" in the liberation of Cambodia from French rule. The formal transfer of power took place in Phnom Penh on November 9, which has since been celebrated as Independence Day in Cambodia.

But no sooner had the celebrations ended than Sihanouk found himself faced with a renewal of internal political dissension. He was anxious to capitalize on his successful negotiations with France by holding new elections. The small parties, however, opposed the holding of elections because they feared another Democrat victory. The Democrats also protested, for they foresaw that, with his newly gained popularity, King Sihanouk would influence the outcome of the elections.

Sihanouk then made two radio broadcasts in which he threatened to abdicate unless the opposition accepted its responsibility.[88] He claimed that the opposition, by accusing him of weakness before the French, and belittling his role in the negotiations for independence, was undermining his prestige among the people and his control over the army. The parties responded to his threats with declarations of loyalty but did not come to agreement on elections.[89]

---

et des Conférences, *Accords, Protocoles, Conventions et Echanges de Lettres relatifs au transfert de toutes les compétences par le Gouvernement de la République Française au Gouvernement Royal du Cambodge* (Phnom Penh: Imprimerie Albert Portail, 1954), pp. 5–37.

[88] Radio Phnom Penh, Dec. 1 and 2, 1953.

[89] *Ibid.*, Dec. 5, 1953.

In a move to discredit the parties and to organize personally the military operations against the rebels and the Viet Minh, Sihanouk suddenly departed for Siem Reap. This action had the remarkable effect of bringing most of his opposition to heel. Two Khmer Issarak chiefs, Chantarangsey and Savangvong, began negotiations for the surrender of their combined force of some five thousand men. This left two dissident groups still holding out.

One was led by Son Ngoc Thanh. In February, 1954, his lieutenant, Ea Sichau, arrived in Phnom Penh to negotiate the terms of Son's surrender. These negotiations dragged on into the spring only to be caught up in the larger issue of the Geneva Conference of April–July, 1954. The other group was the Viet Minh's Khmer People's Liberation army, which later pressed its claims in Cambodia at Geneva. In April, 1954, the Viet Minh invaded northeastern Cambodia and occupied the town of Voeunsai. Sihanouk ordered a general mobilization and, himself assuming command of the Cambodian forces, succeeded in expelling the enemy.

During May–June, 1954, the spotlight was shifted to Geneva and attention was centered on an international solution of the whole Indochina problem. Thereafter the main trend in Cambodian politics was toward a consolidation of power in Sihanouk's hands.[90]

[90] For further details concerning internal political developments in Cambodia see Roger M. Smith, "Cambodia," in George McT. Kahin, ed., *Governments and Politics of Southeast Asia* (2d ed.; Ithaca, N.Y.: Cornell University Press, 1964), and Philippe Preschez, *Essai sur la démocratie au Cambodge,* Centre d'Etudes des Relations Internationales, Fondation Nationale des Sciences Politiques (Paris, 1961).

CHAPTER III

The Geneva Conference and the Development of a Foreign Policy

HAD the French in 1952–1953 been more sensitive to the predicament of King Sihanouk, whose continued popular influence depended upon his wresting the leadership of the nationalist movement from the increasingly vociferous antiroyalists, it is likely that today the French and the Cambodians would enjoy the same bond of friendship that unites the Philippines and the United States, and Malaysia and Great Britain.[1] For the Cambodians, while politically dominated by the French, had not been unduly oppressed or exploited by them and consequently did not dislike them with the fervor that marked Vietnamese sentiments.

Disillusionment with the West

Sihanouk's desire to retain French amity was frankly expressed in a letter to President Auriol of France in March, 1953.

---

[1] A close, friendly association has been maintained between Cambodia and France since 1953, but this has not included any specific commitments by France to Cambodia's defense such as those which characterize the relations between the United States and Great Britain and their former colonies.

The history of recent years . . . demonstrates that the new member-states of the Commonwealth have remained freely within the orbit of England, that each day Libya and Syria ask earnestly for the aid of French technicians, businessmen and industrialists, and that the Philippines, having become independent, accepted the installation of extremely powerful American bases on its territory without any recrimination.

I am convinced that independent Cambodia would follow these examples, as it would be in its interests to do so. It already appears, moreover, that no protests would be raised— quite the contrary—with regard to the presence of French personnel in our Services or in our Army, subject to our authority.[2]

A few months later in an interview accorded to the *New York Times,* he again revealed his hope that a postindependence alliance with France would be possible.

In case of a massive Viet Minh invasion [he said] we will count on the aid—material and armaments—of the United States of America. . . .

Moreover, we would welcome, with pleasure, whether we are within or outside of the French Union . . . action by France benefiting us with a military pact [and] some military bases.[3]

The French, however, appeared determined to fight to the finish for their stake in Indochina. It was only as the military superiority of the Viet Minh became evident that the French began to accede to some of the lesser demands of the Indochinese nationalists. In August, 1953, France agreed to transfer her rights in judicial and police matters to Cambodia. But it declined to yield to Cambodia's de-

[2] Gouvernement Royal du Cambodge, *Livre jaune sur les revendications de l'indépendance du Cambodge, I* (Paris: Imprimerie Centrale Commerciale, 1953), p. 13.

[3] *Ibid.,* p. 203.

mands for the return of military authority. In defense of this position France argued that to do so would leave Cambodia vulnerable to aggression by the Khmer Issarak and the Viet Minh. The United States, which appeared to Sihanouk to be "blinded by the morbid fear of communism," [4] took the French side in this issue. The defeat of Communism in Southeast Asia was to the United States a matter of greater priority than the increasing restlessness of countries which yearned to divest themselves of foreign control.

To deprive France of her remaining objection to the complete relinquishment of authority in Cambodia, Sihanouk in September instructed Penn Nouth to warn the Khmer Issarak to surrender to the government lest they be punished as traitors and to call upon the Viet Minh to quit Cambodia. Penn Nouth's message in part read as follows:

Vietminh! You who operate in the Kingdom under the pretext of aiding our country to realize its independence, the Royal Government wishes to inform you that we have obtained it by our own means, as has been shown to you by the events of this week.

Although we are not communists, we have no quarrel with communism as long as it does not seek to impose itself on us by force. . . .

Vietminh, it is incumbent upon us not to contest your right to occupy Vietnam. We ask you only to let us live our life and leave our national soil.[5]

---

[4] Norodom Sihanouk, *La monarchie cambodgienne et la croisade royale pour l'indépendance* (Phnom Penh: Imprimerie Rasmey, 1961), p. 94. See also *Livre Jaune, I*, pp. 209–210.

[5] Gouvernement Royal du Cambodge, *Livre Jaune sur les revendications de l'indépendance du Cambodge*, II (Phnom Penh: Im-

In this message Cambodia for the first time publicly asserted her position on the issue of Communism. The reaction of the West, especially of the United States, was swift and harsh. The United States threatened to terminate its aid, which since 1951 had totaled $25 million.[6] The Cambodians were accused of committing themselves to a neutral policy that would hamper the prosecution of the war against the Viet Minh.

At this time the Cambodians were still trying to win acceptance by the West. In a reply prepared by King Sihanouk during his exile in Siem Reap, Penn Nouth denied that Cambodia was embarking upon a neutral policy. He reiterated:

I have said, and I repeat, that the realization of our independence should confound the Viet Minh, and that if, despite this, the Viet Minh persist in tormenting us, we should be authorized by our People to fight to the death against this enemy.[7]

Further on in the text he said:

The fact that we cannot receive aid directly from the United States, the fact that one wishes to cut off economic aid to us if we refuse to fight against the communists outside of Cambodia, the fact that one will not grant us the right in principle of considering a priori communism and communist governments other than as mortal enemies, when outside of

---

primerie du Palais Royal, 1954), p. 57. Hereafter cited as *Livre Jaune, II.* [Italics added.]

[6] American aid to Cambodia was channeled via France. For the details of this arrangement, see "Economic Cooperation Agreement and Notes between the United States of America and Cambodia, Sept. 8, 1951," *Treaties and Other International Acts Series 2343* (Washington, D.C.: Government Printing Office, 1952).

[7] *Livre Jaune, II,* p. 62.

Cambodia one admits communist representatives in his own National Assembly and one permits himself to maintain diplomatic relations with those towards whom one pushes us to fight to the death, when, moreover, one reserves to himself the right to sign armistices with them, without taking into account the will of the people that one pushes into war, the fact that small countries have only the right to execute what their larger "allies or friends" have ordered, these "major powers" reserving to themselves the right to begin or end a war in the small countries, ignoring the opinion of the latter —all these facts *trouble* me.

We, the inhabitants of this small country, who worry as must as our "friends" and who are perhaps going to die for our "idealism" that no one tolerates, we ask ourselves if there is justice on this earth, if the small peoples are permitted to live freely and to cooperate on an equal footing with the large powers, and if it is normal that a small nation be condemned to die, condemned as malevolent because it refuses to buy its life at the shameful price of abdication of a free and conscious people.

I pose this case of conscience to the world, in the hope that it will accord its attention to the problem of my country and my people, who are at the point of death because of the incomprehension or the malice which surrounds them, for this problem is perhaps one of the elements of the larger problem, the solution to which humanity has up to now searched for in vain: that of peace and concord among men on earth.[8]

On the same day, at a conference with Senator William Knowland, who happened to be visiting Indochina at the time, and the American ambassador to Saigon, Donald Heath, Penn Nouth declared that Cambodia would not participate in the fight against Communism until it had been granted independence from France and direct aid

[8] *Ibid.*, p. 64.

from the United States.[9] Penn Nouth reported, "The Americans were unable to furnish me with a satisfactory response on this point."[10]

With independence finally won in November, 1953, the Khmer Issarak disbanded, and only a few hundred among them chose to continue lending their loyalty to Son Ngoc Thanh, reportedly in hiding in the northwest. There remained, however, the Khmer resistance government that had been set up in the south by the Viet Minh and its military arm, the Khmer People's Liberation army, which is believed to have drawn its recruits from local Vietnamese. While this "rival government" never seriously threatened the legitimate one, it nevertheless served the purpose intended by the Viet Minh: as a symbol of the widespread popular support claimed by Viet Minh propaganda.[11] In the spring of 1954 a Viet Minh invasion of Stung Treng province, launched from southern Laos, prompted Cambodia to appeal for direct military aid from the United States.

The Cambodian request for military aid came at a time when the deteriorating military situation in Vietnam had aroused alarm in the United States over the possible loss of Indochina to Communist forces. The decision of France to settle the war at a conference in Geneva did not meet with the full approval of the United States, which felt that compromise with the Communist powers would place Indochina on the same pathway taken by Czechoslovakia and the other Soviet satellites.[12] Moreover,

[9] "Compte-rendu de S.E. Penn Nouth à Sa Majesté le Roi sur son entretien avec le Sénateur Knowland," *ibid.*, pp. 68–69.

[10] *Ibid.*, p. 69.

[11] See *Viet Nam Information* (Viet Nam News Service, Rangoon, Burma), various numbers during Mar.–June, 1954.

[12] Undated news bulletin, Royal Embassy of Cambodia, Washing-

with the battle of Dien Bien Phu it had become evident that the West could not negotiate from a position of strength. On March 29, 1954, Secretary of State John Foster Dulles alerted the world to a sharp turn in American policy when he said:

Under the conditions of today, the imposition on Southeast Asia of the political system of Communist Russia and its Chinese Communist ally, by whatever means, would be a grave threat to the whole free world community. The United States feels that possibility should not be passively accepted but should be met by united action. This might have serious risks. But these risks are far less than those that will face us a few years from now if we dare not be resolute today.[13]

In subsequent talks with Congressional leaders, the Eisenhower administration apparently considered intervention in Vietnam without allied support,[14] but the reluctance of Congress as well as of the President and certain American military personnel [15] to undertake unilateral action

---

ton, D.C. See also *New York Times,* May 21, 1954, and U.S. Department of State, *American Foreign Policy, Current Documents, 1956,* (Washington, D.C.: Government Printing Office, 1959), p. 790.

[13] See Department of State *Bulletin,* XXX (Apr., 1954), no. 772, pp. 539–549, for the text of Dulles' statement.

[14] See the statement of John W. McCormack, Democratic leader of the House of Representatives, in *Congressional Record,* Feb. 22, 1955, p. 1655. See also Chalmers M. Roberts, "The Day We Didn't Go to War," *The Reporter,* XI, no. 14 (Sept. 14, 1954).

[15] See Robert J. Donovan, *Eisenhower: The Inside Story* (New York: Harper & Bros., 1956), pp. 262–263; Miriam Farley, *United States Relations with Southeast Asia, with Special Reference to Indochina, 1950–1954* (New York: Institute of Pacific Relations, 1955), p. 10; Jean Lacouture and Philippe Devillers, *La fin d'une guerre, Indochine 1954* (Paris: Editions du Seuil, 1960), p. 71; Roberts, *op. cit.,* pp. 31–35; and *Soldier—The Memoirs of Matthew B. Ridgway* (as told to Harold H. Martin) (New York: Harper & Bros., 1956), pp. 276–277.

obliged Dulles to seek the commitment of the other Western powers. On April 4, President Dwight D. Eisenhower approved a proposal by Dulles that an effort be made to persuade Britain to join with the United States, France, and friendly Asian powers in opposing Communist forces in Indochina.[16] During the next few days, Dulles met with the Washington representatives of the nations likely to be concerned: Great Britain, France, Australia, New Zealand, the Philippines, Thailand, Cambodia, Laos, and Vietnam.[17]

Britain and France rejected the American proposal. The French, economically exhausted by the Indochina war, had now resigned themselves to a negotiated solution, and they like the British feared that American entry into the conflict would only enlarge and prolong it.[18]

---

[16] See *The Memoirs of Anthony Eden: Full Circle* (Boston: Houghton Mifflin, 1960), p. 103. According to Donovan's account, "in agreeing to submit the proposal for united action to Churchill, the President laid down certain conditions that would have to be met before the United States could move into Indochina with its allies. Prominent among them was that Congress must first authorize American participation in any military action. The other conditions were these: (1) Britain must participate. Implicit in this, in the American view, was participation also by Australia and New Zealand. (2) France and the Associated States—Vietnam, Cambodia and Laos—must invite the United States and the allies to join them in their struggle. (3) France must agree to stay in the war and see it through. (4) France must go beyond her previous efforts in granting unequivocal independence to Vietnam, Laos, and Cambodia so that American entry into Indo-China would not have the taint of colonialism." See Donovan, *op. cit.*, p. 265. Quoted by permission of Harper & Row, Publishers.

[17] *New York Times*, Apr. 7, 1954.

[18] See France, *Journal Officiel, Débats*, Apr. 10, 1954, pp. 1972–1973. By the beginning of 1954, it had become clear that French opinion was averse to the continuation of the war. The only question then seemed to be whether the war's end should be on the

In the United States, Congress also displayed reluctance to support America's entry into the Indochina war.[19] An informal poll of Congressmen conducted by the administration revealed "no more than five men at most" who unequivocally voiced their approval of quick and decisive action.[20] Congress reflected the mood of 85 per cent of the American people as assessed by the Gallup poll in March.[21]

At a press conference on April 29, the President clearly indicated the United States had now resigned itself to accomplishing less than it wanted to in Indochina.[22] The reversal of policy required a discounting of the previously inflated estimates of the strategic importance of Indochina to the rest of Southeast Asia. Thus, on May 11 Dulles asserted that Indochina was not vital to the defense of

---

basis of bilateral French–Viet Minh talks, or in the framework of a larger conference. See *ibid.*, Mar. 6, 1954, pp. 713–715, and *Le Monde*, Mar. 31, 1954. For an indication of British opinion, see Eden, *op. cit.*, pp. 103–108; *The Times* (London), Apr. 9, 1954, and the *Manchester Guardian*, Apr. 10, 1954. The reaction of the Indochina states at this time is not known.

[19] See *Congressional Record*, Apr. 6, 1954, pp. 4401–4410.

[20] *Christian Science Monitor*, Apr. 29, 1954.

[21] See *U.S. News & World Report*, May 7, 1954, pp. 25–26. Several "trial balloons" were raised by the Eisenhower administration during late March and April in order both to persuade the public of the danger of American security stemming from Indochina and to test its reaction to the possibility of U.S. intervention. These soundings included Dulles' speeches of March 29 and April 5; Eisenhower's press conference of April 7, in which he used the analogy of a line of falling dominoes, saying that the American defense system based on a chain of islands from Japan to the Philippines would be imperiled if Indochina were lost; and Vice-President Nixon's speech of April 16, in which he linked Indochina to Japan's importance as an industrial center and said that in the unlikely circumstance of French withdrawal the United States would have to send troops to Indochina.

[22] *New York Times*, Apr. 30, 1954.

Southeast Asia.[23] The initial reaction of France and the Indochina states to the new American position was that of dismay, for to them it signified that the United States was prepared to abandon Indochina. That this was not the case was explained by the chief American delegate to the Geneva Conference, Under Secretary of State W. Bedell Smith, who revealed that the United States was now planning to set up a collective defense system in Southeast Asia which would defend the area from further Communist incursion. The participation of the Indochina states in this system would be crucial to its success, he said. What Dulles meant, he went on, was that if for unforeseeable reasons Indochina were to fall to Communist forces, the United States would not renounce in a desperate gesture the defense of the rest of Southeast Asia.[24] The interpretation of observers at Geneva of the American position was as follows:

For the United States, Indochina is still important but it has ceased to be essential. . . . The fate of Indochina being decided altogether on the battleground, at Geneva and at Paris, or in places out of American control, the United States cannot and does not want to undertake any firm commitment on this subject.

The American attitude seems to be that so long as France does not abandon Indochina, the United States will support her as much as it can. If France gives up and Indochina falls into Communist hands the United States would attempt to limit the damage by a system of collective security. The United States is not disposed to abandon the Associated States but its attitude depends in a great measure on the will of resistance

---

[23] See *Ibid.*, May 11 and May 13, 1954. Cf. U.S. Department of State *Bulletin*, May 24, 1954, p. 782.

[24] See Lacouture and Devillers, *op. cit.*, pp. 172–173.

of the interested parties. They will help those who do not abandon themselves.[25]

The Geneva Conference on Indochina, 1954

The Geneva Conference on Indochina convened on May 8, 1954.[26] Represented at the conference were the United States, France, Great Britain, the Soviet Union, the Chinese People's Republic, Cambodia, Laos, the Republic of Vietnam, and the Democratic Republic of Vietnam. Following the initial French statement of its position, that the situation in Vietnam was one of civil war, and that in Cambodia and Laos it was a matter of Viet Minh invasions, the delegate of the Democratic Republic of Vietnam (DRV), Pham Van Dong, posed what was to become one of two major issues at the talks: should the resistance government set up by the Viet Minh-supported Cambodian Communists be regarded as the undertaking of local elements or should it be viewed as the work of foreign forces? To settle this issue, he strongly urged representation at the conference of the Cambodian Communists. His demand was opposed by the Cambodian delegates, Tep Phan, Nong Kimny, and Sam Sary, as well as by the United States, France, and Great Britain. The Cambodians argued that the only legal government in Cambodia was the royal government, which had been instrumental in secur-

[25] *Ibid.,* p. 173.

[26] The major documents of the conference are Great Britain, *Documents Relating to the Discussions of Korea and Indo-China at the Geneva Conference, April 27–June 15, 1954.* Cmd. 9186, Misc. No. 16 (London: H.M. Stationery Office, 1954; hereafter cited as *Documents, Cmd. 9186)* , and *Further Documents Relating to the Discussion of Indo-China at the Geneva Conference, June 16–July 21, 1954.* Cmd. 9239, Misc. No. 20 (London: H.M. Stationery Office, 1954; hereafter cited as *Further Documents, Cmd. 9239).*

ing independence from France.[27] Replying to DRV charges of American imperialism in Indochina, which menaced the peace in Southeast Asia, Tep Phan asserted:

The United States wishes to conform to its tradition of liberty, to protect my country against foreign aggression. The United States does not wish to create a colonial empire. It wishes simply to furnish us with the means of preserving our independence and to prevent our country from becoming a colony of communist imperialism.[28]

Vyacheslav Molotov and Chou En-lai added the support of the Soviet Union and China to the DRV proposal, but both suggested that the matter be settled in private discussions. The question was not disposed of until late in June, when Chou En-lai recognized the legitimacy of the Sihanouk government and acknowledged that it alone had obtained Cambodia's independence.[29]

The second major issue grew out of the DRV demand that a cease-fire be made contingent upon the acceptance by the conference of its terms for a political settlement.[30] Chou En-lai again supported his Vietnamese colleague, arguing specifically for the demilitarization and neutralization of Cambodia. Cambodia refused to accept the DRV

[27] See *Conférence de Genève de 1954: Compte rendu sténographique provisoire* (unofficial), F/I.C./PV.1, May 8, 1954. See also *Documents, Cmd. 9186,* pp. 107–114.

[28] *Conférence de Genève,* F/I.C./PV.2, May 10, 1954, and F/I.C./PV.3, May 12, 1954. See also *ibid.,* F/I.C./PV.4, May 14, 1954, and "Observations de la Délégation cambodgienne sur le plan présenté par le Viet-Minh," *ibid., Documents,* IC/11, May 14, 1954.

[29] Molotov apparently played a key role in resolving this difference. See Eden, *op. cit.,* pp. 130, 131–132, 136, 140.

[30] See *Conférence de Genève,* F/I.C./PV.4, May 14, 1954, and *Documents, Cmd. 9186,* pp. 116–118.

proposal, insisting that while it did not intend to authorize the establishment of foreign military bases on its territory or to use its armed forces for aggressive purposes, it would not countenance any restrictions on its right to act in accordance with the United Nations Charter or to solicit military aid in the interests of its own defense.[31] On June 16, after discussions with Anthony Eden on the future of Cambodia, Chou proposed that all foreign troops be withdrawn from that country and military talks be held between Cambodia and the DRV. He agreed that Cambodia should be permitted to receive arms aid up to the level required for defense but stipulated that it should not become a base for the United States. It was not openly admitted that the Viet Minh had in fact invaded Cambodia, but there was little doubt that they were meant to be included among the "foreign troops" which Chou was prepared to see withdrawn.

At this point, the first phase of the conference was concluded, and the delegates were permitted to return to their respective capitals.

Following the reconvening of the conference on July 12, agreement was quickly reached on the composition and functions of the International Commissions for Supervision and Control, which were to oversee the implementation of the Geneva decisions in each of the three Indochina states. Before this was accomplished, on July 18, a series of restricted meetings were held by the British, Russian, and Chinese delegates at which assurances on the status of Cambodia and Laos were traded. Chou En-lai's main concern was the Five-Power talks, then being held in Washington, on the advisability of establishing a defense

[31] See *Conférence de Genève*, F/I.C./PV.17, June 8, 1954, and F/I.C./PV.20, June 9, 1954.

system in Southeast Asia. Chou told Eden that he would guarantee withdrawal of Viet Minh troops from Cambodia and Laos, and that China would recognize their governments, provided that there were no American bases established in their territories.[32] Eden gave his unofficial assurance to Chou that the three states would remain free of foreign military bases [33] and agreed to the neutralization of Cambodia and Laos as buffer states between Vietnam and Thailand. Their defense would be assured by France within the French Union, but they would be prohibited from allying themselves with other nations. From this point, the conference moved rapidly toward a successful conclusion.

By the evening of July 20 the agreements were almost complete. However:

The Cambodians skillfully held out till last, when we were exhausted. Molotov and I, as joint-chairmen, together with Mendès-France, held a long meeting with them and the Viet Minh. At two o'clock on the morning of the 21st, after hard bargaining and some surprising last-minute concessions by Molotov, we succeeded in resolving the remaining differences between them.[34]

Cambodia's delegates had refused, categorically, to associate their country with the general agreements, for in

[32] Eden, *op. cit.*, p. 145.

[33] *Ibid.*, p. 158. These personal agreements between Eden and Chou were never written into the Geneva accords, but they were later referred to by both leaders. See Great Britain, *Parliamentary Debates. House of Commons, Official Reports,* 5th Series, Vol. 530, 1954, col. 1571 (July 22, 1954), and *New China News Agency,* July 21, 1954, in *Survey of China Mainland Press,* no. 853 (Hong Kong, U.S. Consulate-General), pp. 6–7.

[34] Eden, *op. cit.* p. 159. Quoted with permission of the publisher, Houghton Mifflin Co.

spite of the concessions made by Chou En-lai to her position, the final agreement was still judged to be incompatible with Cambodia's sovereignty. When after a delay all of the key members of the Cambodian delegation arrived at the meeting at Eden's residence, the Villa des Ormeaux,[35] they were asked to sign the documents which would have made their country neutral in international affairs. They refused, much to the exasperation of Molotov, who was impatient for the conference to end. Cambodia would not add her signature, they said, until their demands were met. They reiterated their right to engage in any military alliance in conformity with the principles of the United Nations Charter and the right to permit the establishment of such foreign bases as they considered to be essential to their security. To the surprise of everyone present, and over the angry protests of Pham Van Dong, Molotov declared suddenly that he would accept this amendment.[36]

Second, Cambodia insisted on her right to have arms and foreign military personnel introduced into Cambodia at any point on the Cambodian frontier. The Viet Minh

[35] The meeting had been scheduled for 9 P.M., but the Cambodians did not arrive until nearly 11:30 because they had been awaiting word on the outcome of the Cambodian–Viet Minh military talks which were proceeding simultaneously with the political negotiations, and because the delegates' chauffeur, unfamiliar with Geneva's streets, had become lost on the way. This account is based on private communications to the author from Cambodian sources he regards as reliable. See also Sam Sary, *Conférence publique sur les accords de Genève et les Elections générales au Cambodge, 23 août 1955* (Phnom Penh, 1955), pp. 59–60, and Lacouture and Devillers, *op. cit.,* p. 270.

[36] This discussion of Cambodia's position and Viet Minh reaction is based on private communications to the author from Cambodian sources he regards as reliable.

had wished this to be restricted to a few points of entry. The conference submitted to the Cambodian demands.

Third, Cambodia wanted prior agreement on the total withdrawal of the Viet Minh forces and disarmament of the resistance elements. The Viet Minh had proposed that the Cambodians who had collaborated with the Viet Minh should be allowed to retain their arms and to regroup themselves in a specified zone in Cambodia until national elections were held. Faced with Cambodian opposition to this demand, the Viet Minh then proposed the establishment of a mixed commission, composed of representatives of the Cambodian government and the Cambodian resistance movement, which would "study the means of treating the elements of the resistance movement, their incorporation into the national community, the decision of the Commission being supervised by the International Control Commission." [37] On this issue Molotov, despite the protests of the Viet Minh, again sided with the Cambodians, who were unwilling to bestow any form of recognition upon the resistance government.

The Cambodians also rejected Russia's proposal that the International Control Commissions be coordinated by a special organization. They feared that under such an arrangement, Cambodia would again find her affairs being directed from Saigon, headquarters of the former Federation of Indochina and the site proposed by Russia as the seat of the special organization.

At 2 A.M., July 21, 1954, with all of her demands met, Cambodia lent her signature to the agreement. [38] The only

---

[37] Sam Sary, *op. cit.*, p. 62.

[38] For the text of the Cambodian agreement, see *Further Documents, Cmd. 9239*, pp. 13–14.

restrictions to which Cambodia submitted herself were as follows:

The Royal Government of Cambodia will not join in any agreement with other States, *if* this agreement carries for Cambodia the obligation to enter into military alliances *not in conformity with the principles of the Charter of the United Nations,* or, *as long as its security is not threatened,* the obligation to establish bases on Cambodian territory for the military forces of foreign powers.[39]

Cambodia Seeks an American Commitment

Thus, at Geneva, Cambodia displayed the same perseverance in negotiating for a cease-fire and for international recognition of her freedom of action in foreign affairs that Norodom Sihanouk had revealed in his dealings with France. To be sure, American, British, and French opposition to the Communist powers helped to make her task easier. But it was the insistence of the Cambodians themselves which won for them two major concessions: evacuation of Viet Minh troops within ninety days of the armistice and agreement that Cambodia would exercise her sovereign right to enter into alliance and receive such foreign aid as was deemed necessary for her security.

Less successful were Cambodia's efforts to obtain a definite American guarantee of her defense in case of attack. The events of April, 1954, had convinced Cambodia that the prospective Geneva agreement would allow her only a brief respite before the Viet Minh would assume control of all Vietnam and then direct their efforts toward the subjugation of Cambodia and Laos. Feelers issued by Cambodia to test United States reaction to a formal request for a commitment to her defense revealed that

[39] *Ibid.* (Italics added.)

the United States believed she could not undertake such a commitment without violating the unofficial assurances given by Eden to Chou En-lai that Cambodia would abstain from participating in any alliance with a Western power. Cambodia then sought acceptance into the Southeast Asia regional defense system which the United States was about to organize, but again she was informed that her participation in the alliance would undermine the Geneva negotiations. W. Bedell Smith, the American Under Secretary of State, tried to assuage Cambodia's anxieties by assuring her that she would be sheltered by an "umbrella of protection" provided by the new Southeast Asia defense system.[40]

On July 20, the Cambodians, who were about to sign the final Geneva agreement, tried to press the United States into specifying how far she would be willing to

[40] The foregoing is based on private communications to the author from official Cambodian and American sources. During July an Anglo–American "working group" was organized to consider the form which a Southeast Asian defense agreement might take, and also the form of a possible international guarantee to underpin the Geneva agreement (*New York Times*, July 2, 1954). On the problem of whether Cambodia and the other Indochina states were eligible for inclusion in the pact, Dulles was reported to have taken the view that it was "not clear" whether they could become members, but that they could be included in the area of its protection (*New York Times*, July 24, 1954). Britain was believed to consider that there could be no question of Cambodia's membership, since the sense of Eden's agreement with Chou En-lai had been that they should be neutralized, but she did not regard this as preventing the alliance from being so drawn as to safeguard Cambodia. In his report to President Eisenhower after the Manila conference, Dulles wrote that "the Indochina situation was considered by some of the treaty signatories as creating obstacles to those three countries [Cambodia, Laos, Vietnam] becoming actual parties to the treaty at the present time." See U.S. Department of State *Bulletin*, XXXI, no. 805 (Nov. 29, 1954), p. 823.

commit herself in Cambodia's behalf, especially if their country should yield to the proposal of France and the Communist powers that she be included in the buffer-state plan already accepted by Laos.[41] Would the United States, for example, commit her troops to Cambodia in the event of Communist aggression or subversion? According to high official Cambodian sources, Under Secretary Smith's response was to turn to a map of Southeast Asia and indicate that troops might be sent into—Thailand. As one might expect, this answer did not satisfy the Cambodians.

A protocol of the Southeast Asia Collective Defense Treaty, which was signed in Manila on September 8, 1954, included Cambodia within its area of protection, and provided that the signatories would come to her defense in case of foreign aggression.[42] Secretary of State Dulles

[41] The Laotian delegates had already accepted the limitations imposed on Laos' foreign policy by an unofficial agreement between Eden, Mendès-France and Chou En-lai. These prohibited Laos from permitting the establishment of foreign military bases in Laos, entering into political or military alliances, and allowing the introduction of foreign troops and armaments. To Cambodians, this meant that Laos was to be a neutralized buffer state.

[42] The Protocol of the Treaty reads: "The Parties to the Southeast Asia Collective Defense Treaty unanimously designate for the purposes of Article IV of the Treaty the States of Cambodia and Laos and the free territory under the jurisdiction of the State of Vietnam."

Article IV reads: "1. Each Party recognizes that aggression by means of armed attack in the treaty area against any of the Parties or against any State or territory which the Parties by unanimous agreement may hereafter designate, would endanger its own peace and safety, and agrees that it will in that event act to meet the common danger in accordance with its constitutional processes. Measures taken under this paragraph shall be immediately reported to the Security Council of the United Nations.

"2. If, in the opinion of any of the Parties, the inviolability or

was explicit in his description of the type of military commitment the United States envisaged for the treaty area. He wrote:

The responsibilities of the United States are so vast and far-flung that we believe we would serve best not by earmarking forces for particular areas of the Far East but by developing the deterrent of mobile striking power plus strategically placed reserves.[43]

Underlying this persistent unwillingness to offer a specific guarantee of security in Southeast Asia was the same reluctance to act unless supported by her European allies which the United States had displayed during the Dien Bien Phu crisis. There was now an extremely strong

---

the integrity of the territory or the sovereignty or political independence of any Party in the treaty area or of any other State or territory to which the provisions of paragraph 1 of this Article from time to time apply is threatened in any way other than by armed attack or is affected or threatened by any fact or situation which might endanger the peace of the area, the Parties shall consult immediately in order to agree on the measures which should be taken for the common defense."

The United States appended an "understanding" to the treaty which stipulates that "its recognition of the effect of aggression and armed attack and its agreement with reference thereto in Article IV, paragraph 1, apply only to Communist aggression, but affirms that in the event of other aggression or armed attack it will consult under the provisions of Article IV, paragraph 2." See U.S. Department of State *Bulletin*, XXXI, no. 795 (Sept. 30, 1954), pp. 393–396.

[43] U.S. Department of State *Bulletin*, XXXI, no. 805, p. 882. Some of the SEATO members were displeased by the American reluctance to commit the United States. See Roger M. Smith, "The Philippines and the Southeast Asia Treaty Organization," in Roger M. Smith and Mary F. Somers, *Two Papers on Philippines Foreign Policy,* Data Paper no. 38, Southeast Asia Program, Department of Far Eastern Studies, Cornell University, Ithaca, N.Y., Jan., 1960, pp. 9–22.

aversion to deploying American troops in circumstances considered less favorable than in Korea, where a military stalemate had turned American opinion against similar ventures.

Although in 1955 the United States agreed to provide Cambodia with military aid and instituted a large-scale economic aid program in the kingdom, there was little disposition to risk her troops beyond her perimeter of defense, extending from the Aleutian Islands southward through Japan and Formosa to the Philippines. Significantly, at the Manila conference, the only SEATO member to which the United States was prepared to offer a firm commitment was the Philippines, which was conveniently situated at the end of the United States western Pacific defenses, and to which she had a very special relationship. At the Bangkok meeting of the SEATO Council in February, 1955, the United States continued to refuse to commit her forces specifically to the treaty area.[44]

Apart from the unwillingness of SEATO's strongest member to make specific commitments in Southeast Asia, SEATO's organization suggested another failing that may have prompted Cambodia's reservations concerning the protection it offered. In the Indochina crisis, the United States had displayed her unwillingness to take action without the cooperation and support of her principal allies, Great Britain and France. Having differing concepts of priority, these powers failed in 1954 to demonstrate solidarity with the United States. The history of SEATO since its formation has been marked by such divergence of opinion. A well-informed observer of SEATO affairs has remarked:

[44] Smith, *op. cit.*, pp. 21–23.

A major determinant of the . . . effectiveness of the organization is the degree of cooperation between the three major powers. Whenever they disagree, SEATO is powerless and the separate policies of the three partners in Southeast Asia cannot prosper. American and British policies toward Communist China have diverged for at least a decade, with noticeable effect on all SEATO operations.[45]

It is not suggested here that American reluctance and the shortcomings of SEATO were the sole factors influencing Cambodia toward an independent foreign policy. These were only part of the picture. Other possible contributing factors will be considered shortly.

Development of a Neutral Foreign Policy

The first public indication that Cambodia was prepared to adopt a neutral foreign policy was given in November, 1954, following King Sihanouk's return from a state visit to Burma. Speaking before a welcoming crowd in Phnom Penh he urged that

in order to safeguard themselves, the large and small nations of Southeast Asia should deploy all of their good will in order to create a center of pacific resistance to all pacts or alliances susceptible to provoking world conflicts. That is to say, a large group of nations should observe neutrality strictly.[46]

The policy of neutrality was formally declared on Decem-

[45] George Modelski, "SEATO: Its Function and Organization," in George Modelski, ed., *SEATO: Six Studies* (Melbourne: Cheshire, 1962), p. 5. It was partly in response to this shortcoming that in 1962 the United States, in an agreement with Thailand, transformed SEATO into a virtual bilateral mutual defense alliance. See the declaration of Secretary of State Rusk and Foreign Minister Thanat Khoman on March 6 in Department of State *Bulletin*, XLVI, no. 1187, (Mar. 26, 1962), p. 498.

[46] *La Liberté*, Nov. 24, 1954.

ber 23, when Premier Penn Nouth announced that Cambodia would thenceforth assume a neutral position in the cold war. While his government would continue to welcome aid from the United States and France, he explained, it would be unwilling to sign any aid agreement which would compromise Cambodia's freedom of action in foreign affairs.[47]

It is clear that at this time the Cambodian government still regarded North Vietnam as the most serious threat to its independence. Nor did it have any illusions about China, which had backed the Viet Minh's demand at Geneva for recognition of the Khmer resistance government. Thus despite the American refusal to commit herself to Cambodia's defense, it was to the United States and France that Cambodia continued to look for economic and military assistance. The decision to abandon attempts to gain a defense commitment from the West was only in part due to the disappointing American reaction. Growing unrest among the country's politicians necessitated a careful revaluation of Cambodia's foreign policy in terms of its domestic implications. Since January, 1953, when he dissolved the National Assembly on grounds that it was obstructing negotiations with France for independence, King Sihanouk had enjoyed absolute powers. But now that independence had been won and the Viet Minh had been expelled, his political opponents were agitating for new elections. Beginning in the summer of 1954, there were reports of increasing political activity, of which the most alarming to King Sihanouk was a rumor that Son Ngoc Thanh, from his headquarters in the forests of Siem Reap, was organizing a "popular movement" through

[47] Radio Phnom Penh, Dec. 24, 1954.

which he planned to participate in the elections. Sihanouk is said to have feared Son Ngoc Thanh more than any other person, for the latter's widespread popularity made him a formidable opponent. Moreover, the leadership of the Democrat party, which had won over two-thirds of the seats in the National Assembly in the two previous elections, was believed to be dominated by men loyal to Son. In the early part of Son Ngoc Thanh's career as a nationalist, he had been befriended by Sihanouk.[48] But when, in the early 1950's, Son organized rebel forces against the French and disseminated charges that Sihanouk was a servant of France, he incurred the latter's lasting enmity.[49] In an attempt to prevent another Democrat victory, the king assigned to his trusted adviser, Yem Sambaur, the task of effecting a coalition of all the parties which would participate in the elections as the Sahapak (Union) party. The plan was that the candidates would run on a single platform, with the agreement that after the election the cabinet portfolios would be distributed equally among the parties.[50] It is possible that at this time Sihanouk and his advisers saw that a foreign policy of neutrality was the least likely to meet with the resistance of those whose cooperation was sought. A neutral policy would not only facilitate

[48] It was partly as a result of Sihanouk's intervention in 1945 that Son's sentence to death by a French military tribunal was changed to one of exile in France.

[49] See Sihanouk's reply to Son Ngoc Thanh's petition in 1954 for a royal audience, as published in *Kampuchea* (Phnom Penh), Jan. 20, 1955.

[50] Sambaur succeeded in organizing the united front, without, however, the participation of the Democrats. Later domestic political developments led to the dissolution of the Sahapak party before the elections. See Roger M. Smith, "Cambodia," in George McT. Kahin, ed., *Governments and Politics of Southeast Asia* (2d ed.; Ithaca, N.Y.: Cornell Univ. Press, 1964), pp. 619–624.

unification of diverse parties but would also deprive those who chose to remain in opposition of an important political issue. A policy of alignment, adopted so soon after the struggle for independence, would almost certainly have placed in the hands of the adversaries a lethal propaganda weapon. By espousing a neutral policy, however, the king forced into a defensive position those who would have tried to use foreign policy as a campaign issue.[51]

If King Sihanouk was in need of reassurances that in committing his country to a neutral policy he had performed a wise act, he probably received many from U Nu during his visit to Burma in November and in his talks with India's Prime Minister, Nehru, in Phnom Penh a few days later. Nehru in particular, during this period, had openly expressed concern about the growing bipolarization of power in the world and had sharply criticized the formation of SEATO. He argued persuasively that the former Indochina states should remain unaligned and thereby "form part of the area of peace." [52] He warned that SEATO, by renewing old fears and feelings of insecurity, would stimulate actions which would undermine the Geneva agreements.[53] In the light of Nehru's convictions, it would not be surprising if he had taken advantage of his visit to Cambodia to extol the merits of a policy of nonalignment.

It is important to note that the Cambodian government's initial statement of neutrality implied no more than a decision to abstain from alignment with the West. The

51 This discussion reflects in part the views of official Cambodians to whom the author talked.

52 Quoted in the *Statesman* (New Delhi), July 31, 1954.

53 See the Lok Sabha, *Debates*, Vol. VII, Part 2, no. 30 (Sept. 29, 1954), col. 3672. See also the *Hindustan Weekly Review* (New Delhi), Aug. 30 and Sept. 13, 1954.

neutrality to which she committed herself was passive; the king did not at that time seek to counterbalance Western influence in Cambodia with that of the Communist bloc.[54]

In March, 1955, shortly after abdicating the throne and forming his own political movement, the Sangkum Reastr Niyum (People's Socialist Community),[55] Sihanouk

---

[54] At this time, relations with France were conducted through the French High Commissioner in Phnom Penh. The United States did not establish its embassy in the Cambodian capital until early 1955. Relations with the Soviet Union were entered into in 1956. Although Cambodia negotiated an economic aid agreement with China in 1956, diplomatic recognition of the People's Republic was not accorded by Cambodia until mid-1958.

[55] On Mar. 2, 1955, Sihanouk relinquished his crown and appointed his father, Prince Norodom Suramarit, king. He gave as the reason for his abdication his desire to work more closely with his people, a desire that he found difficult to fulfill on the throne because of the traditional distance between the king and his subjects. (See Sihanouk's address to the nation, Mar. 15, 1955, in *Agence Khmère de Presse* (Phnom Penh, Mar. 15, 1955). The people, however, have continued to regard him as their ruler. His abdication occurred a few weeks before the 1955 elections, when it appeared that the Democrats would again be the victors. Believing that the legislature rather than the executive should be the seat of real power, the Democrats had persistently opposed urgent measures for economic and social reform put forward by the government and had brought about one cabinet crisis after another. One of Prince Sihanouk's first actions upon stepping down from the throne was to organize the Sangkum Reastr Niyum, through which he hoped to prevent another victory by the Democrats. He set its objectives so broad that he was able to attract to its fold diverse political groups which until then had been competing with one another. In the election, which was postponed to September, the Sangkum appeared on the ballot as the only major contender against the Democrats, and having the advantage of Sihanouk's name associated with it, the Sangkum succeeded in realizing an overwhelming victory. Because of Prince Sihanouk's own efforts, the Sangkum is the first and only political organization in Cambodia

visited Prime Minister Nehru in New Delhi, where, on the eighteenth, he "expressed his appreciation of India's general approach to world problems and desire for the maintenance of peace." [56] The two leaders agreed to support the principles of peaceful coexistence, which they believed to be the best guarantee for peace in the world.

The lines of Cambodia's foreign policy began to emerge more clearly in April, 1955, at Bandung, Indonesia, where twenty-nine Asian and African nations registered a protest against the efforts of the United States and the Sino-Soviet bloc to induce bipolarization of the international system.[57]

In Sihanouk's opinion, one of the most important problems deserving discussion at the Bandung conference was the danger of Chinese and North Vietnamese expansion. With the cooperation of Thailand's chief delegate, Prince Wan Waithayakon, Sihanouk sought to focus the conference's concern on this problem. He said that Cambodia

now finds herself on the separating line of two civilizations, of two races, of two political worlds . . . and as such, she has the dangerous privilege of standing the test and the application of the principles of Pancha Shil.

My country has adopted these principles and wishes to apply them to the fullest extent. In so doing, she only requests

---

which can boast support and participation at the grassroots level. A result of this movement has been the disintegration of the Democrat party, most of whose members have found it politically expedient to defect to the Sangkum. For further details, see Smith, "Cambodia," pp. 621–631.

[56] "Nehru–Sihanouk Joint Communiqué of March 18, 1955," *Foreign Affairs Reports* (New Delhi), I, no. 3 (Mar., 1955), p. 49.

[57] For a discussion of the conference, see George McT. Kahin, *The Asian-African Conference, Bandung, Indonesia, April 1955* (Ithaca, N.Y.: Cornell University Press, 1956).

that her independence, her integrity, her security, her traditions and political ideology be not threatened.

It will be the task of more powerful nations to set the example, to give proofs and guarantees to smaller nations.[58]

Later, during the political committee session on April 22, the Prince elaborated on his fears of China and North Vietnam. He asserted that most non-Communist countries, including those favoring coexistence, distrusted the Communist bloc. He suggested that the solution to the problem of coexistence lay in the hands of the Communist countries, whose policy should be that of reassuring the rest of the world of their peaceful intentions. He concluded by proposing adoption of the following resolution:

The Asian-African Conference, being of the opinion that peace is threatened by fear and mistrust, and that the restoration of confidence is necessary for peaceful co-existence, recommends that each participating country should scrupulously respect the independence of all other countries, particularly of those which, like Cambodia, are either by their situation or by agreements, neutral and determined: (a) to remain neutral so long as their security is not threatened; (b) not to be used as a base of aggression.[59]

For Cambodia, probably the most significant event at Bandung was a private meeting between Sihanouk, Chou En-lai, and Pham Van Dong. At this meeting potential problems between Cambodia, on the one hand, and China and North Vietnam, on the other, were frankly discussed. Chou En-lai reportedly requested clarification of Cam-

[58] *Ibid.,* p. 13. For the full text of Sihanouk's speech, see Asian–African Conference, Bandung, Indonesia, April, 18–24, 1955, *Speeches and Communiqués* (Kementerian Penerangan [Ministry of Information], Republik Indonesia, 1955) , n.p.

[59] Kahin, *op. cit.,* p. 22.

bodia's relations with the United States.[60] Sihanouk took this opportunity to explain that the military aid he had requested would not mean the establishment of an American presence in Cambodia. He also assured the Communist representatives that he had not asked for SEATO's protection. Chou En-lai and Pham Van Dong in turn pledged their countries' respect for Cambodia's independence and territorial integrity.[61] These talks persuaded Sihanouk for the first time that a normalization of relations between Cambodia and her Communist neighbors was possible. He returned to Cambodia satisfied that a policy of neutrality was the best means of averting cold-war tension in Cambodia.

On May 16, 1955, a few weeks after Sihanouk's return to Cambodia from Bandung, a military-aid agreement between Cambodia and the United States was signed.[62] By its terms, the United States undertook to provide money and equipment for the maintenance of Cambodia's armed forces. In addition, a military assistance advisory group (MAAG) was to be established in Phnom Penh to supervise the distribution and use of equipment. In agreeing to consider Cambodia's request for military aid, President Eisenhower, on January 5, 1955, had specified that such aid would be intended by the United States to assist Cambodia in developing and maintaining a strong and viable state, capable of resisting subversion and/or aggression

---

[60] Reported by Sihanouk in an interview with *Le Monde*, June 13, 1956.

[61] Kahin, *op. cit.*, pp. 15, 21.

[62] See "Military Assistance Agreement between the United States of America and Cambodia." Effected by exchange of notes, Phnom Penh, May 16, 1955. *Treaties and Other International Acts Series 3240* (Washington D.C.: Government Printing Office, 1956).

through military means.[63] Soon after the Bangkok meeting of the SEATO Council in February, Secretary Dulles visited Phnom Penh, where he discussed with Sihanouk the terms of the aid agreement. He assured Sihanouk of America's respect for Cambodia's preference to remain outside of SEATO and acknowledged that acceptance of aid would not imply a compromise of Cambodia's neutrality.

In the exchange of notes effecting the agreement, United States Ambassador Robert McClintock asserted that this agreement was based on principles subscribed to by both Cambodia and the United States in December, 1951. The principles are worth quoting, since they were the cause of the heated attacks subsequently directed against the military-aid agreement by the Communist bloc and domestic politicians.

The Government of the Kingdom of Cambodia hereby confirms that it has agreed [with the United States] to—

(a) Join in promoting international understanding and goodwill, and maintaining world peace;

(b) Take such action as may be mutually agreed upon to eliminate causes of international tensions;

(c) Make, consistent with its political and economic stability, the full contribution permitted by its manpower, resources, facilities, and general economic condition to the development and maintenance of its own defensive strength and the defensive strength of the free world;

(d) Take all reasonable measures which may be needed to develop its defense capacities; and

(e) Take appropriate steps to insure the effective utilization of the economic and military assistance provided by the United States.[64]

---

[63] See *New York Times,* Jan. 6, 1955.

[64] These principles constitute the body of the well-known "Sec.

Although on signing the agreement the Cambodian government stressed that a military alliance had not been entered into and that the United States would not acquire bases in Cambodia,[65] the implications of principle (c) in particular aroused the suspicion of the International Control Commission, which was being prodded by the Communist bloc.

On the grounds that the Geneva agreements[66] prohibit Cambodia from participating in any military alliance in violation of the principles of the United Nations Charter and allow her to seek foreign aid only for the purpose of the effective defense of her territory, the Commission undertook an examination of the United States–Cambodian aid agreement. While the Sino–Soviet bloc charged that Cambodia had entered into a "military alliance with the United States, the leader of the SEATO aggressive bloc,"[67] the Commission unanimously concluded that the

---

511 (a) " of the *Mutual Security Act of 1951* (P.L. 165, 82nd Cong., Oct. 10, 1951, as amended). They were subscribed to by Cambodia in an exchange of notes dated Dec. 18 and 28, 1951. See "Military Assistance Agreement," pp. 1–2. "Sec. 511 (a) " was involved in the *cause célèbre* in Indonesia in 1952 when U.S. Ambassador Cochran apparently forced them on Indonesia and thus brought about the subsequent fall of the Sukiman cabinet.

65 See *Le Cambodge*, May 30, 1955.

66 See Art. 7 of the Geneva cease-fire agreement on Cambodia and Point 4 of the Final Declaration in Great Britain, *Further Documents, Cmd. 9239*.

67 Great Britain, *Third Interim Report of the International Commission for Supervision and Control in Cambodia for the Period Apr. 1 to July 28, 1955. Cambodia No. 3 (1955)*. Cmd. 9579 (London: H.M. Stationery Office, 1955), p. 18. See also *International Affairs* (Moscow), no. 11 (Nov., 1955), pp. 155–156. *Izvestia* of Jan. 29 and Mar. 2, 1955, charged that the U.S. was exerting great pressure on Cambodia in order to build military bases. An editorial in

agreement did not compromise Cambodia's obligation under the Geneva agreements and, by taking note of Cambodia's assurances that she would follow a neutral policy, in effect approved the independent position which Cambodia was claiming for herself.[68]

Jen Min Jih Pao (Peking) of June 24 charged the agreement as a gross violation of the Geneva accord. See *Survey of China Mainland Press*, no. 1077 (June 25–27, 1955), p. 39.

[68] See Great Britain, *Third Interim Report . . . Cambodia No. 3 (1955)*, Cmd. 9579, pp. 5–6. In a meeting between the Commission and the Cambodian Foreign Ministry on May 30, the following position was stated by the government and accepted by the Commission:

"(1) The Royal Government of Cambodia is not bound by the provisions of any United States legislation, particularly the Mutual Security Act. No clauses of the 1951 Agreement between Cambodia and the United States govern the present agreement, except paragraph 1 as reproduced in the footnote [i.e., 'Sec. 511 (a)'].

"(2) According to the Royal Government, the term 'free world' includes all freedom-loving nations, and not only the Western bloc. Cambodia has declared that it would not join either the Western bloc or the Eastern bloc; that it would not enter into any military alliance with any country; and that it would not tolerate the establishment of any foreign bases on its territory. This position was known to the United States Government well before the granting of aid under the present agreement. In these circumstances, the Royal Government will not contribute to the defensive strength of the free world unless its own security is dangerously threatened. The commitment . . . is therefore quite illusory so far as Cambodia is concerned until a new situation arises.

"(3) The Royal Government does not consider that the placing of war material and equipment received strictly for the effective defense of Cambodia at the disposal of the United States or other countries in terms of [the agreement] is contrary to the Geneva Agreement, as such aid will be given in accordance with the principles of the United Nations Charter. As regards S.E.A.T.O., Cambodia is not a member of this organization and is not bound under [the agreement] to support any action by S.E.A.T.O. unless it decides to do so to safeguard the defense of its territory. Again, this commitment is subject to mutual agreement and it is open to Cam-

The military-aid agreement predictably gave Sihanouk's domestic political opponents, who had demanded unsuccessfully to be included in the negotiations with the United States, the opportunity to brand the government as having surrendered Cambodia's sovereignty. The government defended its position vigorously in a communiqué issued on May 29 in which it asserted:

The Royal Government intends scrupulously and always to respect the terms of the Geneva Agreement concerning it, as well as the undertaking made in its name at the Asian-African Conference at Bandung by its delegation led by [Prince] Sihanouk; the Government renews its approval of the declaration made by him concerning the neutrality of Cambodia. . . . The Agreement recently concluded with the U.S.A. has therefore for its object the direct grant of American military aid to Cambodia. There is no question of granting military bases nor of a military alliance of any sort nor of the sending of American military instructors to Cambodia.[69]

This and other government statements, as well as public declarations by Sihanouk himself, effectively limited the influence which Cambodia's Democrat party expected to gain through exploitation of the military-aid agreement. The government stated that it would allow criticisms of the agreement as not being in Cambodia's interests, but that if any person said that the government had "sold the country to the United States," he would be prosecuted.[70]

---

bodia to refuse to give such aid. The obligations under [the agreement] are not therefore automatic and Cambodia cannot be compelled to extend aid on all occasions. In view of her present policy of neutrality, Cambodia does not envisage the possibility of giving such assistance unless her national security is involved." (*Ibid.,* p. 10.)

[69] See *Le Cambodge,* May 30, 1955. See also *ibid.,* June 7, 1955.

[70] See Great Britain, *Fourth Interim Report of the International*

After the election of September 11, in which the Sang-kum soundly whipped the Democrats and gained all of the seats in the National Assembly, Sihanouk tried to silence domestic opposition to his foreign policy by explicitly rejecting protection offered by SEATO.[71] Until then he had stated only that Cambodia did not feel bound by the military-aid agreement with the United States to support any actions by SEATO. Sihanouk was probably aware, however, of the possibility that the Democrats and others could in the future make an issue of the military-aid agreement. Thus, at a National Congress [72] held on September 25–26, he promised to submit the general question of foreign aid to the people for discussion.[73] At the second National Congress, December 30–31, 1955, Sihanouk re-affirmed Cambodia's neutrality, her refusal to allow the establishment of foreign bases on her territory, and her willingness to establish friendly relations with all nations on the basis of strict neutrality. He then posed the question of military aid. The participants at the Congress resolved that the government might accept aid "from any

---

Commission for Supervision and Control in Cambodia for the Period April 1 to September 30, 1955. Cambodia No. 1 (1956). Cmd. 9671 (London: H.M. Stationery Office, 1956), p. 12.

[71] See *Agence Khmère de Presse,* Sept. 13, 1955.

[72] The National Congress was conceived by Sihanouk in 1955 as a biannual forum at which the people might discuss current issues with him and his advisers, and air their complaints and grievances against government officials and legislators. Since 1955, twenty Congresses have met on the palace grounds in Phnom Penh for the discussion of important domestic and foreign policy problems. See Smith, "Cambodia," pp. 623–624, 647–648.

[73] See *Bilan de l'oeuvre du premier gouvernement du Sangkum Reastr Niyum* (Phnom Penh: Imprimerie du Palais Royal, 1956), p. 11.

quarter, provided that it does not prejudice the sovereignty and the neutrality of the Kingdom." [74]

Early in 1956, Prince Sihanouk summed up his country's foreign policy as follows:

Our foreign policy is based on neutrality.

It is appropriate to note that we have already been able to realize our national aspirations with respect to obtaining independence, membership in the United Nations, and the recognition of large powers of all tendencies.

Our policy will adapt itself essentially to the circumstances and events of the world and to the position which will be taken in our regard by the various powers.

It will be carried out in perfect accord with the Parliament and the National Congress. [75]

[74] See *Bilan de l'oeuvre du Sangkum* (Phnom Penh: Imprimerie du Ministère de l'Information, 1960), p. 40.

[75] *Les idées du discours-programme présenté par le Prince-Président devant l'Assemblée Nationale lors de l'investiture du 3ème Gouvernement Sangkum, le 29–2–56* (Phnom Penh: Imprimerie du Sangkum, 1956), pp. 6–7.

CHAPTER IV

Cambodia's Relations with the Major Powers

IN her choice of a foreign policy, Cambodia has been guided by four major considerations. She hopes, first of all, to avert a confrontation between the cold-war powers on her soil. Prince Sihanouk has expressed his fears of the consequences of such an encounter by likening Cambodia to the proverbial ant who, having had the misfortune to be present at the scene of combat between two elephants, was trampled to death. Cambodia's apprehensions in this regard have been greatest when cold-war tensions in neighboring Laos and Vietnam have reached near-explosive levels. Second, only recently having shed her colonial status, Cambodia wishes to avoid any relationship with a stronger power which may compromise her independence. Third, she wishes to preserve the sanctity of her borders and the security of her people against what she fears are the imperialistic ambitions of her traditional antagonists— Thailand and Vietnam.[1] Finally, recalling her former greatness and her once dominant position in Southeast Asia, Cambodia would like again to be able to exert some influence upon international events.

[1] For a discussion of Cambodia's relations with her neighbors, see below, Chap. V.

Cambodia's Foreign Policy

In the context of the present cold war, a country as small and militarily as weak as Cambodia is limited to adopting either of two foreign policies. She can join one of the two blocs, or she can choose not to align herself with either. The first alternative was seriously considered by Cambodia in her early days of independence but was dismissed when it became apparent that her interest would not be served by it. In entering an alliance with one bloc, Cambodia's leaders reasoned, she would run the risk of provoking hostile actions by the other bloc. Moreover, in joining an alliance Cambodia would almost certainly be relegated to secondary status within it and would thereby lose some of her independence in international and, possibly, domestic affairs. Furthermore, once committed to a bloc, Cambodia would lose any influence she might have in affairs falling outside the domain of that bloc.

The second alternative, that of remaining unaligned, has been selected by Cambodia, for a study of modern international politics by Prince Sihanouk revealed to him that through nonalignment Cambodia can best realize her objectives. By refraining from joining either bloc, she can maintain the interest of both so that neither one can easily maneuver itself into a position of dominance over her. In this way she makes it much more likely that competition between the blocs within her borders will be of a nonmilitary nature and may even be beneficial to her. Her freedom of action in international affairs is preserved, and in addition because her friendship is courted by both camps, she gains some influence over their actions.

Positions of the Major Powers, 1955

In the post-World War II period, the interest of the United States in Southeast Asia was stimulated in part by two major developments: the rise to power of the Communist regime in China and the almost coincident withdrawal of European powers from their colonial possessions in Southeast Asia. The actions of China in Korea and her support of the Viet Minh in the Indochina war convinced American policy-makers that unless the United States filled the vacuum left by the departed colonial powers, all of Southeast Asia would soon succumb to Communism. How deep was this conviction was revealed in the sudden increase in 1955–1956 in the proportion of total foreign aid assigned by the United States to Asia.[2] In that year 60 per cent of total aid went to Asia. The American concern with defense against Communism was especially evident in the allocation of approximately 75 per cent of aid to Asian countries for direct military assistance and defense support. Of the $3.5 billion allocated by the United States for foreign aid to all recipient countries, only $712,500,000 was intended for purposes of economic development.

The Soviet Union at this time was embarking on her policy of peaceful economic competition with capitalist nations. In many of the underdeveloped countries of Southeast Asia she found a receptive audience. In 1955 agreements were reached with India for assistance in the construction of steel and aluminum plants and a hydroelectric power station; in Burma in the same year arrangements were made for aid in the construction of industrial plants

---

[2] See the "Message of the President [to Congress] on the Mutual Security Program for 1956, Apr. 20, 1955" (House Document 144, 84th Cong., 1st Sess.), in Paul E. Zimmer, ed., *Documents on American Foreign Relations, 1955* (New York: Harper & Bros., for the Council on Foreign Relations, 1956), pp. 33 ff. See also *New York Times*, Apr. 21, May 4, June 5, and July 1, 1955.

and development of agriculture in exchange for Burmese rice.

In total amounts, the aid advanced by the Soviet Union was not large, but its psychological impact was relatively great. The Soviet leaders, it seems, were better tuned to Asian attitudes. While the United States had been regarded by many Asian leaders as pressing "swords into their hands for a crusade against an unrecognized Communism in the name of a Democracy they have never known," [3] the Soviet Union had been usually seen by them as offering "ploughshares." By publicly endorsing the principles of peaceful coexistence propounded at Bandung, Premier Khrushchev and Marshal Bulganin, on their tour of southern Asia in 1955, were partially successful in quelling the suspicions of certain Asian leaders and, perhaps more importantly, in reassuring the new nations that their attempts to make themselves heard were not being lightly dismissed. Of greater practical value to Asians was the fact that the Soviet Union was prepared to grant more favorable terms—low interest rates, long repayment periods, barter deals—than were obtainable from the West. Such terms and the absence of political conditions, which the United States was so frequently prone to attach to its offers, were of course attractive to many Asians.

While the United States and the Soviet Union were trying to establish a foothold in Southeast Asia, China launched a more active program to win the friendship of the governments in this area. This action of the Chinese was probably as much in response to Soviet efforts to extend its influence into what China considered its domain as to American endeavors. At Bandung, Chou En-

[3] "Soviet Political Strategy in Asia," *World Today*, XII, no. 5 (May, 1956), p. 193.

lai tried to overcome historically rooted fears of Southeast Asians of the giant in the north by espousing the principles of peaceful coexistence and by undertaking to discuss resolution of specific issues of concern to several Southeast Asian countries. In subsequent months China undertook a foreign-aid program of her own with the stated objective of supporting the establishment of basic industries in the underdeveloped countries of Southeast Asia.

Foreign Policy Crisis of 1956 in Cambodia

In the early days of her independence, as we have already noted, Cambodia sought a guarantee of her security from the West. The United States discouraged her overtures for reasons cited in the previous chapter. In addition to these considerations American policy-makers probably did not regard the Cambodian request as pressing because of that country's internal stability and because she appeared to be well buffered from China by Thailand, South Vietnam, and would be eventually, it was hoped, by Laos. Shortly thereafter the United States reversed its policy with regard to Cambodia, and began to employ pressure to draw her toward the pro-West camp. This shift in attitude appears to have stemmed from the increasingly cordial relations between Cambodia and the Communist bloc.

The first indication that the United States had changed her policy was highly indirect and was conveyed via one of her closest allies, which presumably viewed Cambodia's position in the same way. This was indicated during Prince Sihanouk's good-will visit to the Philippines in early 1956. There he planned to assert, as he had during a visit to Japan a few weeks earlier, Cambodia's neutral position in the cold war. On February 1, the *Manila Chronicle* reported: "The Philippines and Cambodia restored their historic ties yesterday with the arrival of Prince Norodom Sihanouk for a visit of five days, which may lead Cambodia to join SEATO. Philippine officials last night confirmed that the careful preparation for Sihanouk's visit was part of a movement to impel the neutral state into the East-West fight." On the same day, the *Philippines Herald* wrote: "In a brief interview at Manila International Airport, it was evident that the Vice-President hoped to persuade Cambodia to join with SEATO against Communist aggression." [4]

Faced with these pressures, Prince Sihanouk, in an address before the Philippine Congress, declared that neutrality in international affairs was consonant with "the feelings and deep conviction of all the Khmer people who have learned in the course of the last four years to distrust the quarrels of the great and to rely mainly upon themselves." [5] After Sihanouk's address the *Herald* reported that "the Prince's categorical declaration of [neutrality] . . . was interpreted in certain circles as having chilled the hopes of the . . . government to bring Cambodia into SEATO." On the same day, Vice-President Garcia informed the press that Cambodia would not be asked to join the defensive alliance.[6]

[4] On Feb. 5, after Sihanouk's departure, the *Manila Chronicle* reported that "Philippine officials have confirmed that at the beginning of the Prince's visit, the 'red carpet' treatment reserved for him was part of an attempt to persuade Cambodia to abandon its neutrality and become a full member of SEATO."

[5] "Address of H.R.H. Norodom Sihanouk before a Joint Session of Members of the Congress of the Philippines, Feb. 3, 1956," *Official Text*, Department of Foreign Affairs, Division of International Information (Manila, 1956), n.p.

[6] See *Philippines Herald* and *Manila Times*, Feb. 3, 1956.

According to Prince Sihanouk, however, a direct attempt was then made to influence him into reconsidering his position. A certain Daniel François Baroukh, who had accompanied Sihanouk to Manila from Cambodia, asked the Prince to make a pro-Western statement on the occasion of his visit to Camp Murphy, an American military installation near Manila.[7] He suggested that the Prince commend the efforts of the Philippines and "other free world governments' to obstruct Communist expansion and that he declare that Cambodia would not hesitate to accept American aid against aggression. At Camp Murphy, however, Sihanouk again defended Cambodia's neutrality and explained why Cambodia could not participate in a military alliance. Neutrality, Sihanouk implied, was a natural outgrowth of his belief that peace among nations could best be assured by a policy of noninterference in the affairs of others.[8] At a press conference afterward, Sihanouk was reported as having said, "As soon as the Communists change their policy and our peace is threatened, we will certainly change our neutral policy."[9] The press concluded from his remarks that he preferred to rely on the protection afforded Cambodia indirectly by the SEATO protocol. But when asked for his views on this

[7] The *Manila Times,* Feb. 3, 1956, described Baroukh as Sihanouk's "adviser and interpreter." Sihanouk, however, says that Baroukh, who had come to Cambodia from the Philippines a short time before, had requested permission to return to Manila as a member of his entourage. During the evening of Feb. 3, Sikanouk claims, "M. Baroukh came to entreat me to make a declaration at Camp Murphy which would 'mitigate' the 'rigor' of my address before the Philippine Congress. He told me that the Philippines government, which had sent him, had been placed in an awkward situation by my remarks and he asked me, as a 'personal favor,' to put things in order." See *La Liberté* (Phnom Penh), Apr. 26, 1956.

[8] *La Liberté,* Apr. 26, 1956.   [9] *Manila Times,* Feb. 5, 1956.

position, Vice-President Garcia said that he did not believe that Cambodia would be able to benefit from the protection accorded by the protocol, "at least not as the protocol was ratified." [10]

It is worthy of note that Sihanouk's trip to the Philippines coincided with an invitation issued in Bangkok to SEATO members to participate in a combined "operation-demonstration" to prove "the mobility and effectiveness with which various members of SEATO can cooperate in mutual defense." [11] One of the objectives of the demonstration may have been to impress on Cambodia the attractiveness of alignment with the West. If this was an objective, it was not realized; indeed, in the planning stages of this first SEATO military operation, Cambodia announced that she would not allow aircraft bound for the exercise to fly over her territory.[12]

While the Cambodian leader was in the Philippines he disclosed his acceptance of an invitation to visit China.

[10] *Manila Chronicle,* Feb. 5, 1956. According to Secretary of State Dulles, however, Cambodia was adequately protected by the protocol. On Sept. 15, 1954, he said, "The protocol also extends the treaty benefits to Cambodia, Laos and South Vietnam. The Indochina armistice created obstacles to these states becoming actual parties to the treaty at the present time. The treaty will, however, to the extent that it is practicable, throw a mantle of protection over these young nations." (Department of State *Bulletin,* XXXI, no. 796 [Sept. 27, 1954], p. 432.) In a report to the President on Nov. 2, 1954, Dulles wrote, "The protocol assures that armed attack or indirect aggression against Cambodia . . . will bring into operation the obligations of the parties under [Art. IV]." (*Ibid.,* XXXI, no. 805 [Nov. 29, 1954], p. 823.)

[11] *Bangkok World,* Feb. 2, 1956.

[12] See George Modelski, "The Asian States' Participation in SEATO," in George Modelski, ed., *SEATO: Six Studies* (Melbourne: Cheshire, 1962), p. 152.

Prince Sihanouk arrived in China on February 13. He was acclaimed and feted wherever he went, and his trip was hailed by the Chinese press as another application of the five principles of peaceful coexistence.[13] It also gave the Prince another opportunity to assure China of his neutral position: "We are neither in one bloc nor in the other." [14] At a press conference on February 18, he declared:

Cambodia is neutral. The people themselves request me to remain neutral whatever may happen. The SEATO has told us that we would be automatically protected. We reject such protection which can only bring us dishonor.[15]

He added that Cambodia was prepared to establish direct relations with the Chinese and that she was looking forward to increased economic and cultural relations. As a result of the trip, Cambodia became the beneficiary of a $22.4 million aid grant, the first such grant made by China to a non-Communist country.[16] Several months later at a press conference in Paris, Prince Sihanouk justified his acceptance of Chinese aid by referring to the question of Chou En-lai's, during the Bandung conference, as to why,

[13] See *Jen Min Jih Pao,* Feb. 13, 1956, in *Survey of China Mainland Press* (SCMP), no. 1230 (Hong Kong, U.S. Consulate-General, 1956), pp. 37–39.

[14] *New China News Agency (NCNA),* Feb. 13, 1956, in *ibid.,* p. 37.

[15] *NCNA,* Feb. 18, 1956, in *SCMP,* no. 1233, p. 33.

[16] The signing of the aid agreement was not officially announced until June 22. It was then stipulated that the aid would provide for goods and services over a period of two years and included the construction of a textile mill, cement, paper, and plywood factories, irrigation works, expansion of rural electricity, and the construction of schools, clinics, youth and sports centers, roads and bridges. In addition, a trade and payments agreement was reached a short while later, which provided for $14 million worth of trade for one year. See *NCNA* June 22, 1956, in *SCMP,* no. 1318, p. 45.

if Cambodia were neutral, she received aid only from the West.

It was to answer [this] question that I visited Peking and concluded an economic aid agreement with China. . . . Henceforward, we shall receive assistance equally from Communist and Western countries.[17]

Upon his return from Peking late in February, Prince Sihanouk found Cambodia suddenly confronted with overt hostility from Thailand and South Vietnam. The Thai premier, Phibunsongkhram, charged Cambodia with unlawful arrest of Thais at several points along the border and with "plundering, robbing and kidnapping" Thais.[18] Cambodia retorted that Thai troops had occupied a strategic promontory which overlooks the Cambodian plain and on which an ancient Khmer temple, Preah Vihear, is located; and Cambodia further alleged that Son Ngoc Thanh from a base in Thailand was leading armed raids into her territory.[19] Simultaneously, tension in relations with South Vietnam was heightened: some Vietnamese planes violated Cambodian air space, and several Cambodian fishing boats were commandeered by Vietnamese patrol boats.[20] These incidents were followed by the closure of the frontiers by Thailand and South Vietnam. Cambodia, whose foreign trade then depended upon access to the sea via Saigon and Bangkok, found her economic life disrupted. Amid heated exchanges between the countries, the Cambodian government charged that the United States had entered into collusion with South Vietnam and

[17] *Le Monde,* quoting Sihanouk at a press conference in Paris, June 13, 1956.
[18] *Siam Rath Weekly Review* (Bangkok), Mar. 22, 1956.
[19] *Réalités Cambodgiennes* (Phnom Penh), Mar. 17, 1956.
[20] *Times of Viet Nam* (Saigon), Apr. 17, 1956.

Thailand to coerce Cambodia into joining SEATO.[21] Prince Sihanouk also learned that the American Embassy was displeased with some earlier remarks in which he had apparently disparaged United States aid to Cambodia.[22]

In an attempt to remove misconceptions about his position Sihanouk declared on February 28:

In clear language, it is good always to remain in the middle . . . to observe strict neutrality, dangerously bending toward the left, toward the right. Thus, I first of all accepted an invitation of the Philippines, an anti-Communist nation, then that of People's China. Certain press organs, especially that of the Democrat party, have accused me of "false neutrality." I am not a liar, otherwise my people would not have voted for me during the last general elections. I went to the Philippines, and I was invited by that country to participate in a reciprocal pact, but I did not want it. I went to Communist China with the aim of applying Pancha Shil. This does not mean that Cambodia has become communist . . . that is impossible for a Buddhist country like Cambodia.[23]

In an address to the National Assembly on the following day, he charged the United States with helping only those countries "which accept its supervision" and he contrasted this with the Chinese offer of aid "without any condition." He went on:

The Americans are dissatisfied because I have refused the proposals of the Philippines to adhere to SEATO and because I have declared that American aid is used for enriching those who are already rich. . . . If the Americans want to cut off their aid to Cambodia, we on our part are resolved to remain

[21] These charges were broadcast by Phnom Penh Radio, Mar. 3, 1956.

[22] See Martin Herz, *A Short History of Cambodia* (New York: Praeger, 1958), p. 128.

[23] *Agence Khmère de Presse*, Feb. 29, 1956; hereafter cited as *AKP*.

faithful to our neutrality policy. We will accept neither Soviet nor Chinese aid. . . .

We can assume that, if we ask for economic aid from a foreign country, several nations will hasten to reply to our appeal. . . . If our domestic and foreign policies are well balanced, our country will have full foreign aid like India, and our national sovereignty will be strengthened. We will accept aid from the right, from the left, and from the center in any way which will stabilize our policy.[24]

In a series of speeches and communiqués during the succeeding weeks, the Prince reiterated his complaints against American pressure.[25] Echoing Sihanouk's charges, the semiofficial *Réalités Cambodgiennes* wrote editorially on March 31 that Cambodia's problems with her neighbors resulted from American pressures and her anti-Communist phobia. "Washington's view—classing other people 'good or bad,' 'white or red'—is not only a simple view, but an unjust view, and dangerous for peace in Southeast Asia." While critical of these aspects of American policy, Prince Sihanouk showed that he recognized that the American presence in Cambodia was important to his country's independence. He declared that "we cannot do without American aid without falling into the orbit of the communist powers, an event which would signal the end of our neutrality, and probably our independence. . . . I hope therefore that Khmer neutrality will be maintained . . . by the balance of powers, west and east." [26]

24 See *AKP*, Mar. 1, 1956; *Les idées du discours-programme présenté par le prince-président devant l'assemblée nationale lors de l'investiture du 3ème gouvernement sangkum, le 29–2–56* (Phnom Penh, 1956); see also Herz, *op. cit.*, p. 129; *La Liberté*, Mar. 3, 1956.

25 See *Réalités Cambodgiennes*, Mar. 24 and 31, Apr. 7, 14, 21, and 28, and *La Liberté*, Mar. 30 and Apr. 26, 1956.

26 See *Réalités Cambodgiennes*, Apr. 28, and *La Liberté*, Apr. 26, 1956.

To confirm his assertion that Cambodia's choice of a neutral policy was the immediate cause of harassment by her neighbors, Prince Sihanouk cited statements from two South Vietnamese journals. *Ngôn-Luân* had written:

And what is more legitimate than measures taken by free and democratic nations to protect themselves against the infiltration of such a dangerous policy? The threat even of neutrality is danger enough. We believe nevertheless that the far-sightedness of the Khmer people will never permit Sihanouk and his party to follow a road so spiked with perils.

And *Tu Do Van Nghê* had declared:

The Chinese Communists are preparing to invade us via Cambodia. . . . It is to avoid fissures in our flanks that Vietnam and naturally Thailand must take defensive measures.

The *Times of Viet Nam,* a semiofficial organ reflecting the views of the South Vietnamese government, in its editorial of April 17 noted that Cambodia's troubles started after Sihanouk had broadcast her neutrality in the hope that he could profit "from the East-West controversy."

Things began to go wrong following Cambodia's claims to Preah Vihear and the categorical refusal to open diplomatic relations with South Vietnam, which motivated the closure of both frontiers closing off Cambodia's principal accesses to the sea.

In contrast, the editor of Bangkok's *Siam Rath Weekly Review,* Khukrit Pramoj, commented:

We do not like to think that some kind of pressure has been put upon the Thai and South Vietnamese governments to rope off Cambodia into solitary neutralism. It will be regrettable indeed for the Thai government to carry out the closure of the Cambodian frontier. Americans will certainly be blamed for this.[27]

A few days later, Pramoj noted that similar border incidents with Burma had been dealt with by the Thai government in a sportsmanlike manner. He wondered, therefore, if there was not something behind the Thai government's attitude toward these "minor incidents" with Cambodia. One possible reason might be Cambodia's foreign policy, he said. "To hem in the Cambodian people merely because some prominent Cambodians went on a visit to Red China . . . seems to make them objects of pity and sympathy." [28] He compared Cambodia's position with that of Thailand during King Chulalongkorn's reign. The Thai monarch had made frequent trips to countries which were potential threats to his country in order to buy time during which Thailand could develop its internal strength. Similarly:

What Prince Sihanouk wants is time to build strength against the danger of disturbance and interference from the Viet Minh. The only way by which to make the Viet Minh feel afraid of causing offense is to go and contact the person or persons whom the Viet Minh feel most afraid of. It seems absolutely impossible for any conclusion to be reached that Prince

[27] *Siam Rath Weekly Review,* Mar. 22, 1956. According to David A. Wilson, a well-informed observer of Thai politics, *Siam Rath Weekly Review,* and its Thai-language parent, *Siam Rath,* are probably the most independent of Bangkok's newspapers. Wilson has suggested to the author that Mr. Pramoj's views in 1956, and in 1958 (see below, p. 143), may have stemmed from the position, generally antimilitarist and opposed to Premier Phibunsongkhram, of Thai royalists, of whom Pramoj is one. After the establishment in 1958 of the Sarit regime, which was supported by the monarchy, the royalists abandoned their antigovernment position.

[28] *Ibid.,* Mar. 29, 1956.

Sihanouk is becoming a Communist just because he visited Peking.[29]

At the height of this crisis late in March, Sihanouk resigned as premier. Shortly thereafter, he challenged American policy toward Cambodia. At press conferences held at Siem Reap and Kampot,[30] he declared that if Western-inspired "injustices" continued, he was certain the Cambodian people would call for even closer relations with the Communist bloc.

In any case, the Americans who have so often promised to defend the liberties of small countries, have just shown their real face in Cambodia. It is not exemplary. Let my compatriots be assured, however. We will not permit anyone to trample on our neutrality or our sovereignty. We will not retreat a single step. We have victoriously rebuffed threats of this sort before.

He concluded by announcing that a National Congress would be held on April 21 to consider urgent matters of internal and external policy. Some of the specific issues would be: "Cambodia's attitudes towards foreign powers in relation to the attitude of these foreign powers towards our country. Foreign aid granted or proposed to our country. The problems of national union as posed by the Pracheachon [Communist] party."

Throughout the developing crisis the United States, officially, had remained silent. But Sihanouk's heated statements in April prompted the United States to issue assurances of her respect for Cambodia's neutrality and her

[29] *Ibid.*

[30] See *La Liberté,* Apr. 2, and *Réalités Cambodgiennes,* Apr. 14, 17, and 21, 1956.

desire for the continuation of military and economic aid.[31] In a conference with King Suramarit, the American ambassador said the United States had not questioned Cambodia's neutral policy and did not entertain hopes of establishing bases in Cambodia. He assured the King that American aid was accompanied by no condition prejudicial to Cambodia's neutrality or independence. Later in April, Secretary of State Dulles addressed an open letter to Foreign Minister Nong Kimny.[32] In it he denied the Cambodian charges that the United States had instigated Thai and South Vietnamese actions and expressed his

alarm that statements from various sources are giving increasing publicity to allegations according to which the United States tried to force Cambodia to join SEATO by threatening to withdraw American economic aid and that the United States had obliged independent and friendly nations such as Vietnam and Thailand to impose measures of economic warfare against Cambodia for these same ends. . . .

I regret that these allegations have been made as they are completely false and could damage the friendly relations existing between our two states. . . .

I am certain that this letter will end these false allegations regarding our policy which, I repeat, has no other aim than to help free nations preserve their liberty and independence.

In spite of this letter, and the sudden announcement by the Thai and South Vietnamese governments on April 19 that they had ended the economic blockade and were

---

[31] Ambassador McClintock to King Suramarit, communiqué of the Ministry of Foreign Affairs, quoted in *Réalités Cambodgiennes,* Apr. 7, 1956.

[32] Secretary of State Dulles to Foreign Minister Nong Kimny, Apr. 17, 1956. See *La Liberté,* Apr. 26, 1956, and U.S. Department of State *Bulletin,* XXXIV (Apr. 30, 1956), No. 879, p. 727.

ready to resume normal relations with Cambodia, preparations for the National Congress continued.

During four days of discussion at the Congress, April 21–24, Prince Sihanouk reviewed the hardships caused by the South Vietnamese and Thai blockades and noted the progress being made by Foreign Minister Nong Kimny in bringing about a *détente* with Cambodia's adversaries. In response to the question concerning relations with foreign powers, the participants in the Congress voted unanimously for continuation of a policy of strict neutrality. On the question of foreign aid, the Prince informed the delegates that China had offered a large grant and that negotiations were underway regarding the uses to which the aid would be put. The Soviet Union, he said, had also offered assistance. But, he continued, "If we accept help from these countries perhaps the United States Congress will vote to cut off all American aid." After a vigorous debate of the pros and cons of Communist-bloc aid and of the possible American reaction, it was decided to accept aid from any country provided such aid was offered without conditions. It was further agreed that Cambodia should seek friendship, peace, and cooperation with all nations of good will. On this discussion, *Réalités Cambodgiennes* commented:

This decision has a precise meaning. It means that apart from its traditional friendships, Cambodia wishes to keep or acquire new friends—in the neutralist as well as the eastern bloc. Cambodian neutrality for a long time has not included relations with the eastern bloc. A slight "slide to the left" has taken place. The Kingdom will accord equal treatment to the two blocs. This does not mean Cambodians are becoming pro-communist or that the Prince is throwing himself into the arms of Moscow or Peking as one already hears certain foreign voices, specialists in anti-neutralism and anti-communism, commenting.[33]

The question of national unity was also considered. The Pracheachon, Sihanouk said, desired a coalition government of the Sangkum and the other parties with himself as premier. The Prince objected to the idea, however, on the grounds the Sangkum was not a party, but a movement whose *raison d'être* was the dissolution of parties. In a counterproposal, he called upon the Pracheachon and the Democrat members to join the Sangkum. A resolution was finally adopted which expressed the parties' agreement with the Sangkum's foreign and domestic policies.[34]

Relations with the Communist Bloc

Following the foreign policy crisis of 1956, Prince Sihanouk announced his intention to establish relations with the Communist bloc, "not necessarily to counterbalance western influence, but it will work that way."[35] Shortly thereafter, he paid state visits to the Soviet Union, Poland, and Czechoslovakia. While in Moscow, he defined Cambodia's neutrality in terms much less critical of the West than he had in Peking earlier in the year. In an interview with the *New Times* (Moscow), Sihanouk said:

Ours is a policy of active neutrality, that is, of cooperation with all nations, regardless of their political or social regimes,

[33] *Réalités Cambodgiennes*, Apr. 28, 1956.

[34] The Democrat party dissolved itself in 1957 and many of its members joined the Sangkum. The Pracheachon has continued to exist outside of the Sangkum. See Roger M. Smith, "Cambodia," in George McT. Kahin, ed., *Governments and Politics of Southeast Asia* (2d. ed.; Ithaca, N.Y.: Cornell Univ. Press, 1964), pp. 624, 627–628.

[35] *Réalités Cambodgiennes*, Apr. 21, 1956.

who abide by the same principles in relations to us and are motivated by the same ideal, namely universal well-being and sincere friendship.[36]

Radio Phnom Penh reported that the Prince added: "So long as our present policy is not threatened, we will never reject neutrality." [37]

During Sihanouk's visit to the Soviet Union, the Russian leaders agreed to consider the possibility of assisting Cambodia's industrial development. They also "proposed to construct and equip with Soviet forces and funds a hospital in Phnom Penh." [38] The aid grant negotiated during Sihanouk's visit resulted in the construction of a modern 500-bed hospital costing $10.7 million. Funds for the project were obtained from the sale in Cambodia of commodities and equipment supplied without compensation by the Soviet Union. In addition, Poland promised to contribute the surgical facilities to the new hospital, and Czechoslovakia agreed to send a mission to Phnom Penh to negotiate agreements on trade and technical aid.

Following the signing of the Sino–Cambodian aid agreement, Chou En-lai journeyed to Cambodia in November, 1956, further to cement relations. In Phnom Penh, a joint Chinese–Cambodian communiqué was issued calling for observance of the principles of peaceful coexistence. In the communiqué the visiting premier urged all Chinese residents in Cambodia strictly to "abide by the laws and decrees of the Kingdom of Cambodia, not take part in local political activity and take a practical part in the efforts made by Cambodia to promote its national prosperity

---

[36] *New Times,* no. 29, 1956, pp. 9–10.

[37] Radio Phnom Penh, July 5, 1956.

[38] Joint Russian–Cambodian communiqué, July 7, 1956, quoted in *Pravda,* July 8, 1956.

and its people's welfare." Addressing a gathering of Chinese residents of Phnom Penh on November 27, Chou noted that some of them would eventually become citizens of Cambodia. "Do not think the Chinese government would be displeased with this," he told them. "No, it would absolutely not be. On the contrary, this would enable both countries to become still more intimate and friendly." He warned those who were not citizens to refrain from political activity; they should beware of "big nation chauvinism," he said. Upon his departure on the same day, Chou declared that the Chinese government "will in accordance with its consistent policy . . . encourage the Chinese residents in Cambodia to integrate themselves with the Cambodian people and share the sweets and bitters of life with them, to abide by the law, respect the customs and habits of the country and contribute to the full to its prosperous development." [39]

Motivating this effort to strengthen relations with the major communist powers—to practice, as he put it later, *"la grande diplomatie"* [40]—were Prince Sihanouk's increasing suspicions of the intentions of Thailand and South Vietnam. His anxiety was revealed early in November, when in the wake of the Suez and Hungary crises Sihanouk proposed the establishment of a special commission of neutral nations to investigate conflicts in Asia and Africa.[41] In particular, he had in mind the continued Vietnamese incursions of Cambodia's border and a reported buildup of Thai armed strength along the fron-

[39] Quoted in *NCNA*, Phnom Penh, Nov. 27, 1956, in *SCMP*, no. 1421 (Nov. 30, 1956), pp. 23–29.

[40] Norodom Sihanouk, *La monarchie cambodgienne et la croisade pour l'indépendance* (Phnom Penh: Imprimerie Rasmey, 1961), p. 20.

[41] See *Réalités Cambodgiennes,* special edition, Nov. 3, 1956.

tier.[42] The Prince referred, pointedly, to Cambodia's future as being "clouded and stormy again. . . . The people of the countryside, who compromise 90 percent of the kingdom's population, and who for six centuries have been the victims of injustice, will they understand it when the effects of war impose themselves again?" As if to confirm his fears, South Vietnam again attempted, soon after Chou En-lai's visit, to occupy certain of Cambodia's offshore islands and asserted ownership of them.[43]

In a further attempt to strengthen Cambodia's security, the Prince now sought more firmly to root his policy of neutrality. At the fourth National Congress early in January, 1957, he proposed that the constitution be amended to include a neutrality act. He noted that although China and the Soviet Union had both signed joint declarations with Cambodia recognizing her neutrality,[44] other countries had not, nor did they appear to acknowledge Cambodia's right to neutrality.[45] One delegate to the Congress asked if Cambodia's neutrality did not already have strong foundations. Sihanouk answered, "Yes. Neutrality is our house. But after you have built a house it is prudent to put a fence around it. The Neutrality Act will be our fence." [46] Following a long discussion, in which the wis-

---

[42] See Great Britain, *Fifth Interim Report of the International Commission for Supervision and Control in Cambodia for the Period October 1, 1955 to December 31, 1956. Cambodia No. 1 (1957)*, Cmnd. 253 (London: H.M. Stationery Office, 1958), pp. 19–20, 35–38, and *Sixth Interim .... . for the Period January 1, 1957 to December 31, 1957. Cambodia No. 1 (1958)*, Cmnd. 526 (London: H.M. Stationery Office, 1959), p. 14.

[43] See *Angkor*, Dec. 10, 1956. See also below, pp. 158–159.

[44] *Réalités Cambodgiennes*, Jan. 19, 1957.

[45] See *Angkor*, Jan. 15, 1957.

[46] Quoted in Wilfred Burchett, *Mekong Upstream* (Hanoi: Red River Publishing House, 1957), p. 202.

dom of writing neutrality into the constitution was debated, the Congress unanimously adopted the Prince's proposal. As it was later passed by the National Assembly on September 11, 1957, the act declares neutrality to be the law of the land and requires Cambodia to abstain from all military or ideological alliances. It further states that Cambodia will not commit aggression against other countries, but in the event of foreign military invasion, will reserve the right to (*a*) defend herself with arms (*b*) request aid from the United Nations, and (*c*) appeal to a friendly power.[47]

In the meantime, late in 1956 a large Chinese economic-aid mission arrived in Phnom Penh. Soon after its arrival several heretofore small Chinese-language newspapers received large financial grants from the mission to increase their linage and support wider circulation among Chinese outside of Phnom Penh.[48] As a result of the economic-aid mission's activity, which was taken over by the Chinese embassy in 1958 following the establishment of diplomatic relations, four of five Chinese newspapers adopted a pro-Communist orientation.[49]

[47] See Law 232–NS, printed in *Réalités Cambodgiennes,* Sept. 21, 1957. The Neutrality Act, however, has not been formally incorporated into the constitution.

[48] There are an estimated 300,000 to 350,000 Chinese living in Cambodia. Chinese newspapers have long been the only papers in Cambodia with widespread circulation, due mainly to the fact that they have been carried around the country by the Chinese-controlled domestic trucking and bus firms. As a result, Chinese retail merchants and money-lenders have been the chief source of news for the Cambodian peasant. This is now being countered by the government-subsidized *Neak Cheat Niyum,* which also circulates throughout the country, and by the Ministry of Information.

[49] The fifth paper follows a neutral line and until 1963 received substantial financial assistance from the U.S. Information Service in Phnom Penh.

An attempt was also made by members of the mission to gain control of the Chinese *congrégations* [50] and schools, mainly by manipulating elections to the administrative units of these organizations. During the fourth National Congress, Prince Sihanouk protested very firmly against what he termed the "foreign money" which was subverting the country.[51] Probably because he was then preoccupied by the hostile acts of Thailand and South Vietnam, he did not take action against the Chinese mission's activities.

The increase of Communist Chinese influence in Cambodia during 1957, which included the establishment of an Overseas Chinese Workers Relief Committee to distribute funds donated by the People's Relief Administration of China to unemployed Chinese in Cambodia,[52] so alarmed the Cambodian government that late in the year

[50] During the protectorate, the French had organized the Chinese into five *congrégations,* according to their area of origin in China. Under this system, the Chinese enjoyed extraterritoriality and were granted the same commercial rights as French residents. Self-administering, the *congrégations* facilitated the French task of governing and tax collection. While extraterritoriality and the special commercial privileges were discontinued when Cambodia gained its independence, the *congrégations* themselves remained in existence until 1958.

[51] See *Angkor,* Jan. 15, 1957.

[52] *NCNA,* Sept. 7, 1957, in *SCMP,* no. 1608, p. 43. A law prohibiting foreign nationals from engaging in 18 specified businesses was enacted in Cambodia on Mar. 19, 1956. Designed to encourage greater participation by Cambodians in business and to limit the control by Chinese and Vietnamese over commerce and industry, the law threw many Chinese out of work. (See Law 83–NS, Mar. 19, 1956, quoted in *Angkor,* Nov. 22, 1956.) While many Chinese businessmen managed to sidestep the law by exercising control of their firms behind Cambodian front men, their position in commerce was further undermined in 1964, when all import-export companies were nationalized.

it decided to abolish the *congrégations* on grounds that they constituted a state within a state and as such offered unlimited opportunities for subversion by China. It was also decided to establish certain controls over the Chinese schools (curriculum, number of students, etc.); because of a shortage of competent personnel, and bureaucracy and corruption, however, the government has been unable to exercise a complete check on them.

The government's concern was expressed by Prince Sihanouk during an early 1958 meeting of the National Congress.

If the moment comes [he said] when we must die or be taken over by the Communists, we will accept inevitable death with the conviction of not having betrayed our country.

I want to proclaim in advance that many countries have not believed in the mortal danger of Communism, and when the evidence became clear to them it was too late and impossible for them to come to their senses. Look at Hungary! [53]

In March, in a series of articles on Communism, Sihanouk declared:

I am well aware that the Red Chinese may influence my countrymen through blood ties of "Sino-Khmer." It is also possible that the Chinese Economic Mission, in spite of official warning from Chou En-lai, believes in the necessity of communizing the Chinese and the Khmers. But the general opinion is that, if this Mission doesn't sit on its hands, it keeps its actions very discreet and apparently doesn't exceed the limits of decency.[54]

He then underscored the growing attraction of Cambodia as a target for East-West competition by saying:

[53] *Réalités Cambodgiennes,* Jan. 11, 1958.
[54] *Ibid.,* Mar. 15, 1958.

If, like Paris in the Greek legend, we should have to award the golden apple of seduction, we would be hard pressed to choose between Venus, Juno and Minerva, each of whom casts us beguiling smiles.

We know perfectly well that the "Reds" applaud our neutrality only because it serves their interests. As for the "Blues" who congratulated me for having denounced Communist subversion here, I advised them to temper their enthusiasm. . . . It is not the "friends who wish you well" who saved Cambodia at Geneva from the Viet Minh and from partition. It isn't our "unassailable neighbors" who aid us in protecting our frontiers or in stopping clandestine infiltration of Red agents into Cambodia. . . .

In certain Red countries the leaders told me:
"Continue, Your Highness, on the road of neutrality and your country will know complete independence."

At the time, I couldn't see that our independence wasn't complete. After reflecting, I understood.

According to "Red" terminology, a member country of SEATO or NATO is not independent, a neutral is semi-independent, those who are Red are the only "real independents."

I must say that, according to the "Blues," this is just reversed. A member of the Warsaw Pact is a satellite, a neutral is a public danger, and a true "free country" is a member of SEATO or NATO.[55]

In spite of Cambodia's wariness of China's intentions, relations between the two countries appeared to progress even further with Cambodia's *de jure* recognition of China in July, 1958.[56] This move by Cambodia followed a long series of incidents on the Cambodian–South Vietnamese border, coupled with Cambodian charges that the

---

[55] *Ibid.,* and Mar. 22, 1956.
[56] See joint Sino–Cambodian communiqué in *NCNA,* Aug. 24, 1958, in *SCMP,* no. 1821, p. 37.

United States was trying to use Vietnamese troops to force Cambodia to forsake its neutral position.[57] In the face of these alleged pressures, Sihanouk justified his country's policy:

People can remember that our policy of neutrality is dictated by our necessity to keep the Eastern bloc from menacing or accusing us of becoming an arsenal or base of aggression for the West. We have adopted this policy dictated by the intense desire of all the Khmer people to avoid being menaced and accused by certain neighboring countries or by certain participants in the other bloc. . . .

Nevertheless, despite this and despite our loyalty and our correctness, certain pieces of our territory have been taken away and military measures of intimidation against us have been taken on the fabricated pretext that our territory has served as a den of the Communists and of the enemies of certain regimes.

Under these conditions, we have no reason any longer to sacrifice our national interests and future unnecessarily.[58]

He regretted that "some people" should detect a contradiction between his policy of anti-Communism in Cambodia and a policy of friendship with the Communist powers, China in particular. "This, undoubtedly, shows their entire ignorance of the spirit of . . . Pancha Shil," he said.[59]

Following Cambodia's recognition of China, Sihanouk made a second trip to China, where he extended his per-

[57] These charges were broadcast by Radio Phnom Penh, July 4, 1958. See also below, pp. 159–161.

[58] *Réalités Cambodgiennes,* Aug. 2, 1958.

[59] The Communist press gave wide publicity to Sihanouk's statements, and indicated that the bloc was in full agreement with his views. See, for example, *Novoe Vremya,* Aug., 1958, no. 32, p. 21, and *Peking Review,* I (Dec. 23, 1958), no. 43, p. 28.

sonal thanks for the aid China had given and promised to support China's cause with respect to both Taiwan and the United Nations.[60]

Since 1956, the Communist powers, principally China, have granted generous amounts of aid to Cambodia's economic development. In 1961, China offered additional monies to complete construction of four factories—plywood, cement, paper, and textile—provided for in 1956, and to build a small glass factory and a tool plant. It also agreed to establish a joint Sino–Cambodian shipping company and to provide two 1,500-ton ships for this venture. Russia announced plans in 1961 to build a technical school, and in 1963 signed an agreement with Cambodia to construct a hydroelectric dam on the Kamchay River near Kampot. Under agreements concluded in early 1961, Czechoslovakia committed herself to build a tractor assembly plant, a palm sugar refinery and a tire factory. Finally, in 1963 Yugoslavia extended $6 million in credit, to be repaid over a fifteen-year period at 3 per cent interest, for the construction of three small hydroelectric power plants in the Kirirom mountains. The total amount of economic aid received by Cambodia from Communist countries (including Yugoslavia) during the period 1956–1963 amounted to $114.95 million.[61] Military aid from the major Communist powers has included, since 1963, the provision by the Soviet Union of several MIG aircraft and a control and maintenance system for them, and an offer by China to build two jet airbases and to provide various types of military equipment.[62]

[60] *NCNA,* Aug. 31, 1958, in *SCMP,* no. 1846, pp. 47–48. An account of Sihanouk's trip was broadcast by Radio Phnom Penh, Oct. 22, 1958.

[61] See Table 1 below, p. 123.

[62] See *Réalités Cambodgiennes,* Sept. 6, 1963, *La Dépêche du*

The major Communist powers have also provided important political support in Cambodia's conflicts with its neighbors. A joint declaration issued in Peking during Sihanouk's visit to the Chinese capital in August, 1958, expressed China's concern over "the unfriendly acts of some of Cambodia's neighbors in blockading and invading her territory." [63]

At the end of 1958, in a speech before the National Congress, the Prince charged that the Thai government wished to occupy Cambodia and that it was misrepresenting Cambodia's foreign policy in an effort to arouse fear among the SEATO nations and to create a pretext for "certain nations" to attack Cambodia "so that Thailand can fish in troubled waters." [64] Subsequent communiqués from the Cambodian Foreign Ministry accused Thailand of provocation on the border.[65] Thailand replied with its own charges of "invasions" and "other provocations" by Cambodia.[66] The Prince later charged that South Vietnam and Thailand were backing the dissident Cambodian leaders, Son Ngoc Thanh and Sam Sary, who were intent upon trying to overthrow the government and turning it into "a satellite of the free world." [67] At the peak of this exchange, the Russian Ambassador called upon the Prince and extended his country's

great sympathy for the brave struggle of the freedom-loving people of Cambodia against the intrigues of the imperialist

---

Cambodge, Feb. 17, 1964, and *New York Times,* Feb. 18, Apr. 7, and May 11, 1964.

[63] *NCNA,* Aug. 24, 1958, in *SCMP,* no. 1821, p. 37.

[64] Radio Phnom Penh, Dec. 16, 1958.

[65] *Ibid.,* Dec. 18, 23, 24, and 29, 1958.   [66] *Ibid.,* Jan. 7, 1959.

[67] *Ibid.,* Feb. 4, 1959. See also an interview with Prince Sihanouk in *Réalités Cambodgiennes,* Jan. 6, 1959.

powers that are encroaching on the sovereignty and territorial integrity of Cambodia . . . and that are creating a strained condition in Indochina.[68]

The Soviet Union said that it understood and appreciated Cambodia's foreign policy, which "is finding understanding and broad support" in Asia.

It is having a certain influence on those countries in Southeast Asia that, for one reason or another, have been drawn into aggressive military blocs and that do not have an independent foreign policy. This is clearly not to the liking of the colonial powers because Cambodia's policy makes it difficult for them to carry out their plans for strengthening and maintaining their positions in Asia and for enlisting the countries of this region in aggressive military and political groupings such as SEATO.

The Soviet Government nurtures feelings of steadfast friendship toward Cambodia and is convinced that the Cambodian people and government, supported by other peace-loving countries, will overcome the temporary difficulties created by foreign powers and their agents within the country and will achieve new successes in strengthening the political and economic independence of their state.[69]

The verbal support of the Communist bloc was accompanied in 1959 by persistent Communist Chinese maneuvers in the now defunct *congrégations,* which continued to exist underground, and in the schools. Most success was achieved in the schools where, having gained control of the school boards, the Chinese could dictate to the teachers. In an effort to control this situation, the royal

[68] Text in *Pravda,* Mar. 27, 1959. Reported also on Radio Phnom Penh, Mar. 26, 1959.

[69] *Ibid.* For further Soviet comments, see *New Times,* no. 5 (1959), pp. 22–23, and no. 10 (1959), pp. 19–21.

government arrested several hundred Chinese suspected of illegal activity (allegedly, gambling and the manufacture of false identification cards as well as attempted subversion) and shipped them to a work camp in Kompong Thom province. The government also demanded of the Chinese government the right to deport these persons to China. After extended negotiations, which were concluded during Chou En-lai's second visit to Cambodia in May, 1960, China agreed to accept the deportees; an estimated sixty to seventy actually left Cambodia in 1960.[70]

Prince Sihanouk has been cautious in his relations with the Chinese People's Republic primarily because he feels that one day in the future China will exercise a paramount, and perhaps dominant, influence over Southeast Asia. Good relations now, the Prince believes, are insurance against a time when Cambodia's destiny will be within China's control. He expressed himself frankly in this regard at a press conference in March, 1961, in Phnom Penh when he explained:

China, with its 650 million inhabitants, has become one of the largest world powers. If it continues to progress in its development, within 30 years, with a population surpassing a billion, China will be without doubt the largest world power and its influence in Asia will certainly predominate.

In the light of these considerations, all of Southeast Asia will be at China's mercy, but we have confidence in the Chinese attitude towards us. I think that China has suffered from colonialism too much to itself impose it on weaker nations, and my conviction has been reinforced by the way

[70] This discussion of clandestine Communist Chinese activity in Cambodia and the government's reaction to it has been derived by the author from Cambodian, Chinese, and American sources in Phnom Penh which he considers to be reliable.

China has never failed to support our independence and national sovereignty.

He added:

My confidence in China is limited to the same extent that one should limit his confidence in all large powers, or those more powerful than oneself. Our country has always been the victim of its neighbors and even now, despite its considerable domestic difficulties, South Vietnam dares to claim several of our offshore islands, which have always belonged to us.

Westerners are always astonished that we Cambodians are not disturbed by our future in which China will play such a powerful role. But one should try to put himself in our place: In this jungle which is the real world, should we, simple deer, interest ourselves in a dinosaur like China when we are more directly menaced, and have been for centuries, by the wolf and the tiger, who are Vietnam and Thailand? [71]

For its part, China's behavior suggests that a neutral Cambodia in the midst of what is otherwise a Western stronghold is for the present, at least, worth supporting even though certain repressive measures are taken by her government against alien Chinese residents. Equally important is the likelihood that China wishes to impress Southeast Asia—especially those countries now allied with the Western powers—with the fruits to be gained from association with the Communist bloc.[72] She might also

[71] Press conference, Phnom Penh, Mar. 2, 1961.

[72] See Chou En-lai's address given in Phnom Penh in 1956, quoted in *NCNA*, Nov. 23, 1956, in *SCMP*, no. 1419, p. 14. In this context, China probably hopes to influence Thailand. The fact that until 1963 the United States provided economic and military aid to Cambodia, a country which Thailand appears to consider pro-Communist, elicited pained comments from Thai leaders on more than one

wish to dissociate herself from the stigma of being an aggressive power. China's reported offer in 1956 to guarantee Cambodia's security against harassment by North Vietnam, if actually made, probably served to strengthen the inclination of Cambodians to view China as nonaggressively inclined toward their country.[73] During Chou Enlai's second visit to Cambodia in 1960, which occurred when South Vietnam's claims on Cambodia's offshore islands were being asserted most vigorously, he stated: "If the Kingdom of Cambodia is aggressed upon from whichever direction, the Chinese people . . . and the Chinese government . . . will stand on the side of the Royal Cambodian Government." He added, however:

As to the kind of support, undoubtedly moral and political support as there has always been. As to support in other aspects,

---

occasion in recent years. Neutral Cambodia's position as a recipient of aid from both blocs led some Thai leaders in 1962 to propose a reconsideration of their country's foreign policy. See, for example, the remarks of General Praphat Charusathien, Thai Minister of Interior, made on the occasion of an American grant of additional military aid to Cambodia, quoted in the *Bangkok Post*, Sept. 6, 1962. See also below, p. 186. For a provocative discussion of China's relations with Southeast Asia, see O. W. Wolters, "China Irredenta: The South, "*The World Today*, 19 (Dec., 1963) no. 12, pp. 540–552.

[73] Herz, *op. cit.*, asserts that during Sihanouk's visit to Peking in Feb., 1956, he was assured by the Chinese "that if ever [he] had trouble with the Viet Minh, he need only appeal to Peking" (p. 127). During 1955, Sihanouk had complained to the International Control Commission in Cambodia of hostile North Vietnamese propaganda directed at his government and of alleged North Vietnamese incursions into Cambodian territory; given his forthright manner, it is entirely likely that he raised this matter with the Chinese during his visit in 1956. The Cambodian Foreign Ministry, however, categorically denied that such an assurance was given to the Prince (see *Angkor*, Dec. 7, 1956). For an account of the Cambodian charges against North Vietnam, see below, pp. 167–171.

we will take into consideration the needs of the Royal Cambodian Government, the possibilities at our disposal and the conditions prevailing at the time.[74]

Later in the year, Chou En-lai proposed the establishment of a "peace area" in Indochina,[75] and in December, 1960, during his third visit to Peking, Prince Sihanouk signed a treaty of friendship and nonaggression with China.[76]

China's good will is valued by Cambodia for another reason, less often mentioned but of great importance. Viet Minh designs on Cambodia during the Franco–Vietnam

[74] This statement was made at a press conference in Phnom Penh on May 11, 1960, and was quoted in *NCNA*, May 11, 1960, in *SCMP*, no. 2260, p. 41. See also *Cambodge d'Aujourd'hui*, no. 5 (May, 1960), p. 21.

[75] *NCNA*, Sept. 2, 1960, in *SCMP*, no. 2334, p. 31.

[76] For the text of the treaty see *NCNA*, May 3, 1961, in *SCMP*, no. 2491, pp. 35–36. The key articles of the treaty are as follows:

"Art. 1. The People's Republic of China and the Kingdom of Cambodia will maintain a lasting peace between them and develop and consolidate their friendly relations.

"Art. 2. Each contracting party undertakes to respect the sovereignty, independence, and territorial integrity of the other.

"Art. 3. The contracting parties undertake to settle any dispute that may arise between them by peaceful means.

"Art. 4. Each contracting party undertakes not to commit aggression against each other and not to take part in any military alliance directed against the other.

"Art. 5. The contracting parties will develop and strengthen the economic and cultural ties between the two countries in accord with the principles of equality and mutual benefit and of non-interference in each other's internal affairs.

"Art. 6. Any difference or dispute that may arise out of the interpretation or application of the present treaty or one or several articles of the present treaty shall be settled by negotiation through normal diplomatic channels."

For the texts of the declarations and communiqués issued on the occasion of the signing of the treaty, see *AKP*, Dec. 22, 1960, and *NCNA*, Dec. 19, 1960, in *SCMP*, no. 2404, p. 21.

war have not been forgotten by Prince Sihanouk. Indeed, this and more recent Viet Minh-supported activities in Cambodia make it likely that he considers the North Vietnamese to be a more serious threat to his country than the Thai and the South Vietnamese. It is probably for this reason that he has kept a watchful eye on the advancements of the Viet Minh-supported Pathet Lao in Laos. He fears that a decisive Pathet Lao victory would permit the Viet Minh to extend their influence into Laos and from there into Cambodia.[77] On her own Cambodia could not for long withstand concerted Viet Minh aggression, and the American experience in Laos and South Vietnam, according to officials close to Sihanouk, has convinced him that to appeal to the United States would only involve his country in protracted and futile bloodshed. On the assumption that China still exercises some influence over North Vietnam, a friendly China would be able to intervene on Cambodia's behalf to restrain the Viet Minh.

Prince Sihanouk's reasoning on the implications of Chinese–North Vietnamese relations was indicated in statements made in 1961; despairing that the big powers would ever agree to a peaceful settlement of the Laotian crisis, he predicted a Pathet Lao victory and warned that in such an event he would have to "entreat China to make North Vietnam confine itself to South Vietnam." [78] Later in 1961, the exposure of a Viet Minh-sponsored plot to subvert Prince Sihanouk's regime prompted him to state:

Since we have become wedged between two SEATO countries,

[77] This information was conveyed to the author by Cambodian sources which he considers to be reliable. See also Sihanouk's interview with *Nice-Matin* (France), May 16, 1961.

[78] These remarks were broadcast by Radio Phnom Penh, May 3, 1961.

the socialist bloc not only supports us diplomatically, but also will order (I suppose) the Viet Minh to suspend (temporarily, without doubt) its activities in support of the Pracheachon.[79]

This statement, while questioning the sincerity of Communist professions of respect for Cambodia's neutrality, may also have been designed to pressure China into taking an unequivocal stand on the issue of Viet Minh infiltration into Cambodia and to assess the degree of influence which China actually exercises over North Vietnam.

In May, 1963, Chinese President Liu Shao-chi visited Cambodia to endorse China's previous assurances of support for her independence. At that time Liu also emphasized that China was not interested in using Laos as the site of armed confrontation with the West. It is of significance that shortly before Liu's arrival in Phnom Penh, North Vietnam publicly renounced Vietnamese claims to Cambodian islands in the Gulf of Siam. Earlier, Prince Sihanouk's efforts to determine North Vietnam's reactions to South Vietnam's claims to these islands had evoked only noncommittal replies.[80] It was perhaps in return for this support that Cambodia in 1963 and 1964 proposed that the United Nations give China's seat in the General Assembly to the People's Government.

[79] Quoted in *Réalités Cambodgiennes,* July 14, 1961. In early 1962, the government disclosed that it had arrested 15 members of the Pracheachon, including its leader, Non Suon, upon discovering that they were carrying North Vietnamese directives for subversion of the Sangkum, and Cambodia's teachers, Buddhist monks, and the military. See Norodom Sihanouk, *Le Cambodge et ses relations avec ses voisins* (Phnom Penh: Imprimerie du Ministère de l'Information, 1962), pp. 59–61.

[80] See the *Washington Post,* May 22, 1963, for an account of an interview with Prince Sihanouk during which this subject was discussed. See also *Réalités Cambodgiennes,* July 19, 1962, and below, pp. 188–189.

Cambodia's Foreign Policy

Relations with the United States

Cambodia's relations with the United States have oscillated between periods of warm friendship and coolness bordering on hostility. Strains on Cambodian–American relations, when they have occurred, have usually been traceable to harassments of Cambodia by Thailand and South Vietnam. It has been the Cambodian view that, while the United States may not be the instigator of these hostile actions, she is guilty of tacit approval of them, for economically, politically, and militarily the regimes of these two countries are so dependent upon American support that the United States could easily restrain them if she chose to do so. But in spite of frequently outspoken criticisms of American policy in Southeast Asia, Cambodian leaders did not until 1963 question the importance of permitting the continuation of the American presence in their country through its economic- and military-aid programs. For while withdrawal of American assistance was seen as probably stimulating offers of increased aid from the Communist bloc, the fact that the Communist presence would no longer be checked by a countervailing influence would undermine Cambodia's independence.[81]

As of 1963, the total aid granted to Cambodia by the United States since 1955 amounted to $403.7 million, of

[81] In 1959, Sihanouk portrayed the role of economic aid in maintaining a balance of power between the blocs in Cambodia as follows: "By keeping ourselves in the golden mean, by accepting economical and technical aid from Communist countries, we succeed in neutralizing the American prevalence. . . . The contrary is also true. The influence of the Communist countries must similarly be neutralized; on that account we ought to preserve American friendship." Quoted in François Nivolon, "Cambodia—The Universal Beneficiary," *Far Eastern Economic Review*, XXVII (July 16, 1959), no. 3, p. 73.

which $94.0 million was directed toward military and defense support. United States economic aid was directed principally toward long-range programs for the improvement of Cambodia's primary industries and the development of her educational and health facilities. The United States also undertook one "impact project,"

Table 1. Foreign aid (economic and military) to Cambodia, 1955–1964 (in millions of U.S. dollars)

Foreign Country	1955–1960	1960–1961	1961–1962	1962–1963	1963–1964	Total
United States *						
Economic	179.2	23.1	33.2	20.0	6.9	309.7
Military	64.0	3.2	6.5	10.3†	10.0†	94.0
People's Republic of China ‡	22.4	25.7				48.1
France §	18.8		1.8		32.6	53.2
Soviet Union ‡	28.8	.5			20.0	49.3
Japan ||	4.3		4.1			8.4
Czechoslovakia ‡	1.4	8.0†				9.4
Poland ‡	1.9	.3†				2.2
Yugoslavia #					6.0	6.0
United Kingdom ** Australia New Zealand Canada	3.0					3.0
United Nations ††	1.0	.4	1.7	‡‡	‡‡	3.1

* Agency for International Development, Mission to Cambodia, *Termination Report, American Economic Aid Program in Cambodia* (Phnom Penh: U.S. AID, 1964); *U.S. Economic Assistance*

the $32 million, 130-mile highway linking Phnom Penh with the port city of Sihanoukville. Built to enable Cambodia to become less dependent on Saigon and Bangkok for the conduction of foreign trade, the road also has stra-

_____

Program in Cambodia, 1963–1964 (Phnom Penh: U.S. AID, 1963); *U.S. Foreign Assistance and Assistance from International Organizations: Obligations and Loan Authorizations,* July 1, 1945–June 30, 1961, revised (Washington, D.C., Mar. 21, 1962). The total for economic aid includes cash grants and other items not listed by year.

† These figures are estimated.

‡ Most of the data on Communist bloc aid were obtained from its members' embassies in Phnom Penh. The amount listed in 1963 is a loan, repayable in 12 years at an unspecified low interest rate. *See L'oeuvre du Sangkum Reastr Niyum: Bilan de décembre 1962 à juin 1963* (Phnom Penh: Imprimerie du Ministère de l'Information, 1963), p. 103.

§ These figures were supplied by the French Economic Aid Mission, Phnom Penh. The amount listed in 1964 is a long-term loan.

‖ This information was supplied by the Japanese Embassy, Phnom Penh.

Yugoslavia's aid was in the form of a loan, repayable in 15 years at 3 per cent interest. See *Réalités Cambodgiennes,* July 26, 1963.

** Since 1953, most aid has been furnished through the Colombo Plan. In 1961, the United Kingdom proposed to provide a civil aviation school for the training of ground specialists and to train the cadre of teachers for the school. Australia has offered scholarships for secondary and university technical training. The value of this aid is unknown. Source: Embassies of the United Kingdom and Australia, Phnom Penh.

†† Agency for International Development, Statistics and Reports Division, *U.S. Foreign Assistance and Assistance from International Organizations: Obligations and Loan Authorizations,* July 1, 1945–June 30, 1961, revised (Washington, D.C., Mar. 21, 1962). In 1961–1962, United Nations Technical Assistance had 59 technicians in Cambodia and was offering 24 fellowships for study in various foreign countries. In addition, the International Labor Organization offered to establish, jointly with the Cambodian government, a center for the training of skilled workers. The estimated cost of this center was $2.1 million.

‡‡ Unknown.

tegic importance, as an access route for troops and supplies should Cambodia be subjected to Communist aggression.[82] Prior to 1962, American aid for Cambodia's industrial development consisted only of loans to small private industry; the United States resisted Cambodian suggestions that she assist further by constructing larger, state-owned industrial facilities which would permit the country to reduce its imports. In 1962, however, the United States offered to help Cambodia secure an international loan which, together with local investment, would pay for the erection of a jute-bag factory. It was suggested by the United States that such a new industry could result in the development of a new marketable crop in Cambodia, a large net annual savings in foreign exchange, and make Cambodian rice, which is now shipped in bags imported from Calcutta, more competitive in world markets.[83]

American military aid [84] allowed Cambodia to divert its own funds to necessary public services. This aid helped to maintain Cambodia's army at a 30,000-man level, deemed by American officials in Cambodia adequate for defense and internal security needs. From the beginning of the military-aid program, the United States was explicit in its intentions not to do more to develop

[82] See U.S. House of Representatives, Committee on Government Operations, *Hearings before a Sub-Committee of the Committee on Government Operations, Part I: Cambodian Port Highway,* 87th Congress, 1st Session, Feb. 9–June 20, 1961 (Washington, D.C.: Government Printing Office, 1961), pp. 1–41.

[83] See *Aide économique américaine au Cambodge en 1962* (Phnom Penh: U.S. Agency for International Development (AID), 1962), pp. 28–30.

[84] The United States contributed an average of $12.2 million each year in military aid. In 1962 alone, the amount of aid, exclusive of military equipment, totaled $12.4 million, or 32.6 per cent of Cambodia's budget for its armed forces and police.

the armed forces "unless [Cambodia] believes that [the] application of the principle of collective security will better assure its independence." [85] From time to time, Cambodia sought an increase in arms aid, but the United States did not fulfill her requests entirely to her satisfaction, presumably, Cambodian leaders are convinced, because Americans are critical of her neutral policy, which fails to "see Red China as its principal enemy." [86] In 1961–1962, however, at the peak of the Laotian crisis, the United States increased aid to Cambodia to enable her to improve her defenses along the troubled Laotian–Vietnamese frontiers.

Aid from other Western sources has included the provision of military training and, in 1964, a small quantity of military equipment, credits for the development of education, and various engineering and construction projects, including the seaport of Sihanoukville and the international airport at Pochentong near Phnom Penh, by France; improvements in the Phnom Penh water system, a bridge across the Tonlé Sap River, and several small agricultural projects by Japan; the construction of a technical high school by West Germany; and diverse Colombo Plan aid, in which Great Britain, Australia, New Zealand, and Canada have been among the major contributors. In addition, all of these countries are cooperating with sev-

---

[85] Letter of Secretary of State Dulles to Foreign Minister Nong Kimny, Apr. 19, 1956.

[86] See U.S. Senate, Committee on Appropriations, Hearing, *Report on United States Military Operations and Mutual Security Programs Overseas,* by [Senator] Dennis Chavez, 86th Congress, 2d Session (Washington, D.C.: Government Printing Office, 1960), p. 86. This statement was made by Senator Chavez, who added, "Cambodian officials are still oriented against the historically traditional threats from other countries."

eral others in the extensive Mekong River development project, which is, however, still in the surveying stages.[87]

But while the United States was the principal donor of economic and military aid prior to the end of 1963, Cambodia was troubled by suspicions that the United States was lending covert encouragement to efforts to supplant Sihanouk's Sangkum regime with one that would be unequivocally oriented toward the West.

In June, 1958, it was reported that two South Vietnamese battalions crossed the Cambodian frontier near Bokéo in Stung Treng province, occupied a village for several hours, and left only after moving the border markers to favor South Vietnam.[88] Because he believed that United States support maintained the South Vietnamese government in existence, Prince Sihanouk appealed to Washington to intervene on Cambodia's behalf. The American response, which counseled moderation to the South Vietnamese, appeared halfhearted to Prince Sihanouk, and led him to conclude that Cambodia required the concrete support of other powers. A week of urgent discussion with his advisers resulted on July 13 in the initiation of diplomatic relations with China. The decision to recognize China took the United States by surprise. Ambassador Carl Strom was called for consultation to

[87] In 1963, it was announced in Phnom Penh that a Mekong project dam would be completed in northwestern Cambodia in 1967–1968. See *Réalités Cambodgiennes*, Aug. 2, 1963. For a discussion of the Mekong project, see C. Hart Schaaf and Russell H. Fifield, *The Lower Mekong: Challenge to Cooperation in Southeast Asia* (Princeton: Van Nostrand, 1963).

[88] See Great Britain, *Seventh Interim Report of the International Commission for Supervision and Control in Cambodia for the period January 1, 1958 to December 31, 1958. Cambodia No. 1 (1959),* Cmnd. 887. (London: H.M. Stationery Office, 1960), pp. 20, 24–29, 30–43. See also below, pp. 159–161.

Washington, where he reportedly learned that a threat of aid suspension was being considered as a first step toward removing Sihanouk from power.[89] The Ambassador was said to have argued convincingly that this tactic, which had recently been employed successfully against Premier Souvannaphouma in Laos, would fail in Cambodia. He persuaded the State Department that Cambodia had not abandoned her neutral position and that the possibility of her doing so in the future could most effectively be forestalled by urging South Vietnam to utilize peaceful means of settling differences with Cambodia. The United States then consulted with President Ngo Dinh Diem, and soon thereafter he sent his brother, Ngo Dinh Nhu, to Phnom Penh, where talks with Prince Sihanouk resulted in a *détente* in the relations between the two countries.

During September, 1958, Prince Sihanouk flew to the United States to preside over Cambodia's delegation to the thirteenth session of the United Nations General Assembly and to confer with President Eisenhower, Secretary of State Dulles, and Assistant Secretary of State for Far Eastern Affairs Walter Robertson. Although they expressed disapproval of his policy—Robertson took the opportunity to remind the Prince that the Chinese could not be trusted [90]—the American leaders assured Sihanouk that the United States would use its good offices to try to ameliorate Cambodia–South Vietnam relations.[91] Sihanouk re-

---

[89] This information about Ambassador Strom's actions is derived from American sources which the author considers to be reliable.

[90] See *Réalités Cambodgiennes*, Oct. 25, 1958.

[91] At this time Prince Sihanouk also made known his uneasiness about heightened cold-war tension in Asia which had been precipitated by the issue of Quemoy and Matsu, and he offered to mediate the dispute with China. His services were not accepted. Sihanouk wrote about this incident in an article entitled "Comment nous voyons la Chine," *Réalités Cambodgiennes*, Sept. 27, 1963.

turned to Cambodia convinced that ties of friendship with the United States had been tightened and that the equilibrium between the powers in Indochina, "without which our neutrality would disappear, and with it, our very independence," would be continued.[92]

A few months later, he told an American correspondent:

We cherish American friendship, not only because it is, itself, precious, but also because it is indispensable to us to counterbalance the inevitable influence of Eastern countries.

We know perfectly well that our neutrality and, therefore, our independence would be in danger if the leaders of the West would break off with us. We would have no alternative but to depend on ourselves or to slip, little as we are, toward those who, in the East, open their arms to us.

We are critical, not of America but of certain aspects of its policies. We wish to remain neutral and friendly with all. Our only immediate difficulties come from neighbors bugling their indefectible adhesion to the American bloc and which take turns at causing serious troubles for us, thanks to the considerable aid and numerous arms given by their American allies. We wish to remain neutral [but] we are the object of much pressure to join the "free world front" where we would be only a pawn.[93]

It soon became evident to the Prince that *rapprochement* was only apparent. Early in 1959, relations with the United States were again threatened when several prominent Cambodian personalities were implicated in a for-

[92] Remarks made in an address upon his arrival in Phnom Penh, Oct. 26, 1958, quoted in Royaume du Cambodge, *Principaux discours et allocutions de S.A.R. le Prince Norodom Sihanouk . . . en 1958* (Phnom Penh: Imprimerie du Ministère de l'Information, n.d. [1959?]), p. 88.

[93] *Réalités Cambodgiennes*, Feb. 7, 1959.

eign-supported plot against the government.[94] At a meeting of the Jeunesse Socialiste Royale Khmère on March 2, the Prince left no doubt of his conviction that Thailand, South Vietnam, and "certain American services" (i.e., the Central Intelligence Agency) were involved. In the course of disclosing the details of the plot, he said:

Finally, we should mention the declarations of Dap Chhuon's brother, the ex-deputy Slat Peou, revealing that he was charged with making regular contacts with an embassy of a "grande nation seatiste" [i.e., the United States]. . . . I have written to President Eisenhower to ask for United States intervention in order to stop this illegal "patronage" of our neighbors.[95]

Two months later, on May 7, 1959, President Eisenhower wrote to Sihanouk to reaffirm American support of Cambodia's policies; [96] this period was characterized by a cessation of provocative acts by Thailand and South Vietnam.

To appreciate Cambodia's nonalignment policy it is necessary to understand her fear of her more powerful neighbors, Vietnam and Thailand. Americans who have been critical of Cambodia's relations with China fail to realize that the Chinese have never posed a direct threat to Cambodia's territorial integrity. The Thai and the Vietnamese, on the other hand, in addition to engaging in numerous border provocations and attempted subversion, have laid claims to territory over which Cambodia has historically exercised jurisdiction. In the light of the threat to her security which is posed by her stronger neighbors, Cambodia feels that a friendly China can be of in-

---

94 For the details of this plot, see below, pp. 163–166.

95 See Royaume du Cambodge, *Principaux Discours,* pp. 24–25.

96 See Sihanouk's address to the eighth National Congress, July 4, 1959, in *ibid.,* p. 43.

valuable assistance in helping her to maintain a balanced relationship with them. The important lesson she asks the United States to learn from Cambodia's continuing disputes with her neighbors is that the division of the world into Communist and anti-Communist camps is not a realistic one for many countries who, for reasons peculiar to their own history, find it more practical to partition the world in other ways.[97]

Prince Sihanouk recognizes the right of Cambodia's neighbors to assure their security in an alliance with the United States. But he is unable to understand America's apparent failure to differentiate her commitments against Communist imperialism from similar attempts at expansion by her allies. In his appraisal of the situation, Thailand and South Vietnam are exploiting American backing, given either through SEATO or directly, to encroach upon Cambodia, on the pretext that she is pro-Communist. According to the Prince, continued American support of these countries in the face of aggressive acts committed by them completely disregards the security needs of the United States and those of Southeast Asia.[98]

In early 1960, as antagonism between Cambodia and her neighbors was intensified,[99] the Prince again voiced his concern over what he felt was misguided American policy. Writing of the "three-way conflict among com-

[97] For an elaboration of this idea, although not including a direct reference to Thailand and Vietnam, see Prince Sihanouk's address to the thirteenth Session of the United Nations General Assembly, Sept. 24, 1958, as extracted in Royaume du Cambodge, *Cambodge*, edited by Charles Meyer (Phnom Penh: Imprimerie du Ministère de l'Information, 1962), pp. 71–72. See also Norodom Sihanouk, "Cambodia Neutral: The Dictate of Necessity," *Foreign Affairs*, XXXVI (July, 1958), no. 4, pp. 582–586.

[98] See *Réalités Cambodgiennes*, Feb. 28, 1959.

[99] See below, pp. 145, 159.

munism, neutrality and Western anti-communist democracy," [100] he described what he felt is the most important cause of instability in Asia: "The existence of certain white powers behind certain Asian governments, whose policies and activities respond to the interests of their foreign allies."

In one word [the Prince continued], this . . . cause has been born of the colonialist sequels (if we employ the communist vocabulary). These are sequels which now embarrass certain Asian leaders who, either lacking a conscience or because of carelessness, refuse to understand that the powers, which have had the habit of dominating and exploiting Asian nations of diverse hues, and which, at the present time, should recognize the independence of Asian nations, seek only to advance their interests by utilizing new means to exploit us. Their policy is founded on the principle of divide and rule, by which they seek to smash the solidarity of Asian nations by rendering them enemies of each other.

During the succeeding months South Vietnam laid claims to several of Cambodia's offshore islands, and the propaganda activities of the dissident Khmer Serei (Free Khmer) movement, led by Son Ngoc Thanh and Sam Sary—Sihanouk alleged with Thai and American support —were increased. In addition, certain articles in the American press seemed to the Sihanouk government designed to justify to the American people a United States-supported subversion of royal authority.[101]

The government took particular exception to the remarks of Tillman Durdin, the Far East correspondent of the *New York Times,* who wrote:

[100] *Neak Cheat Niyum,* Jan. 9, 1960.
[101] Among the American press singled out for criticism were the *New York Times,* and *Time* and *Newsweek* magazines.

In Cambodia, mercurial Prince Norodom Sihanouk runs still another form of authoritarianism. He maintains his dominance through a mass party that exercises a monopoly of political activity and demagogy. Prince Sihanouk remains widely popular but his abridgments of democracy, his neutralism and his tolerance toward communism are disliked in some quarters and there have been sporadic flareups of violence against his regime.[102]

Prince Sihanouk's riposte came in a caustic *"Lettre ouverte aux milieux impérialistes,"* published in *Neak Cheat Niyum* on May 21, 1960.

You have met with humiliating defeats and the weakness of your policy in your Asian satellite nations is a well-known fact.

Now you are trying to justify and minimize your errors in the eyes of the people and the youth of your country.

The Prince asserted that the United States was trying to justify her mistakes in Asia by "foolishly accusing neutral Cambodia of not practicing a democratic system such as in South Korea, Thailand, Pakistan, South Vietnam [and] Taiwan." He charged that American officials, lacking integrity, had contracted to produce such "propaganda" as *Cambodia, Its People, Its Society, Its Culture,*[103] and the work of Martin Herz,[104] "with the sole aim of sullying my

---

[102] *New York Times,* May 1, 1960, Part 4, p. 3.

[103] David J. Steinberg *et al.,* revised for 1959 by Herbert Vreeland (New Haven, Conn.: Human Relations Area Files Press, 1959). Cambodians objected to this revised edition because of its antineutral bias and because of the many errors of fact contained in the political and foreign relations chapters.

[104] In *A Short History of Cambodia* (New York: Praeger, 1958), Herz, a foreign-service officer assigned to Phnom Penh from 1955 to 1957, displays a marked pro-Western sentiment in his discussion of Cambodia's relations with the United States, Thailand, and South Vietnam.

reputation, of weakening our neutrality and of glorifying Son Ngoc Thanh."

These dishonest books and writings have been distributed by you in all the schools and universities all over the United States. Today young Americans know Cambodia, its policies, its efforts and its achievements only by the deformations of unscrupulous authors.

The American ambassador, William Trimble, took Sihanouk's letter to be a direct attack on the United States government, and in a personal reply, written on May 23, Trimble informed the Prince that the writings to which he objected "are those of writers free to think and say what they will, and . . . they are expressing their own views, not those of the Government of the United States." [105] He reminded the Prince that he and his colleagues in nearby countries "have made continuing efforts to improve relations between Cambodia and its neighbors." Although some progress had been made toward this goal, complete success was hampered by differences which were rooted deeply in the past. His government's respect for Cambodia's independence and neutrality should be evident, he said, from the continuing American military and economic aid, which amounted to more than twice what Cambodia received from all other countries. He concluded by declaring that "the function of this aid is to strengthen Cambodia's ability to maintain its independence and to carry out national policies."

Was the anger revealed in Sihanouk's letter simply a reaction to recurrent troubles with Cambodia's neighbors

[105] Ambassador William Trimble, letter to Prince Norodom Sihanouk, May 23, 1960. The letter has not been published, but a copy of it was made available to the author by the American Embassy, Phnom Penh.

and an unfavorable American press? The real issue was revealed by the government a few weeks later to be an American decision "to increase the armament of the member countries or satellites of [SEATO], on the pretext that People's China has the intention of invading these neighbors." [106] The United States had recently supplied South Vietnam and Laos with modern arms. "Not wishing to be outdone, Thailand, which maintains a well-equipped army, sent [Foreign Minister] Thanat Khoman to Washington to demand American military equipment which will permit it to fight against the communist danger coming from People's China and . . . from Cambodia." [107] Stating emphatically that the real danger to stability in Indochina was not posed by China, but rather by Thailand and Vietnam, the official Sangkum newspaper, *Neak Cheat Niyum*, declared that "these neighbors use American war material to menace our country, to conquer parcels of our territory, and to equip and train groups of traitors and guerillas to ravage our provinces." The paper complained of the outdated arms furnished Cambodia by the United States, which were a greater menace to their users than to Cambodia's adversaries. Furthermore, it asserted that

while we are neither an ally nor a satellite, in that which concerns the problem of military aid we do not have the rights and liberty of an independent or a neutral country, for we are still tied to an agreement with the United States which holds the exclusive contract to furnish arms to our country.

This accord stipulates that the United States will procure aid for Cambodia in order to give it the chance to defend its liberty and independence. In return, Cambodia will not have the right to receive military aid from other powers, and in

[106] *Neak Cheat Niyum*, June 25, 1960.   [107] *Ibid.*

particular, from the socialist countries. Thus, although our country remains outside of the "Free World" the United States has obligations towards us.[108]

If the United States should refuse to provide Cambodia with arms "sufficient to constitute a barrier to the territorial ambitions of our neighbors," then Cambodia should be allowed to appeal to "other powers which are ready to aid us." Alternatively, the editors of the paper proposed an arms moratorium in Indochina.

The government's position, as expressed in *Neak Cheat Niyum*, was viewed with grave concern by the United States, and on June 29 the American chargé d'affaires, Robert Moore, called on the Foreign Minister and thereafter addressed an *aide-mémoire* to the royal government in which he gave assurance of American opposition to rebel activities directed against Cambodia from foreign countries. He said the United States was prepared to consult with Cambodia on the extent and nature of alleged threats as well as on measures to counter them.[109] Publicly the government expressed its disappointment at what it viewed as a noncommittal response,[110] but soon thereafter

[108] This last paragraph suggests that there was either an informal understanding between Cambodia and the United States or a secret protocol, which was not published at the time the text of the military-aid agreement was released to the public in 1955. The allegation has been categorically denied by the State Department. Cambodia was restricted only in her use of consumable material, e.g., American aviation fuel could not be used for MIGs received from the Soviet Union. For the text of the agreement, see "Military Assistance Agreement between the United States of America and Cambodia." Effected by exchange of notes, Phnom Penh, May 16, 1955. *Treaties and Other International Acts Series 3240* (Washington, D.C.: Government Printing Office, 1956). For further comment on this subject by Prince Sihanouk himself, see *New York Times*, Jan. 15, 1964.

[109] *Neak Cheat Niyum,* July 9, 1960.

[110] *Ibid.,* and July 16, 1960. See also *AKP*, July 24 and 29, 1960.

National Defense Minister General Lon Nol left for Washington for talks, which resulted, in 1961–1962, in the provision by the United States of increased military aid to raise the army's strength by three battalions.[111]

With the advent of the Kennedy administration, United States–Cambodia relations greatly improved. The United States policy-makers appeared to have satisfied themselves that a country can be neutral without being pro-Communist. However, Cambodia's clashes with her neighbors, which have continued into the present, were still potential sources of strain on Cambodia's relations with the United States. As Sihanouk said in a press conference in March, 1961:

The capital error of American policy towards Cambodia . . . during the past eight years has been to consider neutrality as an attitude hostile to the United States. The policy of strict neutrality adopted by Cambodia since the achievement of its independence implies a refusal to align itself with either of the blocs, western, socialist or even neutralist, as well as the desire for friendly relations with all the powers which respect our independence and our national sovereignty.

Unhappily, the United States has from the beginning searched for means to bend our neutrality, and even to overthrow our national regime which the Khmer people have charged with applying the neutral policy. However, we have always made a distinction between the imperialist circles who are systematically hostile towards us and the American leaders who, while badly informed of the nature of our neutrality, have supported us with their sympathy and their economic and technical aid.

Another tragic error of American policy is the unconditional aid given to the unpopular dictatorships which for several

[111] See *AKP*, Nov. 6, 1960, and *Réalités Cambodgiennes*, Nov. 11, 1960.

years have not ceased to threaten our territorial integrity. We are particularly distressed to see that not only have certain American circles backed these threats but have even accused Cambodia of being the author of them!

Despite these failures, American diplomacy has never stopped searching for the "strong man" in all Southeast Asian states and of maintaining him in power by all the means at its disposal. This persistence in error which led to the civil war in Laos and in South Vietnam does not win friendship for the United States among Asian peoples.

We have hoped that the change in the American administration would lead to the "painful reappraisal" of which much has been said, but for which the people of Southeast Asia are still waiting.[112]

The shift in American policy in relations with Cambodia was evident in the serious though unsuccessful attempt made by the United States during the period 1961–1963 to mediate the border dispute between Cambodia and Thailand, a conflict which led to a disruption in diplomatic relations between the neighbors and the closure of their border in 1961. The United States also tried to provide Cambodia with a greater sense of security by granting her increased arms aid. As one might expect, however, the conciliatory attitude of the United States toward Cambodia had repercussions among Thai leaders, some of whom appeared to feel that Thailand was being let down by the United States. Because any action of the United States which is intended to keep Cambodia from joining the Communist bloc must be weighed against its consequences, particularly the possibility that it might prompt Thailand to leave the Western camp, it is unlikely that American actions will keep pace with the change in

[112] Press conference, Phnom Penh, Mar. 2, 1961.

American attitude, at least to the degree considered acceptable by Cambodians. As we shall see in a later chapter, the United States during 1962–1963 was to disappoint Cambodia on an issue of great importance to her, i.e., a neutrality treaty by which the Geneva powers and Thailand and South Vietnam would officially guarantee her security.[113]

[113] This and other developments in United States–Cambodian relations are discussed below, pp. 190–216.

CHAPTER V

Cambodia's Relations
with Thailand and Vietnam

THE present cold war between Cambodia and her neighbors, Thailand and South Vietnam, can be traced back to the years when the Thai (in the thirteenth century) and the Vietnamese (in the seventeenth century), in the course of their expansion southward, began to encroach upon Khmer territory. By the mid-nineteenth century, the incursions of her neighbors had reduced the Khmer Empire to a virtual condominium whose kings rendered homage to the courts of Bangkok and Hué. The actual absorption of Cambodia by the Thai and the Vietnamese was forestalled only by the intervention of France and the establishment of its protectorate in 1864.

Relations with Thailand

Since 1953, when Cambodia emerged from the French protectorate as an independent nation, most of her relations with Thailand have revolved around a series of incidents involving press and radio attacks on each other, cattle rustling, piracy, mutual charges of false arrests, armed forays by the police forces of both countries, violations of airspace, and Thai territorial claims. The major territorial issue between the two countries in recent times has concerned the ruins of the ancient Khmer temple of Preah Vihear[1] located on a rocky promontory in the Dangrek mountains, which Thailand had seized during the Japanese occupation of Indochina and was forced to return in 1946 by the Treaty of Washington.

When the French withdrew from Cambodia in 1953, Thai police forces almost immediately occupied the site of the temple.[2] In accordance with the suggestion of the Thai that border problems be submitted to negotiations, Cambodia expressed willingness to discuss the dispute over claims to Preah Vihear. At a meeting between representatives of both governments it was agreed that a mixed commission should be entrusted with the task of examining the topography of the region. The commission's terms of reference, however, proved to be an insurmountable obstacle. Cambodia insisted that a map of the frontier, which was appended to the 1907 Franco–Siamese treaty,[3] confirmed her rights and asserted that Thai actions since 1907

[1] For a discussion of Preah Vihear from a historical and archaeological standpoint, see Lawrence Palmer Briggs, *The Ancient Khmer Empire*, Transactions of the American Philosophical Society, New Series, Vol. 41, Part 1 (Philadelphia: The American Philosophical Society, 1951), pp. 111, 130, 139, 161–163.

[2] See Royaume du Cambodge, *Documents relatifs à la suspension des relations diplomatiques entre le Cambodge et la Thailande* (Phnom Penh: Imprimerie du Ministère de l'Information, n.d. [1958?]), p. 1.

[3] A protocol attached to the Franco–Siamese treaty of Mar. 23, 1907, by which Thailand retroceded Battambang, Siem Reap, and other territory to Cambodia, stipulated that the border would follow the watershed through the Dangrek mountains. A sketch map annexed to the protocol placed the temple east of the watershed and thus, in 1956–1958, Cambodia claimed it as her possession. Thailand, however, claimed that the temple was located west of the watershed and thus was a Thai possession. For the text of the treaty see Protectorat du Cambodge, *Recueil des actes du gouvernement cambodgien* (Saigon: Imprimerie Albert Portail, 1920), pp. 145–149.

implicitly acknowledged Cambodia's sovereignty over the temple area.[4] Thus, in the 1956–1958 negotiations, her representatives refused to concede that the governments could negotiate on anything other than the "treaties and the documents annexed."[5] Thailand's position, on the other hand, was that since the temple area lay on the Thai side of the watershed which, according to the 1907 treaty, demarcated the boundary, it was an integral part of Thailand. Thus, she agreed to negotiate only on the basis of the "treaties and protocol annexed"; to agree to "the documents annexed," Thailand claimed, would open the subject to "wide meaning and might refer to a sketch which has no accuracy."[6]

Preliminary talks continued with little progress throughout 1957 and early 1958. Matters were brought to a head in the summer of 1958, when it was announced that Prince Sihanouk would pay a private visit to Bangkok for the purpose of holding a "man-to-man" discussion with the Thai leaders. The visit resulted in an agreement to con-

[4] These actions included the public use of a map by Thailand which shows Preah Vihear to be in Cambodian territory; the confirmation of the 1907 border agreement in 1925 and 1937 treaties of friendship, commerce, and navigation between France, on behalf of the Indochina states, and Siam; the publication by Thailand in 1937 of a map showing Preah Vihear as lying in Cambodia; statements made in 1941 by the Thai, after having occupied northern Cambodia, that Preah Vihear had been "retaken"; failure to raise the issue in the Washington conference of Nov., 1946; and acts by Thai national and provincial officials, especially in 1930, acknowledging Franco–Cambodian sovereignty over the temple. See "Case Concerning the Temple of Preah Vihear (Cambodia v. Thailand), Merits, Judgment of 15 June 1962," *International Court of Justice Reports,* 1962, pp. 22–36.

[5] Royaume du Cambodge, *Documents relatifs,* pp. 7–8.

[6] Ministry of Foreign Affairs, *Relations between Thailand and Cambodia* (Bangkok: Prachandra Press, 1959), pp. 20–21.

duct negotiations at the ministerial level, but Sihanouk's visit to Peking on August 14 and the announcement by Cambodia of her recognition of the People's Government of China was interpreted by the Thai as an attempt to intimidate them.[7] The Bangkok government immediately declared a state of emergency in six provinces and one district situated along the Cambodian frontier. In Bangkok the Thai charged that "communist infiltration into this country became very active, and conclusive evidence was received by the . . . authorities showing intensified contacts between leftist elements in Cambodia and certain aliens in Thailand.[8] The Thai Prime Minister, General Thanom Kittikhachon, stated at a press conference that with Cambodia's recognition of Communist China, "all 260,000 Chinese in Cambodia will become Communists without question."[9] Upon arriving in the Thai capital in mid-August, the Cambodian delegation to the ministerial conference was greeted with a violent anti-Cambodian campaign conducted in the Bangkok press.[10]

The *Siam Rath Weekly Review* stood alone in counseling a more objective view.[11] Its editor, Khukrit Pramoj,

[7] See *ibid.*, p. 7. That part of the Sino–Cambodian declaration objected to by Thailand read as follows: "Le Premier Ministre Chou En Lai a exprimé ses regrets que la territoire du Cambodge a été victime à plusieurs reprises de violations et du blocus des pays voisins, et estime que c'est là un acte extrêmement inamical. Le Gouvernement Chinois espère que les pays asiatiques intéressés coexisteront pacifiquement avec le Royaume du Cambodge conformément aux résolutions de la Conférence de Bandoeng sans se laisser guider par la politique colonialiste étrangère."

[8] See *ibid.*, p. 6. A Thai communiqué to this effect was reprinted in Royaume du Cambodge, *Documents relatifs,* p. 9.

[9] Quoted in *Siam Rath Weekly Review*, Aug. 7, 1958.

[10] See Royaume du Cambodge, *Documents relatifs,* pp. 9–15.

[11] See *Siam Rath Weekly Review*, Aug. 7, 1958.

urged his countrymen to seek an understanding of the behavior of modern Cambodia through a study of her history, much of which revolved around attempts of Siam and Annam, and finally France, to subjugate her. He suggested two reasons to explain Cambodia's move toward China. First, the Cambodians may feel a need for external political support of their independence. Second, they may be in need of economic assistance over and above that which the United States was prepared to give.

Relations between the two countries rapidly deteriorated after Cambodia's recognition of Peking and there followed demonstrations outside the Cambodian embassy in Bangkok [12] and campaigns of mutual recrimination in the Bangkok and Phnom Penh press. On November 24, Cambodia suspended diplomatic relations with Thailand. The next day, Thailand recalled her ambassador from Phnom Penh and closed her border with Cambodia. Before troops, which had been massing on both sides of the border, could be drawn into the dispute, diplomatic relations were restored in February, 1959, through the mediation of Baron Johan Beck-Friis, a retired Swedish diplomat, who was sent to Bangkok as the special representative of the United Nations Secretary-General.[13] The reduction in tension, however, did not last long, for Cambodia's exposure of the so-called Bangkok plot [14] a few weeks later

[12] See Royaume du Cambodge, *Documents relatifs*, pp. 13–15, and Ministry of Foreign Affairs, *Relations between*, pp. 7–8.

[13] See Royaume du Cambodge, *Livre blanc sur la rupture des relations diplomatiques entre le Cambodge et la Thailande, le 23 octobre 1961* (Phnom Penh: Imprimerie du Ministère de l'Information, n.d. [1962?]), p. 3. The details of the Secretary-General's good offices were reported in *The Annual Report of the Secretary-General, 1958*, United Nations Document A/4132.

[14] The plot allegedly involved an attempt by Thailand and South

occasioned verbal attacks by the radio and press of both countries.[15]

During 1959, Cambodia suggested two possible solutions of the Preah Vihear problem: the joint administration of the temple by the two countries, or the presentation of the case to the International Court of Justice at The Hague.[16] The failure of the Thai to respond to her proposals prompted the royal government in October to submit the matter to the Court.

Thailand reacted to this move with displeasure and charged that Cambodia was acting under the influence of the Communist bloc.[17] In spite of its recognition of the Court's compulsory jurisdiction, the Thai government sought to test the competence of the tribunal on this matter. In May, 1961, the Court rejected Thailand's exceptions, ruled that it possessed full competence, and undertook formal hearings on the case.

In the meantime, further Cambodian–Thai talks were

Vietnam, acting through dissident Cambodians, to overthrow the Sihanouk regime. See below, pp. 163–165.

[15] See Royaume du Cambodge, *Livre blanc,* pp. 4–16, and Ministry of Foreign Affairs, *Facts about the Relations between Thailand and Cambodia* (Bangkok: Prachandra Press, 1961), p. 2.

[16] See the Cambodian *aide-mémoire* of June 13, 1959, in Royaume du Cambodge, *Aide-Mémoire sur les relations khmero-thailandaises* (Phnom Penh: Ministere des Affaires Etrangères, n.d. [1962?]), p. 27.

[17] See Royaume du Cambodge, *Livre blanc,* pp. 7–13, and Royaume du Cambodge, *Petite anthologie de la presse thaie* (Phnom Penh: Imprimerie du Ministère de l'Information, 1960), *passim.* It was widely believed in Phnom Penh that Thailand's maneuvers were designed to hold the case in abeyance until May, 1960, when Thailand's commitment to recognize the compulsory jurisdiction of the International Court would have ended. Cambodians interpreted Thailand's charges as a Thai reaction to having been outsmarted. See *Cambodian Commentary* (Phnom Penh), nos. 1–3, Nov. 1, 15, and Dec. 1, 1959.

held in New York on the questions of political refugees, extradition of criminals, and the enforcement of law in the border regions, and on the problem of press and radio attacks. Substantive agreement on these topics was reached in December, 1960, with the mediation of Hans Engen, a representative of the United Nations Secretary-General, and on December 15 accords were signed in the presence of Dag Hammarskjöld.[18] Less than two weeks later, however, each country again claimed that the other had engaged in invective through its radio and news media.[19] Throughout 1961, the newspapers and radios of Bangkok and Phnom Penh thundered at each other constantly and were ably abetted by officials of both governments who supplied these media with disparaging statements concerning their adversary's foreign policy, domestic conditions, and the mental state of each other's chiefs of government. By October, 1961, there was a complete breakdown in relations between the two countries.

During his return trip from the fifteenth session of the United Nations General Assembly, Prince Sihanouk held a press conference on October 6 in Tokyo at which he said

in 1956, when we decided to establish normal relations with the People's Republic of China, certain western agents and certain neighboring governments allied with the west combined in an attempt to subvert our neutrality. However, other western nations, Great Britain, for example, had been able to recognize . . . China well before us without attracting the least criticism from her allies. Her action was excusable, for Britain had to safeguard its interests in Hongkong. For Cam-

---

[18] See *Agence Khmère de Presse*, Dec. 23, 1960. Hereafter cited as *AKP*.

[19] See Royaume du Cambodge, *Aide-Mémoire*, pp. 44–45, and Ministry of Foreign Affairs, *Facts about the Relations*, p. 2.

bodia, who wished only to survive, no. And this is why we have had to face plots, attempted secession, the corruption of political leaders and of a general officer, armed incursions, menaces, totally unjustified territorial claims on our islands, etc. . . . All this has been done by pro-western troops, not by the Viet Minh. . . . If we listen to the voices coming from Thailand we find them [not only] badly disposed in our regard [but also] insane.[20]

The next day, the *Japan Times* reported that Sihanouk had said that "Cambodia would fight—not so much against communism—as against 'pro-western neighboring countries.' " According to the interpretation by the *Japan Times,* these countries "undoubtedly include Thailand."

Thai reaction was published two weeks later, at a time when charges and countercharges concerning alleged Communist bases in Cambodia were being flung back and forth between Saigon and Phnom Penh. On October 20, Marshal Sarit Thanarat, the Prime Minister of Thailand, declared that Sihanouk's words in Tokyo

clearly indicated that there was a plan which may serve as an intermediary and a bridge to induce the Communists to harm neighboring nations, which would be treacherous to the region of Southeast Asia. . . .

The world knows very well that his country alone is not sufficiently strong to triumph in battle with Thailand. The declaration indicates the existence of a plan making his country a jumping-off place for attacks on neighboring nations by Communist armed forces.

The government should pay careful attention to dangers coming from this region and, at the same time, we can ignore

---

[20] Norodom Sihanouk, *Le Cambodge et ses relations avec ses voisins* (Phnom Penh: Ministère de l'Information, n.d. [1962?]), pp. 96–97, 98.

his arrogance by reflecting, by way of consolation, on the old tale of a pig who provoked a lion into combat.[21]

Enraged by Sarit's allusion to a pig, Prince Sihanouk went before the National Assembly during the morning of October 23 to call on the deputies for their advice.[22] In reviewing the situation, he added that Sarit's declaration was part of an attempt to pressure Cambodia into the Communist bloc and thus induce the United States to grant Thailand more aid; he further asserted that the Thai government had plans to take over Kôh Moul, a large island near the Cambodian–Thai border, as well as the provinces of Battambang, Siem Reap, and a part of Kompong Thom. On the same day, the Assembly voted to break off diplomatic relations. Immediately thereafter, Thailand closed the frontier and both countries alerted their armies.

Relations between the two countries were further aggravated early in 1962, when, in the course of hearings on the Preah Vihear case in the International Court, Thailand's counsel questioned Cambodia's ability to exercise

[21] Quoted in Ministry of Foreign Affairs, *Facts about the Relations*, p. 4. See also *Bangkok World*, Oct. 21, 1961. Sarit's adviser, Luang Vichitr Vadakarn, confirmed that the Prime Minister was referring only to Prince Sihanouk. He said, "The third danger spot in Southeast Asia is Cambodia, whose chief of state and government pursues policies and ideas which are difficult to understand. Lately, at a press conference in Tokyo, he declared that he would not fight communism but Thailand. Let's be thankful for his frankness. We know exactly who our enemy is and we will prepare ourselves for any eventuality.

"In the meantime, an idea has just occurred to me: Is it a sane and wise policy of the United States to give military aid to Thailand to fight the Communists and to give the same aid to Cambodia in order to fight Thailand?" Quoted in *Bangkok World*, Oct. 21, 1961.

[22] See *AKP*, Oct. 24, 1961.

sovereignty over the disputed area. "Facts, gentlemen," he said, "speak louder than maps. It has not been possible for the Cambodian army to maintain sovereignty over this small pied à terre." [23] It was on the basis of this and other remarks made by Thai leaders that Cambodians concluded that Thailand's attitude toward their country would henceforth be based on the principle that "rights should follow the evolution of facts dictated by force." [24]

On June 15, 1962, the International Court rendered the following judgment in the Preah Vihear case:

The Court, by nine votes to three, finds that the Temple of Preah Vihear is situated in territory under the sovereignty of Cambodia; finds in consequence, by nine votes to three, that Thailand is under an obligation to withdraw any military or police forces, or other guards or keepers, stationed by her at the temple, or in its vicinity on Cambodian territory; by seven votes to five, that Thailand is under an obligation to restore to Cambodia any objects . . . which may, since the date of occupation of the temple by Thailand in 1954, have been removed from the temple or the temple area by the Thai authorities.[25]

Thai authorities condemned the ruling as a "miscarriage of justice" and as "contrary to usage and international law." [26] Concern was expressed that the chief justice of the Court, Bohdan Winiarski, was a Polish Communist and that some of the judges represented colonial powers. The motives and objectives of the United States, which had refrained from commenting on the case, were bitterly criticized. And it was suggested that former Secretary of

[23] Quoted in Royaume du Cambodge, *Aide-Mémoire*, pp. 28, 70.
[24] *Ibid.*, pp. 30, 72.
[25] "Case Concerning the Temple of Preah Vihear," pp. 34–35.
[26] Quoted in *Bangkok Post*, June 18, 1962.

State Dean Acheson, who pleaded the Cambodian case, had been specially posted to that task by the President of the United States. Foreign Minister Thanat Khoman stated, "It was curious that an American official was allowed to take the side of a neutralist, even pro-communist nation in a territorial argument with an ally of the United States." And he alleged that the United States had undermined Thailand's case by nominating Professor Philip Jessup to the Court, thus depriving Thailand of his services as counsel.[27] It was then announced by other officials, "We will defend our country to the last drop of our blood"; and any Cambodian who tried to enter Thai territory (i.e., Preah Vihear) would be shot on sight.[28]

Following the visits of American Ambassador Kenneth Young and Australian Minister of External Affairs Sir Garfield Barwick to Prime Minister Sarit, Thai tempers appeared to abate. On June 21, Sarit announced that Thailand would honor her commitments under the United Nations Charter because" the communists hope to touch off clashes along the Burma, Thai and Cambodian borders." Armed conflict with Cambodia, he said, would only serve Communist objectives.[29] On July 6, Thanat Khoman addressed a note to the United Nations Secretary-General in which he expressed Thailand's official position:

I wish to inform you that, in deciding to comply with the decision . . . His Majesty's Government desires to make an express reservation regarding whatever rights Thailand has,

[27] See *Bangkok World,* June 17 and 20, 1962. Jessup had been retained as counsel by Thailand. Upon his nomination to the Court, he withdrew from the case.

[28] *Ibid.,* June 19, 1962.

[29] Quoted in *Bangkok Post,* June 22, 1962. See also Sarit's address to the nation on July 4, 1962, in *Foreign Affairs Bulletin* (Bangkok, Ministry of Foreign Affairs), I (June–July, 1962), no. 6, pp. 125–127.

or may have in the future, to recover the Temple of Phra Viharn by having recourse to any existing or subsequently applicable legal process, and to register a protest against the decision of the International Court of Justice awarding the Temple of Phra Viharn to Cambodia.[30]

A result of this reaction was that the Cambodian government was "led to consider the Bangkok Government's 'reservation' as a future threat and a serious manifestation of contempt for existing treaties and international obligations." [31] In seeming confirmation of this conclusion, before Thai troops were removed from Preah Vihear, Thailand erected barbed-wire barriers around the temple, an act which Cambodia has since interpreted as being in contempt of the Court's decision.

Prince Sihanouk officially took possession of Preah Vihear for Cambodia on January 4, 1963,[32] but Thailand's attitude and action, which, Cambodians declared, "is to consider that law must follow the changing facts . . . dictated by force," remain for Cambodia a "striking epitome of Thailand's policy of annexation." [33]

Thailand's claim to Cambodian territory has led Cambodians to believe that the Thai seek a redefinition of the boundaries between the two countries. Consequently, Cambodia has demanded, as the *sine qua non* for the re-

---

[30] *Foreign Affairs Bulletin*, I, no. 6, p. 130. A full discussion of the Preah Vihear decision from the Thai point of view will be found in Prayat S. Nākhanāt and Čhamrāt Dūangthisān, *The Khao Phra Viharn Case* (in Thai: Khwan Mŭang Rŭang Khao Phra Wihān) (Bangkok: Sānsawan Press, 1962); see especially pp. 952–968.

[31] See Royaume du Cambodge, *Aide-Mémoire*, pp. 33, 75.

[32] See *Réalités Cambodgiennes*, Jan. 11, 1963, and *Cambodge d'Aujourd'hui*, special number (Sept.–Dec. 1962), nos. 48–51, pp. 34–35.

[33] Royaume du Cambodge, *Aide-Mémoire*, pp. 35, 36, 77, 78.

sumption of friendly relations, Thailand's formal and unconditional recognition of the present frontiers.[34] Both countries again availed themselves of the good offices of the United Nations Secretary-General, who sent his special representative, Nils Gussing, to Phnom Penh and Bangkok in late 1962. But in attempting to mediate their differences, Gussing was criticized by Cambodians for favoring Thailand's position.[35] It was to appease Cambodia that Secretary-General U Thant in mid-1963 sent another of his aides, C. V. Narasimhan, to work with Gussing on another approach to settling differences between the two countries.

Meanwhile, certain Thai actions along the border were viewed by Cambodians as preparations for eventual takeover of Cambodian territory. Not only were the Thai massing troops along the frontier, but according to Prince Sihanouk in his address to the National Assembly on July 20, 1963, Thai secret agents were informing the inhabitants of Kôh Kong that Thailand would soon occupy the province. The people had been warned by the Thai, Sihanouk charged, that if they did not possess Thai identity cards they would be "severely punished or expelled by the new occupiers." [36] Thailand's Foreign Minister, Thanat

[34] See *Réalités Cambodgiennes,* July 12, 1963.

[35] The author has been informed of this matter by a Cambodian source which he considers to be reliable. As an index of Gussing's position, Cambodians note that he supports Thailand's proposal for talks between the Cambodian chief of state and the Thai prime minister, or between the Cambodian prime minister and the Thai foreign minister. The proposal is seen by Cambodians as insulting as well as deviating from normal protocol, which would require that a meeting be held between men of similar rank. For the Thai position, see Ministry of Foreign Affairs, *Facts about the Relations between Thailand and Cambodia,* III (Bangkok, Mar. 1, 1963).

[36] *Réalités Cambodgiennes,* July 26, 1963.

Khoman, replied on July 23 that Sihanouk's charges were "lies designed to entice world opinion." [37] Thailand, he said, was ready to repel Cambodia if she chose to adopt a policy of confrontation.

Relations with Vietnam

South Vietnam. Cambodia's relations with South Vietnam in the postindependence period have been profoundly affected by her historically rooted suspicions of Vietnamese motives in foreign affairs. The fact that the fertile Mekong delta region, which today comprises a large part of South Vietnam and sustains most of her population, was until the mid-eighteenth century an integral part of Cambodia continues to rankle in the minds of certain Cambodian leaders. Indeed, Cambodians have continued to refer to the area as Kampuchea Krom (South Cambodia), and a large, distinct Cambodian minority, estimated at 600,000, still reside there. So important was Kampuchea Krom to Cambodia that when Annam secured control of it in the nineteenth century, King Ang Duong was moved to seek the assistance of Napoleon III in regaining it. Cambodia's hopes were never realized, for with France's defeat of the Annamese in 1859 Kampuchea Krom was not returned to Cambodia but was ruled directly by the French under the name of Cochinchina.[38]

[37] Quoted in *ibid.*, Aug. 2, 1963.

[38] France was assisted by Cambodia in its subjugation of southern Annam. During the siege of Saigon in 1859, Cambodian troops supported France in battles in the provinces of Meat Chrouk (Chaudoc), Krâmuon Sâr (Rachgia), Srok Treang (Soctrang), and Preah Trapeang (Travinh). Under the Franco–Annamese treaty of 1862, Annam transferred to France three Cambodian provinces which it had occupied since the eighteenth century: Bienhoa, Giadinh, and Mytho. In 1867, on grounds that Annam had violated the 1862 treaty, France occupied three more provinces: Long Ho (Vinh

Requests for its return, voiced as late as 1948 by King Sihanouk, were apparently ignored.[39] In 1949 the transfer of
Cochinchina to the Bao Dai regime of Vietnam evoked
vigorous protests from King Sihanouk and Cambodia's
representatives to the French Union Assembly.[40] In 1954,
at the Geneva conference on Indochina, Cambodia once
more took the opportunity to remind the world that Co-

Long), Meat Chrouk, and Peam (Hatien), as well as the rest of western Cochinchina. The French occupation was completed with the
taking of Kôh Tral (Phu Quoc Island) and formalized in 1874 with
a new Franco–Annamese treaty.

[39] See Permanent Mission of Cambodia to the United Nations,
Cochinchina–Cambodian Territory (New York, n.d. [1958?]), p. 7.

[40] One of the major difficulties involved in negotiating a definitive
treaty of independence with France was the question of the future
status of the Cambodian minority in Cochinchina. In the provinces
of Rachgia, Soctrang, and Travinh, Cambodians formed the majority of the population, but among the estimated 5.5 million people
in Cochinchina the Cambodians at this time numbered only some
450,000. Cambodia had often asked for the restoration of the three
provinces on grounds of historical right but had generally recognized the unlikelihood of getting any satisfaction in this respect.
Cambodians frequently complained, however, that their compatriots
in Cochinchina were persecuted by the Vietnamese, and they feared
that France's withdrawal from the area might seriously aggravate
their plight. (See *La Liberté*, Apr. 7, 18, and *La Démocrate*, Apr. 22,
1949.) In the spring of 1949, the imminent unification of Cochinchina, Annam, and Tonkin brought Prince Monireth to Paris and
elicited protests from King Sihanouk and his delegates to the French
Union Assembly. (See *La Liberté*, Apr. 18 and June 15, 1949.) Dis-
appearance of Cochinchina's colonial status, they argued, would
mean an end to the political and cultural guarantees of special
treatment for the Cambodian minority in that area. When the
French finally came to terms with Bao Dai, in the Elysée Agreements
of June, 1949, the unitary state of Vietnam was organized without
consultation with the Cambodian government. Cambodian protests
were to no avail; in the Franco–Cambodian treaty of Nov., 1949,
however, the Cambodian government stated that it would not relinquish its claim on Cochinchina.

chinchina was rightfully hers. Speaking for Cambodia, Foreign Minister Tep Phan emphasized that any agreement concerning the territorial integrity of Vietnam could not be held to "imply the abandonment of such legitimate rights as Cambodia might assert with regard to certain regions of South Vietnam about which Cambodia made express reservations." [41]

While Cambodia has not pressed her claims to Cochinchina, she has taken advantage of every opportunity to keep her interest in the area before the public. From time to time the Cambodian government has charged that the Cambodian minority in Kampuchea Krom are being subjected to frequent harassments by the Saigon government. During 1960–1961 Prince Sihanouk tried to underscore these alleged discriminatory acts by inviting foreign news correspondents and diplomats to interview a large group of Cambodians who had fled their homes in South Vietnam to seek shelter in Cambodia. It is difficult to determine whether the refugees and their compatriots in Vietnam have actually been singled out for persecution by the Vietnamese government or whether they, in common with Vietnamese peasants in the area, have been caught between the cross pressures exerted by progovernment forces and Viet Cong guerrillas to coerce them into cooperation.[42] In any case, Prince Sihanouk, addressing the

[41] See Great Britain, *Further Documents Relating to the Discussion of Indo-China at the Geneva Conference, June 16–July 21, 1954.* Misc. No. 20 (1954), Cmd. 9239 (London: H.M. Stationery Office, 1954), p. 6.

[42] For the Cambodian position see the letters of Cambodia's representative to the United Nations and Ambassador to the United States to the Secretary-General and the Secretary of State, respectively, of Mar. 8, 1961, in *La Dépêche du Cambodge,* Mar. 27, 1961. The author interviewed some of the Khmer Krom refugees in Phnom Den, a refugee receiving center in Takéo province, in Mar.,

United Nations in September, 1961, condemned what he
called South Vietnam's deliberate policy of cultural ex-
tinction. For its part, South Vietnam has steadfastly denied
these allegations.[43] In 1959 her observer at the United Nations, Mme. Tran Van Chuong, dismissed Cambodian
charges as being "absolutely baseless" and asserted that
there were no Cambodians in Vietnam, only Vietnamese
of Cambodian origin. Therefore, she continued, Cambodia's statements represented an "unacceptable encroachment on Vietnamese sovereignty." [44] In 1961, in the wake
of further Cambodian charges of discrimination, the South
Vietnamese government retaliated by declaring that the
exodus had been organized by Communists, and accused
the Cambodian government of hostile acts against local
Vietnamese.[45]

The withdrawal of the French from Indochina awakened fears among some Cambodian leaders that an independent Vietnam would resume the annexationist policies
of the court of Hué. In particular they have been concerned that the Vietnamese still nurture hopes of some
day absorbing the open and sparsely populated plain of

1961, in an attempt to ascertain for himself the veracity of Cambodia's charges. In brief, according to the refugees, their flight to
Cambodia was precipitated by the lack of security in South Vietnam
and by fears that if they were fortunate enough to escape recruit-
ment or repression by the South Vietnamese army, they would surely
be pressed into the service of the Viet Cong. See also *La Dépêche
du Cambodge,* Mar. 9 and 11, 1961.

[43] See Secrétariat d'Etat aux Affaires Etrangères, *Le Vietnam et ses
relations internationales* (Vietnam in World Affairs), III (Dec.,
1958), nos. i-iv, pp. 1–27.

[44] Quoted in *News from Viet-Nam* (Washington, D.C., Embassy
of Vietnam) V (Dec. 4, 1959), no. 17, pp. 10–11.

[45] See *La Dépêche du Cambodge,* Mar. 13, 15, 27, and Aug. 5 and
8, 1961.

the rich Mekong–Tonlé-Sap–Bassac basin, which today constitutes central Cambodia. Partly for this reason Vietnamese residents in Cambodia, who number between 400,000 and 450,000 and thus constitute the largest minority group in that country, are subjected to strict surveillance by the Cambodian government, and their traffic between Cambodia and South Vietnam is restricted. At the peak of the dispute between South Vietnam and Cambodia on the issue of the Khmer Krom (Cambodians residing in Kampuchea Krom) in 1960–1961, the Cambodian government undertook mass displacement and deportation of a large number of Vietnamese who had settled along the river bank in Phnom Penh suburbs. These actions prompted the countercharges from Saigon of persecution of Vietnamese residents by the Cambodian government.[46]

During the immediate postindependence period Cambodian fears of South Vietnamese designs were accentuated by her dependence upon the port of Saigon for most of her commerce with the outside world. Thus during the Quadripartite Conference of 1954 she demanded the internationalization of the Mekong River and interstate control of the port of Saigon.[47] She succeeded in obtaining

[46] In response to the Vietnamese countercharges, the Phnom Penh press has occasionally threatened reprisals against Vietnamese in Cambodia in return for repression of the Khmer Krom. See, e.g., *Réalités Cambodgiennes*, Sept. 15 and 29, 1961.

[47] See Royaume du Cambodge, *Accords et conventions signés à l'issue de la conférence quadripartite de Paris (du 26 août au 29 décembre 1954)* (Phnom Penh: Imprimerie Khmère, 1955), pp. 58–85. Still another outstanding problem involves the disposition of the assets of the Indochina Federation and the receipts from customs collected at Saigon before 1954. At the time of the Paris agreements, Vietnam was discovered to owe Cambodia the equivalent of $25 million. The procedure agreed upon for distribution of these

agreement to the first demand but failed to win the concession of the South Vietnamese to the second. The result was that South Vietnam retained a position from which she could control traffic to and from Cambodia and attempt to exert indirect political pressure on her. Cambodian apprehensions in this regard proved justified in 1956, when South Vietnam suddenly imposed an economic blockade upon her in reprisal for Sihanouk's visit to Peking. While the blockade has since been lifted, Saigon continues to prohibit entry to ships of Communist nations, with whom Cambodia has been conducting an increasing volume of trade. Fortunately for Cambodia the completion of the port of Sihanoukville in 1959, with the assistance of the French, has averted a potential crisis between the two countries arising from conflict over the port of Saigon. For a certain amount of her trade Cambodia continues to rely on Saigon, but she is currently expanding facilities in Sihanoukville in the hope that her economy will soon become completely independent of South Vietnam.

As Cambodia has striven to make herself less and less reliant upon Saigon, tension between the two governments has arisen on a new front. In 1956, while construction of the port of Sihanoukville was proceeding, South Vietnam attempted to occupy Cambodian islands strategically situ-

---

funds, however, has never been implemented, and the money remains tied up in Paris banks. Cambodia has tried several times to open discussion of this problem, but the major difficulty in resolving the issue appears to be Vietnam's refusal to include the other two members of the former Federation (Laos and France) in the negotiations and her insistence on making the issue an exclusively Cambodia–South Vietnam affair. For a report of Sihanouk's efforts to negotiate the matter with the Diem regime in 1959, see *Cambodia News* (Washington, D.C., Royal Embassy of Cambodia), no. 13, Dec. 7, 1959, pp. 2–4.

ated in the vicinity of the new port, affirmed ownership of them, and harassed Cambodian fishermen fishing in the area.[48] The largest of these islands, Kôh Tral (Phu Quoc), was administered as part of Cochinchina by the French and is at present in South Vietnam's possession. In March and April, 1960, South Vietnam demanded that Cambodia renounce claims to other islands in the group over which Cambodia has always exercised control. These acts of the South Vietnamese government confirmed the suspicions of Cambodian leaders that the Vietnamese were still intent upon keeping Cambodia in a subordinate position and that they hoped to accomplish this by keeping her economically dependent upon Saigon. In the spring of 1960, Sihanouk publicly expressed his fears in his assertion that "the loss of the islands and the territorial waters surrounding them would lead to the stifling of the port of [Sihanoukville] . . . and very soon to the end of our independence." [49]

Relations between South Vietnam and Cambodia have also been marked by Cambodian complaints of numerous border violations by the Vietnamese. In June, 1958, for example, the Cambodian government reported that South Vietnamese troops had crossed the border, occupied a Cambodian village and moved boundary markers.[50] An

[48] See Great Britain, *Fifth Interim Report of the International Commission for Supervision and Control in Cambodia for the Period October 1, 1955 to December 31, 1956. Cambodia No. 1 (1957)*, Cmnd. 253 (London: H.M. Stationery Office, 1957), pp. 35–38.

[49] See "Le Cambodge face à l'impérialisme sud-vietnamien," *Cambodge d'Aujourd'hui*, Special number (Mar.–Apr., 1960), nos. 3–4, pp. 31–35, 44.

[50] See the letters from the Royal government to the International Commission in Great Britain, *Seventh Interim Report of the International Commission for Supervision and Control in Cambodia for*

investigation by the International Control Commission verified Cambodian charges.[51] Indignant denials were issued by the Vietnamese government, which accused Cambodia herself of having conducted repeated forays into Vietnamese territory. It also condemned Cambodia for "deliberately allowing itself to be poisoned by propaganda or by secret agents of enemies of Asian independence" and warned that "this is a dangerous policy which could lead directly to war." [52] Vietnamese officials were referring to Prince Sihanouk's statement reported in *Réalités Cambodgiennes* on May 29, 1958:

As far as these neighbors are concerned, either because they are bound by a debt of gratitude to the greater powers which maintain a hold on them with their money, or because they get substantial foreign aid not only in money but in arms, they profit from this by continuing the only policy which they used to follow during the time of our ancestors.

The Vietnamese further charged at this time that the Cambodians, in their campaign to stir up antigovernment sentiments among the Khmer Krom, were guilty of attempted subversion.[53]

Later, in an analysis of Cambodian–Vietnamese problems, the *Times of Viet-Nam* on August 9, 1958, expressed the government view that the border question was not beyond solution. The government, it was suggested, would be willing to cooperate with a commission which would

---

the Period January 1, 1958, to December 31, 1958, Cambodia No. 1 (1959), Cmnd. 887 (London: H.M. Stationery Office, 1959), pp. 27–29.

[51] *Ibid.*, pp. 3, 20.

[52] See *News from Viet-Nam*, vol. 4 (July 18, 1958), no. 17, p. 4.

[53] See *Times of Viet-Nam*, June 28, 1958; *Viet-Nam Press*, June 24, 1958.

clearly demarcate the border and supervise its maintenance, provided, however,

> solid guarantees . . . be given Viet Nam that Cambodian territory shall not be used as a base for Communist infiltration and subversion against Viet Nam, or as a refuge for Vietnamese outlaws.

The *Times* then went on to intimate that the charge of a Vietnamese invasion was being "used by the Cambodian government as a pretext for the recognition of Red China." [54]

Tension over the border issue declined briefly as a consequence of Prince Sihanouk's visit to Saigon in August, 1959.[55] The major outcome of the visit was a series of negotiations between National Defense and Interior officials of both countries which culminated in an informal agreement that local border officials would cooperate to police the frontier. Clashes between Cambodian and South Vietnamese troops have recurred, however.

Cambodia has continued to complain of incursions by Vietnamese soldiers. These incursions, according to more recent statements by the Vietnamese government, have been accidental, having resulted from pursuit of Viet Cong guerrillas who disappeared into Cambodian territory. At the same time South Vietnam has aroused Cambodia's indignation by charging that Viet Cong bases are concealed within her territory. When the American military mission in Saigon supported these accusations in

[54] Prince Sihanouk was reported later to have said that the establishment of diplomatic relations with China was a direct consequence of South Vietnamese hostility in 1958. See *AKP*, Nov. 2, 1961. See also Denis Warner, "The Prince on a Tightrope," *The Reporter*, XXII (Feb. 18, 1960), no. 4, p. 33.

[55] See *Vietnam in World Affairs*, IV (Sept., 1959), nos. 1–3, p. 94.

1961,[56] Prince Sihanouk was reported to have declared that he had completely lost confidence in the Americans and was prepared to terminate diplomatic relations with the United States.[57] Early in November, however, General Edward Scherrer, chief of the United States military advisory group in Cambodia, categorically denied the existence of Communist bases in the country. Prince Sihanouk invited Western correspondents to tour the frontier region in order to determine for themselves whether or not Cambodia was guilty. The invitation was accepted by Robert Trumbull of the *New York Times*, who, after a four-day exploration of the area on the ground and from the air, repudiated earlier stories in which he had lent credence to the Vietnamese accusations.[58]

The border conflict, which was the principal cause for the rupture of political relations between the two countries in August, 1963,[59] is complicated by the fact that the Viet Cong, over the protests of the Cambodian government, apparently do use parts of northeastern Cambodia as points of entry into South Vietnam. Although Cambodia has taken positive measures to make it more difficult

[56] See the report of Robert Trumbull in the *New York Times*, Nov. 8, 1961. The *Washington Post* correspondent, Keyes Beech, however, was skeptical. See the issues of Oct. 31 and Nov. 2, 1961.

[57] See *Réalités Cambodgiennes*, Nov. 3, 1961.

[58] See *Cambodia News*, IV (Nov. 17, 1961), no. 15; *New York Times*, Nov. 22, 1961, and the *Times* editorial of Nov. 27, 1961. See also Robert Trumbull, *The Scrutable East* (New York: David McKay Co., 1964), pp. 181–185. Careful investigation of South Vietnamese reports of Viet Cong bases in Cambodia has often revealed that they refer to areas in South Vietnam which are not under the army's control.

[59] See "Proclamation du Gouvernement Royal du Cambodge concernant la rupture des relations politiques avec le Sud-Vietnam, 27 août 1963," *Cambodia News*, VI (Aug. 23, 1963), no. 19. Further details are to be found in *Réalités Cambodgiennes*, Aug. 2, 1963.

for the Viet Cong to use her territory as an access way, still the frontier which she shares with South Vietnam is very long and in parts thickly jungled; thus some Viet Cong are able to slip past her guard.

Like the Thai, the South Vietnamese have regarded with apprehension Cambodia's friendship with China. It is possible that accusations directed at Cambodia concerning Viet Cong bases may not be so much a pretext for trespassing on Cambodia's territory as a reflection of genuine concern that the Viet Cong, with Chinese assistance, may maneuver themselves into positions from which they can launch attacks against South Vietnamese troops. Such apprehensions could conceivably induce South Vietnam to attempt to subvert the Sihanouk government as a step toward attaining greater security along her borders.

Sihanouk himself has on several occasions stated that his country's neutral policy is a thorn in the side of her neighbors and that it has been the cause of hostile acts by them. The most serious of these is reported to have been the "Dap Chhuon" plot of 1959. According to Prince Sihanouk,[60] who exposed the plot at a rally of the Jeunesse Socialiste Royale Khmère, the South Vietnamese representative in Phnom Penh, Ngo Trong Hieu (who later became Minister of Social and Psychological Action in the Diem cabinet), succeeded in buying the cooperation of Dap Chhuon, governor of Siem Reap province, for the purpose of felling the Sihanouk regime. Dap Chhuon, a powerful Khmer Issarak leader during the struggle for in-

[60] Radio Phnom Penh, Mar. 2, 1959. See also *Principaux discours et allocutions de S.A.R. le Prince Norodom Sihanouk en 1959* (Phnom Penh: Imprimerie du Ministère de l'Information, n.d. [1960]), pp. 22–25; *La Dépêche du Cambodge*, Oct. 1, 1959, *AKP*, Oct. 2, 1959.

dependence who in ceasing his rebel activities to take up arms on the side of the royal army had won the gratitude of Sihanouk, was subsequently appointed governor of Siem Reap. Distantly removed from the central government of Phnom Penh, Dap Chhuon, with the aid of a personal army, was able to rule the province as a virtual fief. According to charges of the Cambodian government, Dap Chhuon's stronghold was to serve as a base for troops led by Son Ngoc Thanh and supplied by Thailand. A communications network linking Dap Chhuon to Saigon, via Ngo Trong Hieu and one Victor Matsui, a Central Intelligence Agency man attached to the American embassy in Phnom Penh, was reported to have been established. The political arm of the organization was said to be under the direction of Sam Sary, a onetime close adviser of Sihanouk, who had fallen from favor.[61] It was

61 The details of Sam Sary's activities were described on Jan. 13 by Sihanouk in a speech in Kompong Cham (*AKP*, Jan. 21, 1959). During the years of his rapid rise as one of Prince Sihanouk's most trusted advisers, resentment against Sam had grown among government officials who felt that he was exploiting his high positions for his personal profit. At the meeting in Kompong Cham, Sihanouk spoke at length of Sam's contravention of customs regulations and his ill-advised use of government facilities. Sihanouk said he had condoned these transgressions because of Sam's early contributions toward winning Cambodia's independence and the formation of the Sangkum. But when he began advocating the American position on foreign affairs ("on issues pertaining to foreign affairs he preferred to seek the suggestions of the British and American ambassadors"), Sam was sent to London as Cambodia's ambassador. While there he was reported in the press to have beaten one of his servants. In a subsequent interview with reporters, Sam outraged the press by saying that beating one's servants was a common practice in Cambodia and not a subject of the reporters' concern. He was promptly recalled to Phnom Penh. Prince Sihanouk was apparently willing to let the matter rest without taking disciplinary action against his adviser. Sam Sary, however, was offended by Sihanouk's failure to

apparently his activities which alerted the government to the plot and enabled it quickly to move in to squelch it. In the confusion that ensued, Dap Chhuon was killed in flight. Sam Sary in the meantime had escaped, reportedly to South Vietnam. South Vietnam, Thailand, and the United States have denied that they participated in this affair. Cambodia, however, continues to remain unconvinced of their innocence. According to Prince Sihanouk:

We are sincerely grateful for the aid granted to us by the great and rich powers, but we can only accept that aid which contributes to improving the lot of our people, and allows us to emerge from our underdeveloped state. For what many of you are perhaps unaware of, but what many small aided nations are perhaps not unaware of, is that too often a friendly aid, provided for in official agreements, is accompanied by a secret and far less friendly kind of aid. This latter kind of aid, which is never mentioned, and which arouses indignation if one mentions it, can take several forms: either direct subversion, the totally artificial support or the creation of opposition groups, or the purchase of the consciences of men considered strong enough to achieve secession of certain provinces, and torpedo neutrality and the national regime.[62]

---

come to his defense when a demand was made by officials that he be dismissed from government office. Subsequently he formed a political party and founded a newspaper, ostensibly to defend himself against his critics. Instead, he soon began to criticize bitterly Prince Sihanouk and the Sangkum. Alerted by friends that the government had issued an order for his arrest, Sam Sary escaped his captors in Phnom Penh and was reported to have fled to South Vietnam.

[62] See Sihanouk's address to the United Nations General Assembly, Sept. 26, 1960, in *Principaux discours et allocutions de S.A.R. le Prince Norodom Sihanouk en 1960* (Phnom Penh: Imprimerie du Ministère de l'Information, n.d. [1961?]), pp. 189–209. Quotation is from p. 207.

Since the "plot" sporadic outbursts of anti-Sihanouk and anti-Sangkum propaganda have been broadcast from transmitters which appear to be located in the Cambodian frontier regions of Thailand and South Vietnam. After a relatively long period of silence, which coincided with the increase in American military aid to Cambodia during 1961–1962, the Khmer Serei movement in the fall of 1963 again began engaging in its propaganda activities. Broadcasting over transmitters reported to be more powerful than those owned by the Cambodian government, the rebels are seeking to rouse the populace against Prince Sihanouk, who, they charge, usurped the position of leadership from Son Ngoc Thanh and has been working against the interests of the people ever since.[63] They have been especially critical of Sihanouk's policy toward South Vietnam and Thailand, which, they claim, have only friendly intentions toward Cambodia.[64] As in 1959, South Vietnam, with Thailand and the American Central Intelligence Agency, has been charged by Prince Sihanouk with supporting the attempted subversion of his government.[65]

North Vietnam. As far as Cambodians are concerned the most significant aspect of the Viet Minh is not their ideology but the fact that they are Vietnamese. Thus the same historical considerations which color their attitude toward the South Vietnamese also influence their relations with the North Vietnamese. In addition they have

[63] See *Réalités Cambodgiennes*, Oct. 4, 11, 18, and Nov. 8, 1963. That these broadcasts have been made has been confirmed to the author by American officials.

[64] *Ibid.*, Dec. 6, 1963.

[65] *Ibid.*, Oct. 4, 11, 18, and Nov. 8, 1963.

been put on their guard in their dealings with North Vietnam by the latter's attempts to undermine the royal Cambodian government during the Indochina war and at the Geneva conference in 1954.

In the post-Geneva period the activities of North Vietnam in Laos and South Vietnam and the absence of a common frontier between Cambodia and North Vietnam have forestalled any significant conflict between the two countries. Nevertheless, Prince Sihanouk has kept a watchful eye on Viet Minh advances, particularly in Laos, for he fears that a Viet Minh-supported Pathet Lao victory in Laos would leave North Vietnam free to attempt a concerted penetration of Cambodia.

Although the Viet Minh have refrained from armed aggressions in Cambodia since 1954, they have been guilty of harassing the Sihanouk government from time to time with uncomplimentary propaganda and of fanning the dissatisfaction of certain segments of the Cambodian population. Shortly after North Vietnam's Foreign Minister, Pham Van Dong, had given his personal assurances to Prince Sihanouk at the Bandung conference of 1955 that his country would not interfere in Cambodia's affairs, the Cambodian government found it necessary to advise the International Control Commission that "harassment and attacks" by Viet Minh forces had taken place in northeast Cambodia, near the town of Voeunsai. Following an investigation, however, the Commission said it could not uncover evidence that "regular units of the Viet Minh forces" had been in the region; instead, it reported that several former members of the Khmer Resistance Forces and one "allegedly Viet Minh area organizer" had formed a band of men, with a strength variously estimated between 178 and 400, which was spreading antigovernment propaganda and generally creating disturbances in the area.[66] Apparently the Cambodian government was satisfied with the Commission's findings, for no more was heard from it concerning this matter.

Another complaint, voiced in September 1955, was easier to substantiate. For some months Radio Hanoi had been broadcasting in Khmer certain statements which suggested that the royal government was trespassing upon the liberties of the people. Sihanouk declared that North Vietnam was conducting a "campaign of interference in the internal affairs of Cambodia," which was a violation of the Geneva agreements and of the Pancha Shil. Hanoi replied that these broadcasts were merely reports of what had been said in Cambodian opposition newspapers and that "broadcasting of newspaper extracts was a recognized practice in all countries." The International Commission sent a strong protest to Hanoi, reminding the North Vietnamese government that all parties to the Geneva agreements had agreed to find ways and means of abstaining from hostile propaganda. Hanoi answered that the matter was a subject for negotiation. It contended that Cambodia's public charges of Viet Minh aggression while the matter was under investigation had led to misunderstanding, and "consequently the maintenance of harmonious relations between the signatory Governments becomes more difficult." [67]

There the matter rested until early 1956, when Prince

---

[66] See Great Britain, *Fourth Interim Report of the International Commission for Supervision and Control in Cambodia for the Period April 1 to September 30, 1955, Cambodia No. 1 (1956)*, Cmd. 9671 (London: H.M. Stationery Office, 1956), pp. 18–20.

[67] *Ibid.*, pp. 21–22.

Sihanouk, on the occasion of introducing his new cabinet to the National Assembly, charged that:

North Vietnam tries to persuade our people to revolt. It invents all sorts of ways to slander me and to tarnish our Kingdom. . . . It supports the Cambodian Communists, who are opposed to the Cambodian government. By so doing, North Vietnam violates the five principles of peaceful coexistence which it promised to apply at Bandung. . . . It has dared to ask Chou En-lai to contact me to find out whether I would agree to go to Hanoi to study [current problems].[68]

Early in 1958, Sihanouk wrote:

As for the Vietminh, they don't have the same scruples as the Chinese towards us (nor the same sympathies). If they could, they would eagerly and rapidly control our destiny. They utilize all their tenacity, their guile, their craftiness to "guide" those of our compatriots who, through weakness or ambition, accept their counsel. Incontestably, they obtain certain results with a "Mission" or "Representation," with a lone correspondent from Hanoi engaged in numerous subtle and discreet activities.[69]

With the signing of a trade and payments agreement on November 19, 1958,[70] relations between Cambodia and North Vietnam appeared to improve. Then in 1959, Cambodians complained that the Viet Minh were using a portion of northeastern Cambodia to infiltrate into South Vietnam. To forestall further incursions by the Viet Minh, Cambodia carved two new provinces, Ratanakkiri and

---

[68] Radio Phnom Penh, Feb. 29, 1956.

[69] *Réalités Cambodgiennes,* Mar. 15, 1958.

[70] Radio Hanoi, Dec. 3, 1958. See also Y. A. Pavlov, "Ob ekonomicheskom poloschennii kambodschi" (Economic Situation in Cambodia), *Problemi Vostokovedeniya* (Moscow), no. 6 (1959), p. 91.

Mondulkiri, from the extreme eastern parts of Stung Treng and Kratié, and set up military administrations there. To effect better control of the nomadic *montagnards* who live in the area and who are potential targets of subversive propaganda, the government launched a program to move them away from border areas and to settle them in permanent villages.[71]

In 1961, Cambodian suspicions of North Vietnam's intentions heightened when, in a public debate with Prince Sihanouk before a special Congress, Non Suon, the head of the Pracheachon party, was cornered into virtually admitting that he received directions from the Viet Minh regime. Although the Prince succeeded in discrediting the Pracheachon, he reaffirmed his decision, made in July at the eleventh National Congress, to allow the party to continue its propaganda activities, thus avoiding the creation of "communist martyrs." Sihanouk was, nevertheless, seriously disturbed by North Vietnam's attempt to "sow discord in the bosom of the nation."[72] Could China be of assistance to Cambodia in this regard? In answer to his own question, Prince Sihanouk declared, "Since we have become wedged between two SEATO countries, the socialist bloc not only supports us diplomatically, but also will order (I suppose) the Viet Minh to suspend (temporarily, without doubt) its activities in support of the Prachea-

[71] The *montagnards,* called in Cambodia Khmer Loeu (Cambodians of the mountains), and sometimes phnong (savages), are believed to share a common ancestry with the Cambodians but because of their long isolation in the mountainous areas of the Indochinese peninsula their culture and language have developed along divergent lines. There are believed to be about 40,000 Khmer Loeu in Cambodia.

[72] See *Réalités Cambodgiennes,* July 29, 1961; *La Dépêche du Cambodge,* July 31, 1961; *Cambodian Commentary,* no. 11, Sept., 1961, pp. 10 ff.

chon." [73] In early 1962, the Cambodian government revealed that it had arrested fifteen members of the Pracheachon, including Non Suon, upon discovering that they were carrying North Vietnamese directives for subversion of the Sangkum, and Cambodia's teachers, Buddhist monks, and the military.[74]

The minatory actions of neighboring states since his country regained her independence have convinced Prince Sihanouk that Cambodia today faces the very problem of survival which had induced his great-great-grandfather, King Ang Duong, to seek the protection of the French in the nineteenth century. Today, as then, Cambodia is militarily weaker than Thailand and the two Vietnams, and thus she would not by herself be able to withstand aggression by them. Once more, therefore, her security requires that she balance the forces pressing against her by appealing for the protection of a greater power. But this time the actions of her leaders are guided not only by the need for succor but also by the bitter experience suffered under the French protectorate. How to survive without compromising their country's independence has thus been the most pressing concern of Prince Sihanouk and his advisers.

While Cambodia, along with many of the newer, weaker nations, has condemned the tendency toward bipolarization of power into two antagonistic camps, this very situation has brought to the Indochina peninsula the balance of power essential to Cambodian independence. With both camps seeking to extend their areas of influence by

[73] *Réalités Cambodgiennes,* July 14, 1961.

[74] Norodom Sihanouk, *Le Cambodge et ses relations avec ses voisins* (Phnom Penh: Imprimerie du Ministère de l'Information, 1962), pp. 59–61.

competing for the friendship of uncommitted nations, Cambodia, by threatening to seek a greater *rapprochement* with one or the other bloc, has been able to pressure the big powers into attempting to restrain their Southeast Asian allies from aggression against her. Thus in a recent crisis with Thailand and South Vietnam, Prince Sihanouk announced that unless the United States used influence to prevent these countries from flooding her air waves with subversive propaganda, Cambodia would be forced to request the termination of all American aid and to accept only Chinese assistance. Similarly it was apparently the fear that Cambodia might forsake her neutrality for a pro-West alliance that prompted China in 1963 to try to hold North Vietnamese harassments of Cambodia in check.

As long as neither bloc is willing to see Cambodia commit herself to the other side, and as long as both continue to be able to restrain actions of their allies which are inimical to her, Cambodia's security and independence are safe. But on the day Cambodia is limited to the protection of only one of the blocs, Prince Sihanouk has warned, her survival will have been bought at the cost of her independence.

CHAPTER VI

The Crisis in Indochina

CAMBODIA has sought a solution to her problem of survival and independence in the cold war. By courting the protection not of one power, but of two powers which are actively vying with each other to extend their sphere of influence, Cambodia has hoped to lessen the likelihood of an all-out attack by her immediate neighbors and to minimize the possibility that the more distant "protector" will maneuver herself into a position of dominance. This view was underscored by Prince Sihanouk on many occasions after 1956.[1] Speaking before an American audience in 1961 he asserted that

---

[1] See, for example, *Réalités Cambodgiennes,* Apr. 14, 1956, Sept. 7, Nov. 30, 1957; Norodom Sihanouk, "Cambodia Neutral: The Dictate of Necessity," *Foreign Affairs,* XXXVI, no. 4 (July, 1958) pp. 582–586; Royaume du Cambodge, *Principaux Discours et Allocutions de S.A.R. Le Prince Norodom Sihanouk en 1958, 1959, 1960* (Phnom Penh: Imprimerie du Ministère de l'Information, n.d. [1958, 1959, 1960?]), *passim; Réalités Cambodgiennes,* Feb. 7, Apr. 4, 1959; political conference held by Prince Sihanouk at the Maison Cambodgienne, la Cité Universitaire, Paris, May 17, 1959, broadcast on Radio Phnom Penh, May 26, 1959; *Cambodge d'Aujourd'hui,* nos. 4, 5, (May, June, 1959), pp. 28 and 1, respectively; *Neak Cheat Niyum,* Jan. 1, 1960; address by Prince Sihanouk, *The Conference of Heads of State or Government of Non-Aligned Countries* (Belgrade: Publicističko-Izdavački Zavod "Jugoslavija," 1961), pp. 182–196.

we are well aware that [Cambodia's] survival as a free and sovereign nation depends entirely on preserving equilibrium and friendship with these two blocs. The day we find ourselves facing only one all-powerful bloc, the days of our independence —perhaps even of our very existence—will be counted. This is why we are absolutely sincere when we say that we want the United States and our other Western friends to preserve and maintain their influence, their position in our area.[2]

To a Cambodian audience at a special National Congress in Phnom Penh on August 1, 1961, he declared that "our survival depends on the two blocs. The moment one of them is defeated, we should have the other on top of us and they would waste no further time wooing us." [3]

The Crisis in Laos

It was this concern with preserving the balance between the major blocs in Indochina that occasioned Prince Sihanouk's protests against American intervention in Laos in 1958. At the time a truce had been called to the civil war which had racked Laos since the Geneva conference of 1954, and the country was being governed by a coalition of Pathet Lao and royalist leaders.[4] Led by Prince

[2] Kingdom of Cambodia, *Address of H.R.H. Prince Norodom Sihanouk, Chief of State of Cambodia to the Asia Society, New York, September 26, 1961* (New York, Permanent Mission of Cambodia to the United Nations, 1961), p. 18.

[3] Full text in *Cambodian Commentary*, no. 11, Sept., 1961, pp. 10–15.

[4] For details of the Laotian situation see Arthur J. Dommen, *Conflict in Laos, The Politics of Neutralization* (New York: Praeger, 1964); Roger M. Smith, "Laos," in George McT. Kahin, ed., *Governments and Politics of Southeast Asia* (2d ed., Ithaca, N.Y.: Cornell University Press, 1964); Stuart Simmonds, "Independence and Political Rivalry in Laos, 1945–61," in Saul Rose, ed., *Politics in Southern Asia* (New York: St. Martin's Press, 1963); Sisouk na

Souvannaphouma, the Laotian government espoused a neutralist orientation in international affairs. The decision of the United States to force Souvannaphouma from power by withholding economic aid caused alarm among Cambodian leaders, who warned that this act by the United States could lead only to a revival of the civil war and prompt more active Viet Minh support of the Pathet Lao.

Fear that the civil war would become transformed into a major international conflict led Prince Sihanouk to urge in 1959 that the big powers cease their military support of the rival political factions and agree to uphold a neutral Laos.[5] A major confrontation between the cold-war powers in Laos, the Prince believed, would lead inevitably to the victory of one over the other, with a consequent shift in the balance of power in Indochina and a renewed threat to Cambodia's own security. In the eventuality of an American-supported victory, Cambodia would find herself completely surrounded by countries solidly in the Western camp. Thus firmly entrenched in the peninsula, the United States would cease to regard Cambodia as being of strategic significance to her.[6] The South Vietnamese and the Thai, no longer restrained by a United States

---

Champassak, *Tempête sur le Laos* (Paris: La Table Ronde, 1961); Wilfred Burchett, *The Furtive War, The United States in Vietnam and Laos* (New York: International Publishers, 1963).

[5] See *Réalités Cambodgiennes*, Aug. 15, 1959, and *Neak Cheat Niyum*, Sept. 12, 1959. For a more detailed discussion of Cambodia's views see Roger M. Smith, "Cambodia's Neutrality and the Laotian Crisis," *Asian Survey*, I, no. 5 (July, 1961), pp. 17–24.

[6] Perhaps only a coincidence, but interesting to note is that during the period when United States influence in Laos was greatest, American economic and military aid to Cambodia underwent a significant decline, only to increase again as a Pathet Lao victory appeared to be assured. See above, Table 1, p. 123.

impelled to woo Cambodia's friendship, would then be free to resume their expansion at her expense. On the other hand, a Pathet Lao victory would open a direct line between Cambodia and North Vietnam. Of more immediate danger to Cambodia, such an event would probably hasten the conclusion of the war between North and South Vietnam in the former's favor. A united, Communist-dominated Vietnam, released from the burden of a costly civil war, would then be free to direct its efforts against Cambodia.[7]

As had been predicted by Cambodia, Moscow and Peking protested vigorously against the American interference in Laos. The period mid-1958 through 1959 was marked by a notable increase in American military aid to the pro-Western government and intensive training of its army by United States military advisers.

In August, 1960, an unexpected event temporarily restored a neutral regime in Laos. Captain Kong Lê, whose parachute battalion had been bearing the brunt of the fighting against the Pathet Lao, staged a *coup d'état* and reinstated Souvannaphouma at the head of the royal government. With Souvannaphouma once more in power and avowing his determination to pursue a neutral policy, Prince Sihanouk saw the way open to the reduction of cold-war tension in Laos. Addressing a gathering of ambassadors in Phnom Penh in August, he beseeched the big powers to lend their support to a neutral Laos.[8] On this occasion, and again before the United Nations Gen-

[7] This view of Cambodia's position was set forth in detail by Prince Sihanouk in his *Le Cambodge et ses relations avec ses voisins* (Phnom Penh: Imprimerie du Ministère de l'Information, 1962). See also Denis Warner, "Prince Sihanouk and the Four A's," *The Reporter*, Oct. 26, 1961, pp. 39–40.

[8] See *Agence Khmère de Presse (AKP)*, Aug. 24, 1960.

eral Assembly in September,[9] he renewed his proposal for the establishment of a neutral zone in Indochina, this time suggesting the inclusion of Cambodia as well as Laos in it. Acceptance of this proposal would require foreign powers to withdraw their military support and the two countries to abstain from participation in any alliance. The international neutralization of Laos and Cambodia would be affirmed in a treaty signed by all the major powers. The neutralization would be supervised by a commission composed of other neutral nations which would also arbitrate differences arising between either country and its neighbors.[10] This second proposal, like the first, did not receive the serious consideration of the big powers.

In the weeks that followed Prince Sihanouk's plea, the United States became more deeply involved in Laos. Reports of preparations for an American-backed *coup d'état* began to circulate and an economic blockade was imposed upon Vientiane, the Laotian capital, by Thailand. Prince Sihanouk's frantic warnings [11] that the American actions

---

[9] *Ibid.*, Sept. 29, 1960. The text of the Prince's address is found in U.N. General Assembly fifteenth Session, *Report of the 877th Plenary Meeting*, Sept. 26, 1960. See also *La mission aux Nations-Unies de S.A.R. le Prince Norodom Sihanouk, Chef de l'Etat du Cambodge* (Phnom Penh: Imprimerie du Ministère de l'Information, Dec. 26, 1960), pp. 5–8, 37–39, and Norodom Sihanouk, *Rapport au peuple khmer au terme de mission en Amérique et aux Nations-Unies* (Phnom Penh: Imprimerie du Ministère de l'Information, 1961).

[10] These details were given by Prince Sihanouk in a memorandum to U.N. Secretary-General Hammarskjöld, the text of which is to be found in *Réalités Cambodgiennes*, Dec. 9, 1960, and commented upon by the Prince in *Rapport au peuple khmer*, pp. 94–103.

[11] See *ibid.*, and also *Réalités Cambodgiennes.* Oct. 21, Nov. 11, Dec. 9, and *La Dépêche du Cambodge*, Nov. 19, 23, 26, and Dec. 6, 1960.

would result in the entry of Russia and China into the conflict were partially confirmed when the hardships imposed by the blockade induced Souvannaphouma's government to enter into diplomatic relations with Russia and to request economic assistance from that country. In early December, 1960, as the American-equipped and -trained army of General Phoumi Nosavan marched north toward the capital, Russia flew in arms to Captain Kong Lê, whose troops alone bore the burden of defending the Souvannaphouma government.[12] The coup,[13] which occurred a few days later, prompted Prince Sihanouk to renew his attempts to persuade the world of the seriousness of the Laotian crisis. In a letter addressed to thirteen nations having an interest in the fate of Laos, he called for an international conference for the threefold purpose of preventing that country's partition, exploring means to restore peace, and enabling Laotians to regain control of their country's destiny.[14]

The proposal for a conference was immediately supported by the Communist bloc, Russia going so far as to suggest Phnom Penh as the site of it.[15] But President Eisenhower's response was lukewarm and noncommittal;[16]

[12] The swiftness with which Russia responded to Souvannaphouma's call for aid may in part have been prompted by a desire to forestall China's direct involvement in Laos and a possible repetition of the Korean war. The Soviet planes were staged into Vientiane via Hanoi.

[13] A few days before Souvannaphouma had fled to Cambodia, whence he continued to preside over his government-in-exile.

[14] For the text of his letter see *Réalités Cambodgiennes*, Jan. 6, 1961. The nations included the United States, Great Britain, France, Canada, the Soviet Union, China, Poland, North Vietnam, South Vietnam, Thailand, India, Burma, and Laos.

[15] For the texts of Russia's and China's replies see *AKP*, Jan. 11 and 17, 1961, respectively.

[16] *Ibid.*, Jan. 26, 1961.

and Great Britain expressed its preference for a revival of the International Control Commission to resolve the crisis.[17]

In the meantime, Kong Lê's troops had joined the Pathet Lao on the Plaine des Jarres northeast of Vientiane, and Soviet arms assistance was now being directed to both groups. With Soviet aid and increased support from the Viet Minh the tide of battle had turned and the Pathet Lao was daily adding new victories to an already long list. In late January, 1961, following the change in administration in Washington, Prince Sihanouk wrote to President John F. Kennedy to urge his support for the conference.[18] The President replied that a conference at this time would be inopportune since, in the absence of unanimous agreement among its eventual participants, the result would be to "increase international tension rather than reduce it." He proposed instead that the Prince support Laotian King Savang Vatthana's appeal to Cambodia, Burma, and Malaya to establish a commission charged with supervising a cease-fire.[19] Cambodia refused this invitation because she believed that the proposal had originated not in Laos but in Washington and that, in any case, the efforts of such a commission would be wasted inasmuch as the Pathet Lao had not been consulted concerning it.[20]

As the West appeared to be stalling for time, Prince Sihanouk began to despair of the conference achieving what it might have had it been convened when first proposed. For, the longer it was postponed, the more territory

[17] *Ibid.,* Jan. 17, 1961. The Commission had suspended its activities *sine die* in 1958.

[18] *Ibid.,* Jan. 29, 1961.

[19] President Kennedy's letter and Prince Sihanouk's reply are to be found in *Cambodge d'Aujourd'hui,* no. 2 (Feb., 1961), p. 3.

[20] *Ibid.*

the Pathet Lao would gain—and the West would come to the bargaining table in a relatively weak position. Sihanouk's comments on this subject, made in the course of a speech at the Faculty of Law in Phnom Penh on March 14, 1961, are worth quoting at length:

If one had deigned to interest himself in the solutions which I put forward at the [crucial] moments, it would have been possible to have a truly neutral Laos between the two antagonistic blocs. But because of the wish to have Laos aligned, in a "pro-western" neutrality, the germ of *true neutrality* has been killed and the keys of the future have been given to a pro-communist neutrality.

The present (and future) evolution of events in Laos will work only to the advantage of the Pathet Lao and to those who support it. Under such conditions, I am unable to see that the socialist powers will persist in their support of my proposition for the effective and guaranteed neutralization of Laos. If, despite their advantage, these powers continue to support it, one must hope that they will sincerely consent to sacrifice their major advantages in the interest of world peace and for the survival of the Lao people in a free and united nation. But in this world conflict, is it reasonable to hope that the big powers will make a sacrifice gratuitously? [21]

The conference, whose aim was to bring about a ceasefire in Laos and return to Laotians control of their own future, convened in Geneva on May 16, 1961. The nations represented included the United States, Great Britain, France, Canada, the Soviet Union, China, Poland, North Vietnam, Cambodia, South Vietnam, Thailand, Burma, India, and Laos.

[21] For the full text of his speech see Royaume du Cambodge, *Discours de S.A.R. le Prince Norodom Sihanouk, Chef de l'Etat à l'inauguration de la Faculté de Droit* (Phnom Penh: Imprimerie du Ministère de l'Information, 1961). Italics in the original.

Despite his misgivings and a brief period during which he retracted his support for the conference,[22] Prince Sihanouk presided at its opening session and called upon the conferees to give their full attention to a guarantee of neutrality that would allow the Laotian people to live in peace.[23] His earnest plea for a constructive, nonpartisan approach to a resolution of the Laotian conflict impressed the delegates and helped to create a conciliatory atmosphere during the first days of the conference.

The United States at Geneva abandoned her insistence on a pro-Western government and expressed willingness to recognize a neutral regime. Thus on this major point the United States and the Communist powers were in agreement. An Anglo–Soviet compromise solution, allowing the representatives of each faction to enjoy equal status at the conference on the invitation of any of the other thirteen delegations, was accepted by the United States, which initially had been willing to recognize only the Boun Oum–Phoumi Nosavan delegation.[24] To facilitate the discussion on Laos, Cambodia temporarily withdrew her proposal of a buffer zone consisting of Laos and Cambodia. However, the head of the Cambodian delega-

[22] The Prince withdrew his support for the conference upon being told by King Savang Vatthana in Luang Prabang on Apr. 30 that it constituted an unwarranted interference by foreign powers in Laos domestic affairs. The King later changed his mind. For a commentary on what took place in Luang Prabang see *Réalités Cambodgiennes*, May 6, 1961.

[23] For the text of his address see *AKP*, May 24, 1961.

[24] According to H.E. Arthur Lall, head of the Indian delegation to the conference, the compromise was actually reached among all of the powers. Thai and North Vietnamese opposition to the agreement was mitigated by the efforts of the major powers. Thailand was opposed to the seating of the Pathet Lao representatives and North Vietnam objected to the presence of the Boun Oum–Phoumi Nosavan group. Interview with the author, Dec. 13, 1963.

tion, Foreign Minister Nhiek Tioulong, left the way open for some other power to introduce a similar proposal at the conference.

Aware that the conference could not attain its objectives without the cooperation of the three princes who headed the warring Laotian factions, Prince Sihanouk devoted much of his effort during its first weeks trying to instill in them an attitude of compromise and conciliation. When it became evident that he could not prevail upon the princes to agree to a meeting, he sought the assistance of President Kennedy and Chairman Khrushchev, who were themselves preparing for their Vienna parley in June on cold-war tensions.[25] Shortly after the Kennedy–Khrushchev meeting, the three princes met for the first time in Zurich. While they expressed general support of a national union government, in four days of heated wrangling they could not agree on the composition of a coalition cabinet.[26] Prince Sihanouk expressed his disappointment at the outcome of the meeting when he returned to Cambodia in July: "Without a government expressing the Laotian point of view and pledging Laos' responsibility in the elaboration, the declaration and the acceptance of its international position, the conference among thirteen nations can hardly decide on the future of the fourteenth." [27]

[25] For the texts of Sihanouk's letters to Kennedy and Khrushchev and their replies to him see *AKP,* June 3, 14, and 27, 1961. It is not known whether Kennedy or Khrushchev actually used his influence to encourage the princes to meet.

[26] For the text of the so-called Zurich agreement see George Modelski, *International Conference on the Settlement of the Laotian Question, 1961–2,* Working Paper No. 2, Research School of Pacific Studies, Australian National University (Canberra, 1962), pp. 79–81.

[27] *AKP,* July 9, 1961.

In the meantime, Prince Sihanouk had prepared a draft agreement which was intended to incorporate the main features of proposals put forth by the Western and Communist blocs. It provided for an international organization whose immediate tasks would include supervision of a cease-fire and withdrawal of foreign military personnel and whose long-range responsibility would be to regulate the introduction of foreign military advisers and armaments into Laos. The draft, however, never reached the conference table, for, according to Prince Sihanouk:

Cambodia's proposal concerning an international statute for Laos was courteously rebuffed by the Americans and the Sino-Soviet camp, each of which wishes to impose its own plans on the conference. . . . In the service of their interests, they will not permit any changes in their proposals. We were made to understand that our proposal was neither reasonable nor useful, but premature.[28]

As the attempts of the Laotian princes to obstruct the formation of a coalition government became more flagrant during the early summer, Prince Sihanouk declared that he would withdraw from the role of conciliator:

I have used my influence in Phnom Penh, Geneva and Zurich [he said on July 3] as much as possible with my Laotian friends in order to persuade them to compromise their positions, and I have done the same with the major powers. I have received many thanks and compliments, but no one has listened to me nor as yet followed my advice. How can you listen to a neutral who is no one's satellite, who leans neither towards the West nor towards the East, and who, naively, uses the language of simple good sense? The major powers are committed by their egoism, ensnared by their amour-propre, and

[28] *Ibid.*

are certain that they alone can speak for the rest of the world. Those who are under their control share their intransigence. Why should I attempt to play the role of conciliator any longer. It is force which governs the world, not right or justice.[29]

In mid-May, Sihanouk had expressed his stake in a neutralized Laos in the following statement: "In order to remain on good terms with my communist friends, we prefer not to have a common frontier with them." [30] After the Zurich meeting, he became more firmly convinced that the Pathet Lao, and hence the North Vietnamese, would soon achieve a commanding position in Laos. He declared in August:

We can predict that Prince Souphanouvong and the Neo Lao Hak Xat will soon become the (indispensable) "seconds" of Prince Souvannaphouma and his "party" (to be created) until the moment when the "Laos fruit" is ripe and ready for the picking. . . . I may be mistaken. *And I hope that I am mistaken,* for the interests of Laos and Cambodia rest in a sincere and well-developed Laotian neutrality (like ours) in order to repulse all compromise. But I have no illusions in this regard.[31]

While the conference on Laos continued throughout the summer without any detectable progress, fighting went

[29] Statement made at a press conference in Zurich, *AKP,* July 3, 1961.

[30] Interview with *Nice-Matin* (France), May 16, quoted in *AKP,* May 23, 1961.

[31] Norodom Sihanouk, "Le Laos pourra-t-il être neutre et libre comme l'est le Cambodge?" *Réalités Cambodgiennes,* Aug. 11, 1961. Italics in the original. As the paper went to press, Sihanouk added a preface to his article in which he stated that the only alternative which he could see to the communization of Laos was its partition into pro-Western and Communist-controlled areas. He continued to hold these views in 1963. See interviews with him in the *Washington Post,* May 22, 1963, and the *New York Times,* May 31, 1963.

on in Laos, each side apparently trying to improve its bargaining position at Geneva. With almost every confrontation the territory claimed by the Pathet Lao increased. In renewed attempts to alert the world to the seriousness of the Laotian conflict, Prince Sihanouk, speaking before the Belgrade Conference of Non-Aligned Nations and the United Nations General Assembly in September, 1961,[32] entreated the major powers to recognize and guarantee support of a neutral zone in Indochina. The formation of a national union government in Laos in 1962 failed to allay his fears concerning the dominant position of the Viet Minh-supported Pathet Lao.

After the Laotian Settlement

Despite intensive American support of General Phoumi Nosavan's army, by the time the Geneva talks had been concluded in July, 1962,[33] the Pathet Lao had fought its way into control of most of eastern and also parts of southern Laos. In this situation, neutralist Prince Souvannaphouma, who was designated premier of the coalition government, could hardly be expected to exercise a dominant influence. Taking note of this fact, Prince Sihanouk predicted that the international orientations of Thailand and South Vietnam would undergo significant change.[34]

[32] See *Conference of Non-Aligned States*, pp. 188–189, and *Cambodian Commentary*, special number, no. 12 (Oct.–Dec., 1961), p. 39.

[33] For the texts of the Geneva agreements on Laos see Great Britain, *International Conference on the Settlement of the Laotian Question, May 12, 1961–July 23, 1962: Laos No. 1 (1962)*. (London: H.M. Stationery Office, 1962), Cmnd. 1828, pp. 15–23.

[34] Sihanouk's analysis of the results of the Laotian conference was first published in a series of articles in *Réalités Cambodgiennes* during the summer of 1962. These articles have been collected in Norodom Sihanouk, *Le Cambodge et ses relations avec ses voisins*

Cambodia's Foreign Policy

We have come to a point in time when [our] neighbors are preparing themselves, the one voluntarily in accordance with its traditional opportunism, and the other involuntarily by the force of events—the Viet Cong—to change their loyalties. What will be our country's future in the context of this "evolution"? [35]

The failure of the United States to achieve a victory in Laos and her subsequent acceptance of a neutral regime in that country caused the Thai to examine more critically their own dependence upon the United States. According to Prince Sihanouk, Thai political leaders, always alert to the "prevailing wind," began to consider a shift to a neutral policy and a *rapprochement* with the Communist bloc.[36] Contact between Thailand and the Soviet Union, which until the American backdown in Laos had been limited to diplomatic recognition, was expanded in 1960–1961 with negotiations between them on a proposed trade

(Phnom Penh: Imprimerie du Ministère de l'Information, 1962), and it is this work, pp. 5–43, to which reference is made here.

[35] *Ibid.*, p. 26.

[36] Sihanouk illustrated this charge with a brief recital of Thailand's actions in 1941 and during the early postwar period, 1946–1950. See *ibid.*, pp. 5–11. Thai leaders themselves hinted at changes in their country's foreign policy. See addresses by Foreign Minister Thanat Khoman as quoted in Ministry of Foreign Affairs, *Foreign Affairs Bulletin* (Bangkok), I, no. 1 (Aug.–Sept., 1961), pp. 6, 7, 56, 57, and in *SEATO Record*, I, no. 12 (Dec., 1962), pp. 15, 16. See also David A. Wilson, "Thailand: Old Leaders and New Directions," *Asian Survey*, III, no. 2 (Feb., 1963), pp. 85, 87; and *New York Times*, May 11, 1961. Western observers, too have called attention to a certain "flexibility" in Thai foreign policy. See *Collective Defense in South East Asia, The Manila Treaty and Its Implications, A Report by a Chatham House Study Group* (London: Royal Institute of International Affairs, 1956), p. 25, and Stuart Simmonds, "Thailand—A Conservative State," in Saul Rose, ed., *Politics of Southern Asia*, pp. 136–138.

and aid agreement. That preparations for a change in Thai foreign policy were underway was made evident to Prince Sihanouk in a meeting with Mao Tse-tung. "If you wish to punish Ngo Dinh Diem," the Chinese leader was reported to have said, "you can count entirely on our aid and support. As for the Thai, we hope that you will soon realize an entente with them. They deserve to be humored for among themselves they do not want the alliance with the Americans. Those [Thai] who have visited [China] have assured us that they have been constrained to submit to this alliance and would like to disencumber themselves as soon as possible in order to adopt the same neutral policy as Cambodia." [37]

How would a neutral Thailand affect Cambodia's own security? In answer to this question Prince Sihanouk warned that "the United States and the Free World will have suffered a definitive defeat in Southeast Asia" and Cambodia herself will be doomed. He went on to elucidate:

We thus come to the paradox facing America. On the one hand it furnishes our adversaries with all the means necessary to menace our existence, while on the other hand it constitutes, voluntarily or not, by its presence within the borders of our adversaries, a sufficient guarantee for our survival.

When Thailand becomes neutral, we will no longer be able to count on communist assistance. They may offer their good offices, but we have seen, in 1941, how the good offices of a major power work: When one must choose between neutrals, one chooses the most important and the most "compliant." When that day comes, it will no longer be possible for us to call on the west for aid, for the voluntary disengagement of

---

[37] Norodom Sihanouk, *op. cit.*, p. 16.

Thailand will mean that the Free World no longer weighs heavily in the balance of Southeast Asia's destiny.[38]

Control of Laos by the Pathet Lao would also enhance Vietnamese threats to Cambodia, Prince Sihanouk declared. With Laos open to use as a corridor linking North Vietnam to South Vietnam, it would not be long before the South Vietnamese regime would capitulate. In this event, the Prince prophesied, the policy of Ho Chi Minh toward Cambodia would be no different from that of Ngo Dinh Diem. Both have a Cambodian "fifth column," he asserted, with the same aim: the subjugation of Cambodia. To support this allegation he gave the following account [39] of his interview with North Vietnam's Minister of Cultural Affairs, who headed his country's delegation to the sixth World Buddhist Conference held in Phnom Penh in 1961. In a reply to Sihanouk's request for his views concerning South Vietnam's claims on Cambodia's offshore islands, the North Vietnamese official said:

We of North Vietnam disapprove of the unfriendly manner by which the Saigon government has broached the common problems of the two countries. It is true that between neighboring countries there are often conflicts arising from different interpretations of the frontier. But there are several ways of resolving such problems. North Vietnam firmly supports peaceful solutions and friendly negotiations.

"In order to obtain a more precise answer," Sihanouk wrote, "I asked my visitor this point-blank question: 'But, Excellency, when your government will have established its authority over all of Vietnam (and I don't doubt that this will be accomplished in the near future), will this

[38] *Ibid.*, pp. 27–28.
[39] *Ibid.*, pp. 36–38.

same question be raised as it has been by the government of M. Diem?'

"My visitor very coolly gave me an answer which was hardly reassuring: 'Nothing will prevent us from discussing all questions between our two countries in a friendly manner, in a spirit of concord, around the conference table.'

"As one can see," Sihanouk continued, "for Vietnam, whether red or white, Cambodia's future is sealed."

Prince Sihanouk concluded his over-all analysis of Cambodia's future as follows:

We can say that the actual survival of our small country is due in part to the fact that Vietnam is still divided and weakened by a civil war . . . and in part by the impossibility, without doubt temporary, for Thailand to divorce itself from the west and especially from the Americans.

The day when Vietnam becomes reunified with Ho Chi Minh at our doors and when Thailand will have become the "good" friend of the socialist camp, on that day our country will face the danger of death. Even more, it will be surrounded in the north by a Laos controlled and directed by the Pathet Lao and Prince Souphanouvong. This Laos, supported by the Democratic Republic of Vietnam, will be strong enough to claim that Stung Treng and Ratanakkiri are Lao provinces, torn away not long ago by the French colonialists for the Khmers.

We may then be compared to a lamb which finds itself surrounded by three wolves with long teeth. Our Cambodia will have no other choice than to die with honor, fighting alone, for neither the United Nations nor the neutralists (who, in fact, have never interested themselves in us) will be able to afford us the least aid.[40]

[40] *Ibid.*, pp. 29–30. Sihanouk is probably also aware of the long-range plans for Cambodia as expressed in the meetings of the North

Cambodia Seeks an International Guarantee of Her Neutrality and Independence

In anticipation of this dire day when Cambodia would find herself prey to the apparently insatiable appetites of her neighbors, Prince Sihanouk, with even greater determination than before, sought defense commitments from the major powers. In letters to the heads of the nations which had participated in the Geneva conference on Laos, he urged that they lend their support to a treaty which would recognize and guarantee Cambodia's neutrality.[41] The letters left no room for doubt as to the reasons for Cambodia's request. In the communications to the big powers he said:

I have the honor to call Your Excellency's attention particularly to the very serious threat that has for years been hanging over my country, which has constantly been subjected to threats, plots, sabotage, blockades, and aggression by neighboring powers that are very much stronger militarily, concerning whose annexationist aims there is no longer any doubt. Territorial claims supported by the use of armed forces, the crossing of frontiers, flights over our territory, and its recent occupation by foreign troops cause me to fear that, in a short time, an insoluble situation will be created which could

---

Vietnamese Lao Dong party in 1951. See, e.g., Allan B. Cole, ed., *Conflict in Indo-China and International Repercussions: A Documentary History, 1945–1955* (Ithaca, N.Y.: Cornell University Press, 1956), p. 105, and U.S. Department of State, *The Situation in Laos* (Washington: Sept., 1959), pp. 2–3.

[41] Sihanouk's proposal was conveyed on Aug. 20 in identical letters to the heads of state of all these nations, except Thailand, South Vietnam, and North Vietnam. He wrote separately to President Ngo Dinh Diem on Aug. 24. According to the *Bangkok Post*, Sept. 3, 1962, he also wrote separately to King Phumiphon Adunyadet of Thailand. Presumably, a third letter was sent to Ho Chi Minh.

lead to an international conflict with *unforeseeable consequences.*

Cambodia can no longer endure this constant provocation and aggression, or the official or unofficial accusations made repeatedly by these same neighbors to the effect that it is encouraging and promoting subversion in their countries; this is not and has never been true.

Sincerely desiring peace, but resolved to defend its honor and what remains of its national territory after numerous "amputations," Cambodia sees no other reasonable solution of this situation than to claim for itself the benefit of the international protection provisions that have been granted to Laos. . . .

Today, before making decisions of prime importance in order to protect its existence, Cambodia requests of Your Excellency's Government and the other powers which met last month in Geneva *the official recognition and guarantee of its neutrality and territorial integrity.* It is ready to accept any appropriate control for that purpose. . . .

I take the liberty of suggesting that Your Excellency be good enough to take an active interest in our fate and agree that an international conference on Cambodia be held as soon as possible in a large neutral capital or city of your choice (Geneva, New Delhi, Stockholm, etc.).[42]

The Communist countries and France and Laos expressed their support of Sihanouk's proposal. But the United States, whose participation was crucial to the effectiveness of the guarantee, sidestepped the issue. In his reply of August 31, 1962, President Kennedy avoided mention of Cambodia's problems with her neighbors and offered only American assurances of respect for her neu-

[42] The texts of Prince Sihanouk's letter and of President Kennedy's reply are to be found in Department of State press release, no. 532, Sept. 3, 1962. Italics in the original.

trality and independence. There was no indication that the United States would also be willing to *guarantee* Cambodia's neutrality and independence. The key parts of Kennedy's letter are quoted below:

It always gives me great pleasure to receive a personal communication from Your Royal Highness and I only regret that the reason for your letter of August 20 was to express your worry over the security of Cambodia. For, as you know, the fundamental and abiding objective of the United States is that each country, large and small, live in peace and independence so that its people may prosper, enjoy the fruits of its own endeavors, and pursue a course of international relations of its own choosing. This applies especially to countries with which we have such close friendly relations as we have with Cambodia.

In this spirit and in view of the present preoccupations of Your Royal Highness, I assure you that the United States respects the neutrality, territorial integrity and independence of Cambodia. I am sure you will recognize that this attitude is the foundation of United States relations with your Government and people. We recognize and respect the high aims you have set for Cambodia, and we wholeheartedly desire to further them. Our economic cooperation has aimed at supplementing Cambodia's own intensive efforts at economic and social progress, while our military assistance has been designed to help your people maintain the security of their beloved country. . . .

There are various methods by which nations achieve a state of peaceful harmony with each other. One, which you mentioned in your letter, is the idea of an international conference to recognize the neutrality and territorial integrity of Cambodia. Another, which you suggested to Ambassador Sprouse in your conversation with him on August 28, is the issuance of "official letters" by interested governments declaring their respect for Cambodia's independence, neutrality and territorial integrity. This second method appears to me to be a wise suggestion, and a more expeditious and effective means of achieving the objectives cited in your letter. I should be glad to write such a formal letter for the United States. It is my hope that other governments interested in peace and stability in the area would likewise affirm these principles in an appropriate manner. Noting that your letter expresses willingness to accept whatever controls are necessary to insure Cambodia's aims as set forth therein, I would be interested in your ideas regarding the instrumentality for bringing the desired stability to Cambodia's border areas.[43]

On August 24, Sihanouk wrote to President Diem to inform him of his request to the big powers. In his note to Diem he frankly discussed the reasons for the proposals. He tried to persuade Diem that an internationally supervised neutralization of Cambodia would benefit both their countries. It would not only allay Cambodian suspicions of South Vietnamese motives, he declared, but it would also eliminate South Vietnamese fears that Cambodia was serving as a place of refuge or passageway for foreign troops. Cambodia, he continued, would be willing "to submit herself to complete international control," if South Vietnam, in turn, would agree to recognize Cambodia's present borders.[44]

On September 5, President Diem replied that since the stated reason for the Prince's request for an international conference was South Vietnam's "threatening attitude," his country was "morally unable to approve a move which is designed precisely to denounce her as a potential aggressor of Cambodia." He went on to say:

[43] *Ibid.*

[44] The text of Sihanouk's letter to Diem was made available to the author by the Cambodian Embassy, Washington, D.C.

If Your Highness would just read again all his own statements regarding Vietnam, he would easily realize the unity and continuity of views of a policy in which Vietnam only plays the role of a scapegoat. When, for example, the Vietnamese Government makes the remark that Communism abuses Khmer neutrality and territory to organize its subversive activities against our country, we do not accuse the Royal Government of Cambodia of being a "covert ally of Communism." We accuse Communism and propose to the Royal Khmer Government a bilateral control of borders, a proposal which Your Highness has constantly rejected for reasons still obscure to us. There are a certain number of problems between our two countries. Vietnam considers these problems as classic problems arising from decolonization and considers that it is in the interest of neither the Khmer Kingdom nor the Republic of Vietnam to involve the powers of both blocs. We are mature enough to solve these problems ourselves.[45]

Thailand also rebuffed Sihanouk's proposal. On September 3, at a press conference in Phnom Penh, Prince Sihanouk requested that the text of the Geneva accords on Laos be made applicable to Cambodia. If agreement to this proposal were unobtainable, he said, Cambodia would then accept the Kennedy counteroffer, provided letters from the Geneva powers explicitly *guaranteed,* as well as indicated respect for, her neutrality and territorial integrity. The Prince suggested that these guarantees could best be enforced by the International Control Commission, which was established by the Geneva conference, 1954, acting in cooperation with joint British–Soviet inspection teams.

While Cambodia was seeking to attract world attention

[45] The text of President Diem's reply to Prince Sihanouk was released to the press by the Embassy of Vietnam in Canberra on Sept. 13, 1962.

to her predicament, South Vietnamese military forces in September and October, 1962, were reported to have committed a series of border violations, including the bombing and strafing of two villages in Ratanakkiri province.[46] Several days later a draft treaty which formalized the Prince's proposal was delivered to the Geneva powers.[47]

Under this treaty, Cambodia would declare its military neutrality, agreeing to refrain from joining any military alliance and to forbid foreign military bases or, with certain exceptions, foreign troops on its territory. In addition, it calls for the International Control Commission to supervise the implementation of the agreement. The Geneva powers, in turn, would be required to recognize Cambodia's present boundaries with Thailand, Laos, and Vietnam; to promise to refrain from interference in Cambodia's internal affairs; and to respect her territorial and political integrity. They would also agree to extend formal guarantees to defend Cambodia against external aggression. Finally, they would agree to use their good offices to encourage the settlement of Cambodia's disputes with her neighbors, specifically Vietnam, through the peaceful means advocated by the Charter of the United Nations.

The Communist bloc again expressed their support of Sihanouk's proposal. Of the Western powers, only France signified her willingness to adhere to the agreement.[48] The United States, however, did not explicitly reject the proposal.

---

[46] See *Cambodge d'Aujourd'hui*, special number, nos. 48–51, Sept.–Dec., 1962, p. 27. See also *New York Times*, Nov. 2, 7, and 15, 1962.

[47] For the text of the draft treaty see Appendix A.

[48] See *Réalités Cambodgiennes*, Nov. 30, 1962. Laos again indicated its approval. Replies were not received from Thailand, South Vietnam, Burma, and India.

The United States position with respect to Cambodia's entreaties has been made difficult by her own relations with Thailand and South Vietnam. Cambodia, in requesting America's commitment to the defense of her neutrality, is looking ahead to the day when the balance of power in Indochina has shifted in favor of the Communist bloc and she can no longer count upon the American presence to check aggressions by a neutral Thailand and a united, Communist Vietnam. The United States, however, is faced with the fact that Thailand and South Vietnam are still in the pro-West camp and that it is in her interest to maintain their allegiance. To sign a declaration whose expressed purpose is to check aggressions by Thailand and South Vietnam, would alienate these allies, for, as Diem pointed out, this act would be tantamount to confirming Cambodia's allegations. Thus the United States, not wishing to be drawn into the quarrels between Cambodia and her neighbors, has tried to encourage them to negotiate among themselves such border disputes as do exist.[49] Cambodia, however, feels that any border settlements arrived at between herself and her neighbors would be impermanent unless they were enforced by the big powers.

The United States has been under pressure to exercise caution in accepting the Cambodian proposal for still other reasons. The American decision to support a neutral Laos in 1961–1962 caused great consternation among Thai and South Vietnamese leaders, who believed that their own staunch anti-Communist stand had been betrayed. Resentment produced by this reversal in American policy was evident in President Diem's reply to Prince Sihanouk

[49] This information concerning the United States position was conveyed to the author by a high official of the Department of State.

of September 5, 1962, in which he alluded to "the fashion of neutrality which now seems to have gained the favor of the powers of the Free World." He said that "while Vietnam respects the freedom of choice of national and international policies," she could not "encourage the tendency for unilateral neutralization among the countries of the Free World," for such a policy is "unfair and dangerous to herself." Given this attitude of South Vietnamese and Thai leaders, United States support of Sihanouk's request so soon after the neutralization of Laos would have been likely to weaken further their confidence in the United States and possibly would have prompted Thailand to seek a normalization of relations with China. We have seen that after the United States changed its policy on Laos, Thai leaders hinted publicly that consideration was being given to a new international posture for Thailand, which would make her less dependent upon the United States.

The United States may have hesitated also because she and South Vietnam fear that adoption of Sihanouk's proposal would pave the way for the imposition of a similar solution on South Vietnam. It is known that France believes that neutralization of South Vietnam is the only way to end the civil war short of losing the country completely to the Viet Minh.[50]

Opposition by the United States to the draft treaty may also in part be due to her unwillingness to accept the International Control Commission as the instrument for maintaining security of the border. The United States

[50] For a report on French views see *New York Times*, Sept. 2, 5, and 20, 1963. A brief account of French activity in Vietnam was given by Robert Shaplen in "Letter from Saigon," *The New Yorker*, Dec. 14, 1963, p. 210. See also the argument for a neutralized South Vietnam in *The New Republic*, Mar. 12 and Apr. 9, 1962.

feels that the delegation of so much authority to the Commission would necessitate the introduction into Cambodia of more Communist bloc personnel, whose activities, she feels, would not be confined solely to the solution of Cambodian border problems.

Cambodia's failure to obtain American acceptance of her various proposals evidently convinced her that she must look elsewhere for a solution to her problems. On January 18, 1963, the editor of *Réalités Cambodgiennes* wrote:

In order to avoid [subjugation by Thailand and Vietnam] the Khmers are ready to ally themselves with anyone. Only the socialist camp seems disposed to protect us from dismemberment. Only it has proposed to help us and says it is ready to offer us its guarantees. If our national existence is at stake, how can we neglect this sheet anchor?

In response to the comment of an American journalist that such a move would endanger Cambodia's monarchy, traditions, and liberties, the paper's editor declared:

Yes, we have been aware of this danger for a long time, for we are without illusions. . . . [But] we would lose more if we became the slaves of our neighbors. . . . We know that [under the Communists] we would [at least] retain our national entity and our frontiers. We know, finally, that we would retain something as precious to a people as to a man: honor. For the decision would have been neither imposed nor obtained by force.

Further indications that Cambodia was considering a new approach to ensure her security appeared in a speech delivered by Prince Sihanouk to a National Congress on July 1, 1963.[51] Noting that only France and the Commu-

[51] See *Réalités Cambodgiennes*, July 12, 1963.

nist bloc, including North Vietnam, were ready to guarantee Cambodia's security, he said:

The other powers, including certain ones who pretend to be neutralists, have made us understand indirectly that they would rather sacrifice us than alienate their friendship or their complicity with the imperialist dictatorships of Saigon and Bangkok. Our future, therefore, is settled. The accord guaranteeing our neutrality and our present boundaries has no chance of being signed by all the powers solicited. It will be necessary for us to defend this neutrality and these boundaries by our own means and with the aid of the big friendly powers (among the first of which is China [52]), who have accorded us without bargaining their total support in case of aggression.

Our propositions, however, have had great merit: That of unmasking hypocrisies and revealing to us the true sentiments held by countries whose ideals of justice and democracy have shown themselves to be empty of meaning.

Cambodian–American relations received another setback with the resumption in October, 1963, of anti-Sihanouk propaganda by the Khmer Serei movement, which, Cambodians alleged, was broadcasting from South Vietnam and Thailand with powerful transmitters supplied by the United States Central Intelligence Agency.[53] On November 12, Sihanouk announced that unless the Khmer Serei broadcasts ceased Cambodia would renounce all Western economic and military aid.[54] His country would

[52] On a visit to Cambodia in early May, 1963, China's President, Liu Shao-chi, reaffirmed China's support for Cambodia's neutrality and independence. See *ibid.*, May 4, 1963.

[53] For details of the Cambodian allegations see *Réalités Cambodgiennes*, Oct. 4, 11, and 18, 1963. These were repeated by Radio Phnom Penh on Nov. 5, 7, 8, and 11, 1963.

[54] This announcement was broadcast by Radio Phnom Penh on Nov. 12, 1963. See also *Washington Post*, Nov. 13 and 14, 1963.

then turn to China for increased economic and technical assistance and also for military aid. A few days later, upon the confession of a Khmer Serei member, who was captured while trying to enter Cambodia, Prince Sihanouk demanded the immediate termination of American aid and the departure from Cambodia of all nonembassy personnel of the United States government. While China applauded this Cambodian action and offered Sihanouk her support, the Prince's subsequent actions indicated that he was not prepared to deliver his country into the Communist bloc.[55] Still convinced of the need to maintain a Western presence in Cambodia, he invited France to fill the vacuum created by the departure of the United States. At his request the existing French military mission has remained in Cambodia. In addition, the Prince renewed his request for an international conference to decide upon a guarantee of Cambodia's neutrality and independence. In contrast to her position on Sihanouk's first request in 1962, the United States in late 1963 adopted a favorable view of his proposal.[56]

The American interest in restoring good relations with Cambodia was indicated by the relative swiftness with which the United States reached agreement in January,

[55] For a further statement concerning Cambodia's adherence to any bloc, see Norodom Sihanouk, "Une politique de neutralité dans l'Asie troublée," Le Monde Diplomatique (Paris), Oct., 1963, p. 13.

[56] According to official American sources, however, Ambassador Sprouse was unable to gain an audience with Sihanouk and thus could not communicate this view to him. For reports of the new American view, see New York Times, Dec. 3, and the editorial of Dec. 8, 1963. On Dec. 15, 1963, the New York Times reported from Paris that in a meeting with the British and French foreign ministers, Secretary of State Dean Rusk emphasized that "the United States would not participate [in the conference on Cambodia] unless ground rules and objectives of the meeting were clearly defined."

1964, with Great Britain and France on a draft declaration of Cambodia's neutrality [57] and, at the same time, accepted a Philippine compromise formula for the settlement of her differences with Cambodia.[58] Complete *rapprochement*, however, was prevented by the intransigence of Thailand and South Vietnam [59] and the reported fear of the United States that a conference on Cambodia would become a forum for a debate on American policy in all of Southeast Asia as well as seriously affect American relations with Thailand and South Vietnam.[60] In mid-February, Prince Sihanouk announced his willingness to limit participation in the conference to the United States, Thailand, South Vietnam, and Cambodia.[61] This concession was made when tension between Cambodia and South Vietnam reached a new height as a result of a South Vietnamese air attack on a village in Kompong Cham province [62] and of charges by American military officials in Saigon that the

[57] See *ibid.*, Jan. 16, 1964. The *Washington Post*, Jan. 22, 1964, reported that the draft declaration included (1) a declaration of neutrality by Cambodia, (2) a declaration of respect for Cambodia's neutrality by the powers, and (3) an agreement strengthening the powers of the International Control Commission.

[58] *Washington Post*, Jan. 22, 1964. The *New York Times*, Jan. 22, 1964, reported that the Philippine compromise was based on the recognition by the United States of the need for an international confirmation of Cambodia's neutrality. It did not, however, specify American agreement on an international conference.

[59] Negotiations in December between Cambodia and South Vietnam on their border difficulties collapsed on the refusal of the latter to participate in the proposed guarantee of Cambodia's neutrality (see *New York Times*, Dec. 19, 26, 27, 28, and 30, 1963). In early Jan., 1964, the Thai government refused to negotiate with Cambodia, under the auspices of United Nations Secretary-General U Thant, a treaty of nonaggression (see *AKP*, Feb. 1, 1964).

[60] See *New York Times*, Dec. 25, 1963; Jan. 15 and 16, 1964.

[61] See *Washington Post*, Feb. 20, 1964.

[62] See *AKP*, Feb. 6, 1964; *New York Times*, Feb. 12, 1964.

Viet Cong were receiving arms and military equipment through Cambodia.[63] His new proposal was viewed by the American State Department as being "most welcome," [64] and an effort was then made by the United States to persuade the Saigon and Bangkok governments to agree to such a conference. Premier Nguyen Khanh of South Vietnam soon declared his government's willingness to attend a limited conference, but Thailand was reported to be balking at American pressure.[65] The *official* response of the United States to Sihanouk's proposal was favorable but she was reported by the Cambodian and the American press as having set as a precondition for the meeting a redefinition of Cambodia's borders by a commission composed of Cambodia and her neighbors. Prince Sihanouk, anticipating that the American counterproposal would serve only to forestall discussion of Cambodia's neutrality, withdrew his proposal for a restricted conference.[66]

American officials in the State Department whom the

[63] See *AKP*, Feb. 2, 1964; *Washington Post*, Jan. 5, 1964. This charge was based on Cambodian customs statistics (which are readily available), on reports of Cambodian seizure of illegal matériel, and on an analysis of equipment captured from the Viet Cong in South Vietnam.

[64] *Washington Post*, Feb. 22, 1964.

[65] See *ibid.*, Mar. 3, 1964; *New York Times*, Mar. 7 and 8, 1964. Thai Foreign Minister Thanat Khoman was reported to have said his government would consider any proposal to enhance the chances for peace in Southeast Asia, but at minimum Cambodia would first have to cease its anti-Thai propaganda (*New York Times*, Mar. 7, 1964). Thailand was probably also concerned over reports that Cambodia was about to receive arms aid from China and that the Chinese government would soon build two jet airbases in Cambodia (see *Washington Post*, Feb. 18, and *New York Times*, Mar. 15 and 16, 1964).

[66] See *Réalités Cambodgiennes*, Mar. 14, 1964; *New York Times*, Mar. 10 and 11, 1964.

author interviewed denied that the United States had set preconditions for the conference. They stated that the suggestion of the United States for delimiting the borders was submitted as a draft, one to be discussed along with other drafts. They indicated that the United States was agreeable to a conference that would review drafts submitted by all four participating countries. Failure of the conference to materialize was attributed, first, to the fact that the invitation to attend the conference had not been extended to Thailand and South Vietnam until the last moment, with the result that neither country submitted a draft; and, second, to the unacceptability of the Cambodian proposal on which Sihanouk desired action. The United States rejected the Cambodian draft for the following reasons: (*a*) it was submitted with the stipulation that the conference be held by the end of March or Cambodia would call it off; (*b*) it contained references to Franco–Thai treaties which the Thai viewed as humiliating; (*c*) Cambodia demanded that the United States bear all of the expenses incurred by the International Control Commission; and (*d*) Cambodia appended to the draft a "Gentleman's Agreement" according to which South Vietnam would accept full responsibility for border incursions and the United States would accept a major share of the responsibility for previous and future attacks, and pay reparations in a form to be determined by Cambodia.

Yet another setback in progress toward a *rapprochement* occurred on March 19, when an American-supported South Vietnamese air and ground attack on the Cambodian village of Chantrea in Svayrieng province resulted in the death of seventeen villagers. Both the United States and South Vietnam accepted responsibility and offered their apologies for the attack, which was alleged to have resulted from the pursuit by Vietnamese army units of Viet Cong guerrillas across the poorly defined Cambodian frontier.[67] Nevertheless, Prince Sihanouk announced his intention to place the matter before the United Nations Security Council. He also reiterated his insistence on the need for an international conference on Cambodia that would include all the Geneva powers. At Sihanouk's request, President de Gaulle and Chairman Khrushchev undertook to persuade the United States and Great Britain of the need for immediate talks on Cambodia.[68] Before results were obtained from their efforts, South Vietnamese military forces again crossed into Cambodian territory. An immediate apology was offered by South Vietnam; it placed the ultimate responsibility for the attack, however, on Cambodia, which, Saigon charged, was providing sanctuary for the Viet Cong.[69]

The issue of incursions of Cambodia's borders by South Vietnam, which Prince Sihanouk had hoped would be resolved by the Geneva powers, was now brought before the United Nations Security Council, where the Cambodian delegate asked for consideration of the "repeated acts of aggression by United States–South Vietnam forces against the territory and civilian population of Cambodia." Am-

---

[67] *Ibid.*, Mar. 22 and 23, 1964. See *AKP*, Apr. 30, 1964, for the text of the South Vietnamese letter of apology, dated Mar. 21, 1964.

[68] In his letters to de Gaulle and Khrushchev, as well as one to R. A. Butler, Foreign Secretary of Great Britain, Sihanouk also urged that the Geneva powers be convened to "determine the most favorable political solution for all the countries of ex-Indochina." For the texts of his letters, see *AKP*, Apr. 23, 1964. See also *Neak Cheat Niyum*, Apr. 26, 1964; *AKP*, May 10, 11, and 23, 1964; and *New York Times*, May 9, 1964.

[69] See *AKP*, May 12 and *New York Times*, May 10, 1964. See also *La Dépêche du Cambodge*, May 9, and *Phnom Penh Presse*, May 11, 1964.

bassador Sonn Voeunsai asked, also, for the establishment of a United Nations investigation commission to look into South Vietnamese–American countercharges that Cambodia was sheltering the Viet Cong.[70] The matter, however, was exploited by the Soviet Union, whose delegate, Nikolai T. Fedorenko, demanded that the Council "roundly condemn the criminal military aggression" of the United States and take immediate measures not only to protect Cambodia but also to end United States interference in any part of Southeast Asia.

In a reply to the Soviet allegation, the chief American delegate to the United Nations, Adlai E. Stevenson, on May 20 asserted that the United States was involved in Southeast Asia for one reason: "to aid . . . peoples prepared to fight for their freedom and their independence against armed aggression sponsored from outside their borders." [71] When "all states in [Southeast Asia] make and abide by the simple decision to leave their neighbors alone," he said, then there will be no need for an American presence. "Until such assurances are forthcoming, we shall stand for the independence of free peoples in Southeast Asia as we have elsewhere."

[70] The text of the Cambodian complaint is to be found in United Nations, Security Council, Doc. S/5697, May 13, 1964, and *AKP*, May 12, 1964. A "dossier of American–South Vietnamese aggression" against Cambodia was sent to the Security Council by the Cambodian government on Apr. 16. See *AKP*, May 5, 1964. For the official text of the Cambodian complaint see United Nations, Security Council, Doc. S/5666, April 22, 1964. See also, *New York Times*, May 14 and 20, 1964. The South Vietnamese reply is to be found in République du Vietnam, *Memorandum en réponse aux accusations formulés par le Gouvernement Royal du Cambodge contre le République du Vietnam devant le Conseil de Sécurité de l'O.N.U.* (Saigon: Ministère des Affairs Etrangères, 1964).

[71] For the full text of Stevenson's address to the Security Council, see *New York Times*, May 21, 1964.

With respect to the Cambodian question before the Council, Stevenson tried to assure Cambodia that the United States was in complete sympathy with her concern for the sanctity of her borders and the security of her people. While admitting American involvement in the attack on Chantrea, he denied that the United States had any aggressive intent against Cambodia. He went on:

The difficulty . . . has been that Cambodia has not been in a position to carry out with its own unaided strength its own desire to live in peace and tranquility.

Others in the area have not been prepared to leave the people of Cambodia free to pursue their own ends independently and peacefully.

The recent difficulties along the frontier which we have been discussing here in the Council are only superficially and accidentally related to the Republic of Vietnam. They are deeply and directly related to the fact that the leaders and armed forces of North Vietnam, supported by Communist China, have abused the right of Cambodia to live in peace by using Cambodian territory as a passageway, a source of supply, and a sanctuary from counterattack by the forces of South Vietnam, which is also trying to maintain its right to live in peace and go its way.

Obviously Cambodia cannot be secure. Her territorial integrity cannot be assured. Her independence cannot be certain as long as outsiders direct massive violence within the frontiers of her neighboring states.

This is the real reason for troubles on the Cambodian border and this is the real reason that we are here today.

Ambassador Stevenson, however, rejected the contention that a Geneva-type conference could produce an effective agreement to restore security along the Cambodia–South Vietnam border. What was needed, he said, was implementation of the Geneva agreements of 1954 by all the participant states, including those who were not members of the United Nations. (The Cambodian delegate had also made this point, but while Stevenson made specific reference to China and North Vietnam, Sonn Voeunsai had referred to South Vietnam.) Stevenson concluded by taking note of the several suggestions which had been made for restoring stability along the frontier: (*a*) establishment of a commission of inquiry to investigate whether the Viet Cong were actually using Cambodian territory; (*b*) establishment by Cambodia and South Vietnam of a joint military force to observe and patrol the border and to report to the United Nations Secretary-General; (*c*) establishment of a bilateral border police force supplemented by United Nations observers and possibly placed under United Nations command; and (*d*) use of an all-United Nations force to patrol and control the frontier. But, Stevenson said:

We would suggest . . . that whether one of these or some other practical solution is agreed, that it would be useful to ask the Secretary-General of the United Nations to offer assistance to Cambodia and to the Republic of Vietnam in clearly marking the frontiers between the two countries. One of the difficulties is that there are places where one does not know whether he stands on one side of the frontier or the other. Certainly it would help to reduce the possibility of further incidents if this uncertainty could be removed.

There followed several days of discussion of the merits of organizing a United Nations patrol force, as suggested by the United States and supported by South Vietnam, or of reopening the conference among the Geneva powers and entrusting the task of preventing frontier violations to the International Control Commission for Cambodia, as favored by Cambodia, France, and the Soviet Union. Cambodia, the United States, and South Vietnam agreed to a compromise proposal drafted by Morocco and the Ivory Coast in accordance with which the Security Council would establish a three-nation committee to investigate friction along the border. The final Security Council resolution stated:

The Security Council, considering the complaint by the Royal Government of Cambodia in document S–5697,

Noting the statements made in the Council in regard to the complaint,

Noting with regret the incidents which have occurred on Cambodian territory and the existing situation on the Cambodian–Vietnamese frontier,

Taking note of the apologies and regrets tendered to the Royal Government of Cambodia in regard to these incidents and the loss of life they have entailed,

Noting also the desire of the Governments of the Kingdom of Cambodia and the Republic of Vietnam to succeed in restoring their relations to a peaceful and normal state,

1. Deplores the incidents caused by the penetration of units of the Army of the Republic of Vietnam into Cambodian territory;

2. Requests that just and fair compensation should be offered to the Royal Government of Cambodia;

3. Invites those responsible to take all appropriate measures to prevent any further violations of the Cambodian frontier;

4. Requests all states and authorities and in particular the members of the Geneva conference to recognize and respect Cambodia's neutrality and territorial integrity;

5. Decides to send three of its members to the two countries and to places where the most recent incidents have occurred in order to consider such measures as may prevent any recur-

rence of such incidents. They will report to the Security Council within 45 days.[72]

The United States and South Vietnam expressed regret that the Council had not complied with their suggestion that it station a United Nations force on the frontier to prevent further incidents. For his part, Prince Sihanouk rejected an American suggestion that the United Nations commission should become involved in helping to demarcate the border, but he hinted that Cambodia would be amenable to United Nations assistance in this respect when South Vietnam dropped her demands on Cambodia's coastal islands and recognized them as belonging to Cambodia.[73]

On June 11, the village of Tralok Bek in Svayrieng province was bombed and strafed by South Vietnamese aircraft. The International Control Commission, which investigated immediately, reportedly asserted that the border was well marked at this point.[74] According to Prince Sihanouk, in letters to R. A. Butler and Andrei Gromyko, the Geneva co-chairmen, and to United Nations Secretary-General U Thant, "The Security Council resolution has been deliberately violated." He again demanded that the Geneva powers be convened to consider Cambodia's case. "I should like to reiterate," he wrote, "that this latest aggression proves the impossibility of finding a solution to the Khmer–South Vietnam problem outside of the international conference for which we have asked in vain for so long." [75]

---

[72] United Nations, Security Council, Doc. S/5741, June 4, 1964; *New York Times*, June 5, 1964. Brazil, Morocco, and the Ivory Coast were chosen as members of the investigation commission.

[73] *Ibid.*, June 8, 1964.

[74] See *Réalités Cambodgiennes*, June 19, 1964.   [75] *Ibid.*

Meanwhile, the Security Council's special mission had returned from Cambodia with the report that Cambodia and South Vietnam, despite fundamental differences in their foreign policies, were prepared to resume normal peaceful relations and that, moreover, South Vietnam indicated its respect for Cambodia's neutrality. Both countries had suggested to the mission ways in which the border problem could be alleviated. South Vietnam proposed establishment of an international police force, or an observer group with sufficient personnel and resources to keep the frontier area under surveillance. Cambodia, in her turn, suggested that teams of unarmed United Nations civilian observers be stationed on Cambodian territory to observe possible incursions but stipulated that they were not to be allowed to cross the frontier. The mission recommended that the Cambodian proposal be carried out.[76]

Subsequent to the mission's report, however, further attacks by South Vietnamese forces (including American military advisory personnel) on Cambodian border villages led to a renewal of tension between the two countries. Vietnamese and American spokesmen conceded the Cambodian charges but insisted that the attacks had been necessitated by increased Viet Cong activity originating from bases in Cambodia.[77] In the wake of these attacks, Prince Sihanouk threatened to sever diplomatic relations with the United States, to strike back militarily across the border, and to negotiate a border settlement with North Vietnam and the National Liberation Front (the political arm of the Viet Cong). He also invited all governments

[76] See Appendix B for an extract of the mission's report to the Security Council.
[77] See *New York Times,* Oct. 27, 1964. Cf. *Réalités Cambodgiennes,* Oct. 23, 1964.

and parties with interests in Indochina to convene to discuss their common problems.[78]

By mid-November Cambodian-American relations were deteriorating rapidly, and the United States proposed a meeting between the two countries to resolve their differences, to forestall a diplomatic break, and possibly, also, to block a border agreement between Cambodia and North Vietnam.[79] The United States did not intend, however, to discuss Cambodia's relations with South Vietnam. "We would not consider it appropriate," the American embassy in Phnom Penh informed the Cambodian government, "to negotiate on matters involving the interests of third countries without their participation." [80] But each side would be free to introduce any subject relevant to the resolution of Cambodian–American differences.

At the opening of the negotiations in New Delhi on December 8, the chief Cambodian delegate, Son Sann, reviewed the events that had led up to the present crisis in United States–Cambodia relations. He emphasized in particular the plight of Cambodians who had borne the brunt of the South Vietnamese attacks, which, he said, involved American aircraft and personnel. He went on to note that since 1956, when Cambodia established relations with the Communist powers, she had become "progressively the target of the western powers, and particularly of the United States and its Asian allies, who were so ob-

[78] See *Réalités Cambodgiennes.* Oct. 23 and 30, and Nov. 27, 1964. Talks with North Vietnam were entered into in Peking in late November. See also *New York Times,* Oct. and Nov., 1964, *passim.*

[79] See *New York Times,* Nov. 17, 1964.

[80] Note no. 32 of American Embassy to the Cambodian Foreign Ministry, Nov. 25, 1964, reprinted in U.S. Department of State *Bulletin,* LI, no. 1329 (Dec. 14, 1964), p. 857.

sessed by the fear of communism that they discovered and continue to discover it everywhere, even in neutral Cambodia."[81] He denied earlier charges by the United States and South Vietnam that the Viet Cong operated from bases in Cambodia and reminded them that both countries had so far refused to support Prince Sihanouk's proposal to increase the mobility of the International Control Commission and extend its investigatory powers.[82] He concluded by enumerating the terms that Cambodia demanded as part of any agreement between herself and the United States. As a minimum condition, he stipulated that "the U.S.–South Vietnamese forces must no longer attack the frontier villages of Cambodia and must not come and make arbitrary arrests in Cambodian territory."[83] He described the second point as a logical compromise, one that should be acceptable to all parties concerned:

The United States and its allies, particularly South Vietnam and Thailand, must no longer unjustly and slanderously accuse Cambodia of being a transit place for Vietcong troops and for transit of arms for the Vietcong so long as these countries do not agree to provide necessary means and to entrust the International Control Commission with the task of establishing an appropriate control which the Royal Government has always accepted over its territory, including its ports, in conformity with the 1954 Geneva Agreements.[84]

[81] "Text of the speech of H.E. Mr. Son Sann, Head of the Cambodian delegation on opening of U.S.–Cambodia talks in New Delhi on 8 December 1964," Cambodian Embassy, New Delhi, 1964, pp. 4–5.

[82] The substance of Prince Sihanouk's proposal may be found in the *Draft Protocol to the Declaration on the Neutrality of the Kingdom of Cambodia*. See below, Appendix A, pp. 231–236.

[83] "Text of the speech of H.E. Mr. Son Sann . . . ," p. 7.

[84] *Ibid.* In addition to these basic issues, the Cambodian govern-

The chief American delegate, Ambassador Philip W. Bonsal, explained in his reply that American interest in Southeast Asia was based on "the very simple principle that each country has the right to choose the form of government and kind of social organization desired by its people, without foreign interference." [85] He urged Cambodia to try to understand South Vietnam's difficulties in her confrontation with the Viet Cong and to undertake with the Saigon government direct negotiations concerning common border problems.

In offering the apologies of the United States for the loss of life and property suffered by Cambodians in the frontier region, Ambassador Bonsal said:

Neither my government nor the South Vietnamese government has anything to gain by violating Cambodian territory. . . . We are convinced that the South Vietnamese government, under difficult conditions, has increased its efforts to avoid further frontier incidents, and it has in this endeavor the complete cooperation of the American military advisors. The American government will continue and will intensify its measures to minimize the possibility that American personnel are involved in future incidents.[86]

Then, in an apparent allusion to Viet Cong activity in Cambodia, Ambassador Bonsal asserted: "We are convinced that the violations of Cambodian territory have

---

ment was anxious to settle with the United States matters pertaining to compensation for the loss of life and property suffered in the attacks on Cambodian villages, to Khmer Serei propaganda broadcasts from South Vietnam, and to the fate of Cambodian prisoners in South Vietnam.

[85] Quoted in "Réponse de la délégation cambodgienne à la déclaration de M. Bonsal du 8 décembre 1964," Cambodian Embassy, New Delhi, Dec. 9, 1964, p. 2.

[86] *Ibid.*, p. 4.

been committed contrary to the desires and in spite of the energetic measures taken by the Cambodian government to prevent them." [87]

While he welcomed the renewed expression of United States interests in the freedom and independence of Southeast Asian states, Son Sann reminded the American delegates that Cambodia had in fact practiced the principle involved and that as recently as November Prince Sihanouk had suggested that all the people of Indochina meet to express their desires on the subject. He went on:

A policy is judged by the results obtained from it. Those obtained in Cambodia prove that the policy extolled by our Prince and followed by all of the Cambodian people is the best. . . . If the United States were able to reconsider its position in time and revise its policy as a result, such a revision will profit everyone and the United States in particular. But, out of scrupulous respect for the principle of non-interference, Cambodia has until now not asked the United States to revise its policy. In return we have the right to ask you to allow us to follow our policy without suggesting a "cooperation" which is contrary even to the principle of neutrality and which would have as an inevitable consequence our involvement in the disastrous situation in which Laos and South Vietnam now find themselves. [88]

To Son Sann, the Americans by suggesting that Cambodia and South Vietnam negotiate their differences seemed to be ignoring the numerous attempts made by Prince Sihanouk to persuade South Vietnam formally to drop its claims to Cambodia's offshore islands and to recognize the present border—steps that would enable the resumption of friendly relations. Furthermore, Son Sann declared, the Cambodian government would like to have more than

[87] *Ibid.*, p. 5.   [88] *Ibid.*, p. 3.

formal assurances that South Vietnam would never again invade her territory; specifically, Cambodia desired "a formal engagement that [would] guarantee once and for all [her] frontiers and territory from aggression and [her] people from all land, air, sea, and river attacks." [89]

During the course of the next week, according to communiqués issued by the Cambodian embassy, "the two delegations arrived at a better understanding of their respective positions." It was hoped by Cambodia that a partial, if not total, agreement might be reached. On December 16, however, the American delegation announced that the Cambodian proposals required considerable study and that it would have to return to Washington for consultations. In acceding to the suspension of talks, the Cambodian delegation noted that the Americans were returning to Washington "to consult with their Government on subjects which had been officially communicated well in advance of the opening of the talks in New Delhi. [We] wish to note that it is the Government of the United States which had taken the initiative to propose the talks and which now takes the initiative to interrupt them." [90]

In perspective, it is evident that the incidents of 1963 and 1964, though they received much publicity, played a small role in the evolution of Cambodian foreign policy to its present state. More important was the American

[89] *Ibid.,* p. 5.

[90] "Communiqué of the Cambodian Delegation," Cambodian Embassy, New Delhi, Dec. 17, 1964, p. 2. What actually motivated the United States to interrupt the talks at this point is not known. It may be of some interest to note, however, that at about this time negotiations which Cambodia was conducting with North Vietnam in Peking failed to reach a satisfactory conclusion. See *Réalités Cambodgiennes,* Dec. 18, 1964.

persistence in disregarding Cambodia's appeal for a guarantee of her neutrality against *all* threats,[91] which confirmed Cambodian fears that she could neither rely upon the United States to curb Vietnamese and Thai harassment and aggression in the present nor count on her assistance against Vietnam and Thailand in a future period when they might no longer belong to the Western camp.

In contrast to the United States, France in 1963–1964 unequivocally supported Cambodia's desire to pursue a policy of neutrality. Moreover, as the United States position in South Vietnam and Laos appeared to Cambodians to be deteriorating and the probability of an American withdrawal from Indochina appeared to be great, France was expressing an interest in re-establishing her influence in that area. These two developments, together with the fact that France is unencumbered by ties with South Vietnam and Thailand, make her very attractive to Cambodia. With China jealously guarding her position on the opposite side of the balance, Cambodia is assured that the danger would be small that France would once more strive to deprive Cambodia of her independence.

[91] The United States assertion that she was in full sympathy with Cambodia's desire for security and would do all she could to defend Cambodia (and other states) from outside aggression notwithstanding, it was clear to Prince Sihanouk that the United States was referring only to Communist aggression.

CHAPTER VII

Problems of
Cambodian Foreign Policy

IN the preceding chapters we have discussed the principal considerations which have guided the evolution of Cambodia's foreign policy in the postindependence period. The most pressing and persistent of these, we have seen, has been the felt need to minimize threats of aggression against her by Thailand and the two Vietnams. Cambodia's uneasiness concerning their intentions is traceable in part to the history of her relations with them, a history marked by the gradual but steady shrinking of her borders as a result of Thai and Vietnamese encroachments. Partly, too, Cambodia's wariness of her neighbors stems directly from incidents in the present which, though minor in themselves, signify to Cambodian leaders that neither the Thai nor the Vietnamese have abandoned their centuries-old tradition of expansion at her expense. How real are Cambodia's fears in this regard is evident in her relations with states whose power predominates in Indochina, in particular the United States and China. Since independence Cambodia's relations with them have oscillated between warm cordiality and aloofness, according to whether their positions were perceived as abetting or restraining aggression against her by the Thai and the Vietnamese.

These inconstancies in Cambodia's relations with the major powers have led certain American journalists to portray her chief policy-maker, Prince Norodom Sihanouk, as "mercurial," "fickle," and "unpredictable." These observers have evidently overlooked the fact that security against Thai and Vietnamese incursions has been the most immediate and paramount objective of Cambodian foreign policy and that relations with the big powers have turned on their ability and willingness to contribute to this security. When viewed in this light, Cambodian foreign policy has been remarkable for its consistency and predictability.

Does the renunciation of American aid by Cambodia in 1963 portend a departure from her neutralist position? Apparently not, for she has once more appealed for an international conference to guarantee her neutrality and independence. The sudden dismissal of American aid was intended to accomplish what verbal appeals could not do: convince the United States how seriously she regards the potential threats to her independence which are posed by Thailand, South Vietnam, and North Vietnam, and how strongly she is persuaded that neutralization is the course best calculated to ensure her security *vis-à-vis* both her two immediate neighbors and other powers to the north. The harassments to which Cambodia is subjected from time to time may appear relatively minor; but in requesting United States commitment to his defense, Prince Sihanouk is looking ahead to the time when China has replaced the United States as the dominant influence on the Indochina peninsula and the United States is no longer able to exercise a restraining influence on Thailand and South Vietnam. If the war in South Vietnam continues its present course and if, as Prince Sihanouk has predicted, a

Problems of Cambodian Foreign Policy

Communist victory in Vietnam will prompt Thailand to abandon her pro-West policy, this time is not remote. If there is a sense of urgency about the conference, it is because Cambodia wants it held while the United States is still in a position to persuade Thailand and South Vietnam to lend their signatures to the agreement.[1] Their participation is particularly important since a key provision in the 1962 proposed treaty on Cambodia's neutrality called for the recognition and acceptance by Thailand and Vietnam of the Cambodian border as it is presently defined.[2]

The proposed treaty also represented an attempt to protect Cambodia from the machinations of the cold-war powers. In requiring the signatories to respect and guarantee Cambodian neutrality, the treaty has in effect called for a truce to the political competition between the cold-war powers within her boundaries. This would mean that attempts by either bloc to create or encourage groups inimical to a neutral regime would constitute a violation of the treaty. We have seen that China and the United States as well as North Vietnam, Thailand, and South Vietnam have at one time or another been charged with supporting subversive elements.

The treaty, if agreed to by all the big powers and her neighbors, would, her leaders are convinced, bring Cam-

[1] Thus whether or not France replaces the United States as the dominant Western power in Cambodia, American participation in a guarantee of her neutrality is still essential. North Vietnam, along with China and Russia, has supported Prince Sihanouk's previous requests for an international guarantee of Cambodia's neutrality and is expected to react favorably to his most recent proposal.

[2] It is not known whether the draft declarations on Cambodia's neutrality, which were agreed upon early in 1964, mention Thailand and Vietnam.

bodia closer to realizing the primary objectives of her foreign policy: (*a*) freezing the borders which she now shares with Thailand, Laos, and South Vietnam; (*b*) preserving the big-power equilibrium within her boundaries even after it has disappeared in the rest of Indochina; and (*c*) reducing the opportunities for subversion from within, which presumably could not come to fruition without foreign support.

In renewing his request for a guarantee of Cambodia's neutrality, Prince Sihanouk has placed the onus for any shift in his country's foreign policy directly on the United States and her allies. (The Communist powers, including North Vietnam, have already signified their willingness to guarantee Cambodia's neutrality.) Whether Cambodia remains neutral, is forced to ally herself with China, or submits herself to an alliance with the West,[3] will be in great part determined by the American reaction to this final challenge. In leaving to the United States the decisive move, Cambodia is taking a carefully calculated risk, i.e., that the United States will continue to be interested in maintaining her presence in mainland Southeast Asia and to regard a pro-Chinese Cambodia as a grave threat to her interests. Failure of the United States to accept the challenge will probably be taken to mean that she is divesting herself of responsibility for the actions of Thailand and South Vietnam and that she may even be contemplating complete withdrawal of her presence from the whole of Indochina. If this should be the case, then Cambodia, true

---

[3] In this connection, Sihanouk has stated on several occasions that if Thailand and South Vietnam were to become neutral or pro-Communist, Cambodia would probably become pro-West, assuming that the West is willing to give her an unequivocal commitment to her defense.

to her earlier declarations of the need for the presence of a countervailing influence against Chinese power in Indochina, can be expected to seek replacement of the United States with another Western power. Since among the Western powers only France to date has displayed any inclination to support Sihanouk's proposal, she is the most likely successor to the United States.

The presence in Cambodia of a sympathetic France that has openly espoused neutralization of her former colonies as the best means of reducing tension in Indochina may be regarded by Cambodians as more desirable than the presence of a more powerful United States which is unwilling, for whatever reasons, to commit herself to Cambodia's defense and apparently has less understanding of a neutralist position. Moreover, France, in apparently being less vigorous than the United States in her anti-Communist stand in Southeast Asia, may perhaps be viewed as being less likely to try to perpetuate the cold war in Cambodia. While France would not be able to exercise direct influence over Thailand and South Vietnam, she would probably be able to count on the United States to urge moderation in their actions. In the event that Thailand and South Vietnam should leave the Western camp, France, because of her less militant approach to Communism, might be able, through negotiation with China, to effect a peaceful solution of any differences which may then arise.

If France, though willing to support Cambodia's neutrality, is unable to guarantee her defense to the extent deemed necessary by Cambodia,[4] Cambodia will probably

[4] For example, if Cambodia should demand commitment of French troops as part of the guarantee, it is unlikely that France any more than the United States would be willing to do so. More-

depart from her neutral course to pursue a pro-Chinese policy. In undertaking this change she will be motivated not by ideological considerations but by practical concerns, in particular by the hope that in this way she will prevent her partition and absorption by the Thai and the Vietnamese. Chinese protection against her neighbors will be bought with her independence, Prince Sihanouk has admitted, but, he has explained, at least her identity and territorial integrity will be preserved.

Any deviation from a policy of neutrality would almost certainly produce far-reaching effects upon Cambodia's domestic scene. As a result of Prince Sihanouk's own efforts, "neutrality" has become synonymous with "independence" in the parlance of the common people.[5] Prince Sihanouk has been so effective in his political education of the people that today neutrality is regarded by the typical Cambodian as being an essential and desirable state. Those who would advise departure from it would be viewed as traitors by the people. Thus neutrality has deprived potential opponents of Prince Sihanouk of an important political issue: foreign policy. It is significant, in this respect, that on the few occasions when political malcontents have publicly criticized his neutrality, they have done so on the pretext that he was not neutral enough. When the military-aid agreement with the United States was signed in 1955, for example, his chief political antago-

---

over, because she does not have bases in Asia, in the event of a sudden attack France would not be able to send reinforcements to Cambodia as readily as the United States.

[5] On the role of neutrality in domestic politics, see *Réalités Cambodgiennes*, Jan. 15, 1965. On Sihanouk as a domestic political leader, see Roger M. Smith, "Cambodia," in George McT. Kahin, ed., *Governments and Politics of Southeast Asia* (2d ed.; Ithaca, N.Y.: Cornell University Press, 1964), pp. 609–631, 644–648.

nists at the time, the Democrats, accused the Prince of having betrayed Cambodia's sovereignty. Similarly, *"les jeunes intellectuels"* in the National Assembly who have agitated for closer ties with the Communist bloc have condemned him for "delivering the country into SEATO!" On the other hand, the Khmer Serei has charged him with leading Cambodia into the clutches of the Communist bloc. Sihanouk, in turn, has been able to rouse the people's sentiments against the dissidents by accusing them of attempts to sabotage Cambodia's neutrality and independence.

Because of Sihanouk's personal popularity among the people, any serious attempt by his political rivals to remove him from power would require foreign support. By maintaining friendly relations with both major blocs he has minimized the possibility of such an occurrence, for the big powers, by lending their assistance to Prince Sihanouk's enemies, would risk losing Cambodia to the opposing bloc. Thus, his adversaries find themselves in a situation where they must support him if they wish to pursue their political careers within Cambodia. Neutrality, therefore, has served as an important weapon which has enabled Prince Sihanouk to combat political opposition and maintain internal stability. This fact alone would make it unlikely that he would willingly abandon a neutral policy.

The reports in late 1963 of the American reaction to Prince Sihanouk's proposal suggested that the West for the first time was giving it concerted attention. In view of the circumstances surrounding the Cambodian request, there appear to be two considerations weighing in favor of an ultimately affirmative reaction by the United States. In the first place, she is now faced with the possibility of an irreversible loss of her influence in Cambodia and with the implications this event would have for the

Western position in the rest of Southeast Asia. In the second place, continued resistance on the part of the United States may precipitate a break in the Western alliance, at least in Southeast Asia. France, it has been noted, has in the recent past expressed her support of Prince Sihanouk's appeal. Moreover France, in her actions with regard to NATO, SEATO, the nuclear test ban, China, and the European common market, has shown an increasing tendency to act independently of her allies. If it is true that France is interested in developing a sphere of interest of her own and in re-establishing her presence in Indochina, she will probably not feel constrained to side with the United States and Great Britain on the issue of Cambodia.

In agreeing to defend Cambodia's neutrality, the United States is not likely to become involved in another protracted face-losing war, such as that waged in Laos and South Vietnam. Cambodia has what neither Laos nor South Vietnam has had: unity and internal stability stemming from a popular regime which, in the years since independence, has commanded the full support of the people. As long as Prince Sihanouk remains at the head of the government, the loyalty of the people, which he has carefully cultivated in his numerous contacts with them, is committed, and any movement to subvert the government will encounter the active opposition of the populace. Thus if present domestic conditions continue to prevail, the chief menace to Cambodian security will be attack from without, and if this should occur, the people will be in the vanguard of resistance.

Because political power in Cambodia is concentrated in the hands of one individual, Prince Sihanouk, it is difficult to avoid the question of the effect his passing would have on the country's foreign policy. During the political crisis which would be occasioned by his death, the existence of a neutrality treaty would, hopefully, deter foreign aggressors from exploiting Cambodia's weakened position. In past centuries, we have seen, succession rivalries often stimulated the entry of the Thai and the Vietnamese into Cambodia, sometimes at the invitation of one of the aspirants to the crown. With the big powers looking on, each having a stake in Cambodia's independence and neutrality, such a situation is unlikely to recur. Whoever finally emerges at the helm of the government will not immediately have the virtually unanimous popular support that has been the source of Prince Sihanouk's strength.[6] Any attempt by him to ally Cambodia with the East or the West will probably meet with the vigorous resistance of supporters of an opposite alliance and of the peasants, whose political education, personally undertaken by Prince Sihanouk, has persuaded them of the merits of neutrality. The military, by lending or refusing its support, can also influence foreign policy. Many of its leaders are veterans of the struggle for independence and it would thus appear unlikely that they would acquiesce to a policy which would threaten their country's independence. Although the military leaders have not publicly expressed their political sentiments, some Westerners who have been closely associated with them believe that they are anti-Communist.

It thus appears that if the stronger nations are willing now to respect and guarantee Cambodia's right to pursue a course independent of them, Cambodian leaders of the future will also find it within their interests and power to pursue a neutral policy.

[6] Prince Sihanouk has designated his son, Prince Norodom Naradipo, as his successor to lead the Sangkum. He was chosen so that in the event of Sihanouk's passing there would be someone to maintain "l'unité indispensable à la suivie de la nation Khmère." See *AKP*, Nov. 18, 1963.

APPENDIX A

Draft Declaration on
the Neutrality of Cambodia
(November, 1962)

The Governments of the Union of Burma, Canada, the People's Republic of China, the French Republic, the Republic of India, the Kingdom of Laos, the Polish People's Republic, the Democratic Republic of Viet-Nam, the Republic of Viet-Nam, the Kingdom of Thailand, the Union of Soviet Socialist Republics, the United Kingdom of Great Britain and Northern Ireland and the United States of America,

Welcoming the presentation of the statement of neutrality by the Royal Government of Cambodia dated ——— and taking note of this statement, which is, with the concurrence of the Royal Government of Cambodia, incorporated in the present Declaration as in integral part thereof, and the text of which is as follows:

The Royal Government of Cambodia,

Being resolved to follow the path of peace and neutrality in conformity with the interests and aspirations of the Cambodian people, as well as the principles of the Geneva Agreements of 1954, in order to build a peaceful, neutral, independent and prosperous Cambodia,

Solemnly declares that:

(1) It will resolutely apply the five principles of peaceful coexistence in foreign relations, and will develop friendly rela-

tions and establish diplomatic relations with all countries on the basis of equality and reciprocal respect for independence and sovereignty;

(2) It is the will of the Cambodian people to protect and ensure respect for the sovereignty, independence, neutrality and territorial integrity of Cambodia;

(3) It will not resort to the use or threat of force in any way which might impair the peace of other countries, and will not interfere in the internal affairs of other countries;

It is resolved to settle its international disputes, including those with countries which are not yet Members of the United Nations, by the peaceful means advocated in the Charter of the United Nations, in such a manner that international peace and security, and justice, are not endangered;

(4) It will not enter into any military alliance or into any agreement of a military nature which is inconsistent with the neutrality of the Kingdom of Cambodia, and will not allow the establishment of any foreign military bases on Cambodian territory. It will not allow any country to use Cambodian territory for military purposes or for the purpose of inter-ference in the internal affairs of other countries, nor recognize the protection of any alliance or military coalition;

(5) It will not allow any foreign interference in the internal affairs of the Kingdom of Cambodia in any form whatsoever;

(6) Subject to the provisions of article 2 of the Protocol, it will not allow the presence on its territory of any foreign troops or military personnel;

(7) It will accept direct and unconditional aid from all countries that wish to help the Kingdom of Cambodia to build up an independent and autonomous national economy on the basis of respect for the sovereignty of Cambodia;

(8) It will respect the treaties and agreements signed in conformity with the interests of the Cambodian people and the policy of peace and neutrality of the Kingdom, in par-ticular the Geneva Agreements of 1954 and 1962.

This statement of neutrality by the Royal Government of

Cambodia shall be promulgated constitutionally and shall have the force of law.

The Kingdom of Cambodia appeals to all States to recognize and respect the sovereignty, independence, neutrality and territorial integrity of Cambodia, to conform to these principles in all respects, to refrain from any action inconsistent with them and, should they be infringed, to take at the request of the Royal Government of Cambodia all necessary measures to ensure effective respect for them.

To this end, the Kindom of Cambodia, in full enjoyment of its sovereignty, requests that an international commission be entrusted under the terms to be defined in a protocol, with the supervision and control of the implementation of the provisions of the present statement.

Confirming the principles of respect for the sovereignty, independence and territorial integrity of the Kingdom of Cambodia and of noninterference in its internal affairs which are embodied in the Geneva Agreements of 1954,

Emphasizing the principle of respect for the neutrality of the Kingdom of Cambodia,

Profoundly convinced that the independence and neutrality of the Kingdom of Cambodia will assist its peaceful development and the strengthening of peace and security in South East Asia:

1. Solemnly declare, in accordance with the will of the Government and people of the Kingdom of Cambodia, as expressed in the statement of neutrality by the Royal Government of Cambodia of ———, that they recognize, respect and will observe in every way the sovereignty, independence, neutrality and territorial integrity of the Kingdom of Cambodia, and, in the event of a violation of these principles, will take, at the request of the Royal Government of Cambodia, every measure to ensure effective respect for them.

Appendix

2. Undertake, in particular, that

(a) they will not in any way commit or permit any act which might directly or indirectly impair the sovereignty, independence, neutrality or territorial integrity of the Kingdom of Cambodia, and will not in any way participate in any act of that nature;

(b) they will not resort to the threat or use of force or any other measure which might impair the peace of the Kingdom of Cambodia;

(c) they will refrain from all direct or indirect interference in the internal affairs of the Kingdom of Cambodia;

(d) they will not attach conditions of a political nature to any assistance which they may offer to the Kingdom of Cambodia;

(e) they will not bring the Kingdom of Cambodia in any way into a military alliance or any other agreement of a military character which is inconsistent with its neutrality, or invite or encourage it to enter into any such alliance or to conclude any such agreement;

(f) they will respect the wish of the Kingdom of Cambodia not to recognize the protection of any alliance or military coalition;

(g) subject to the provisions of article 2 of the Protocol, they will not permit the presence in the Kingdom of Cambodia of any foreign troops or military personnel, nor will they in any way facilitate or connive at the introduction of any foreign troops or military personnel;

(h) they will not establish nor will they in any way facilitate or connive at the establishment in the Kingdom of Cambodia of any foreign military base, foreign strong point or other foreign military installation of any kind;

(i) they will not use the territory of the Kingdom of Cambodia for interference in the internal affairs of other countries;

(j) they will not use the territory of any country, including their own, for interference in the internal affairs of the Kingdom of Cambodia.

3. Undertake, in the event of a violation or threat of violation of the sovereignty, independence, neutrality and territorial integrity of the Kingdom of Cambodia, within its present boundaries, to consult jointly with the Royal Government of Cambodia and among themselves in order to ensure the observance of the provisions of the present Declaration.

4. Appeal to all States to recognize, respect and observe in every way the sovereignty, independence, neutrality and territorial integrity of the Kingdom of Cambodia, to refrain from any action inconsistent with these principles or with other provisions of the present Declaration and, in the event of a violation, to take, at the request of the Royal Government of Cambodia, every measure to ensure effective respect for them.

At the same time, they recommend the Kingdom of Cambodia, and Viet-Nam which is not yet a Member of the United Nations, to put an end to the present difficulties in their relations, by settling as soon as possible all questions pending between them through recourse to the peaceful means advocated by the Charter of the United Nations.

5. The present Declaration shall enter into force from ———, together with the statement of neutrality by the Royal Government of Cambodia of ———, and shall be regarded as constituting an international agreement. The present Declaration shall be deposited in the archives of the Governments of the Union of Soviet Socialist Republics and the United Kingdom, which shall furnish certified copies thereof to the other signatory States and to all the other States of the world.

Draft Protocol to the Declaration on the Neutrality of the Kingdom of Cambodia

The Governments of the Union of Burma, the Kingdom of Cambodia, Canada, the People's Republic of China, the French Republic, the Republic of India, the Kingdom of Laos, the Polish People's Republic, the Democratic Republic of Viet-Nam, the Republic of Viet-Nam, the Kingdom of Thailand, the Union of Soviet Socialist Republics, the United Kingdom of Great Britain and Northern Ireland and the United States of America,

Taking note of the Declaration of the Royal Government of Cambodia dated ——— and the Declaration of the other Powers on the neutrality of the Kingdom of Cambodia,

Desiring to maintain peace in South East Asia, to safeguard the independence, sovereignty and neutrality of Cambodia and to respect its territorial integrity in accordance with the terms of the above-mentioned Declarations,

Have agreed as follows:

Article 1

For the purposes of this Protocol:

1. The present boundaries of the Kingdom of Cambodia are established:

(a) with Thailand, by the Treaty of 9 December 1937 concluded between France and Siam and confirmed by the judgment of the International Court of Justice dated 15 June 1962;

(b) with Viet-Nam and Laos, by the frontiers traced on the maps of the Geographical Service of Indo-China in use before the Paris Agreement of 1954

2. the term "foreign military personnel" shall include members of foreign military missions, foreign military advisers, experts, instructors, consultants, technicians, observers and any other foreign military persons, including those serving in any armed forces in Cambodia, and foreign civilians connected with the supply, maintenance, storing and utilization of war materials;

3. the term "the Commission" shall mean the International Commission for Supervision and Control in Cambodia set up by virtue of the Geneva Agreements of 1954 and composed of the representatives of Canada, India and Poland, with the representative of India as Chairman;

4. the term "the Co-Chairmen" shall mean the Co-Chairmen of the International Conference of 1954 for the cessation of hostilities in Indo-China and their successors in the offices of Minister for Foreign Affairs of the Union of Soviet Socialist Republics and Her Britannic Majesty's Principal Secretary of State for Foreign Affairs respectively;

5. the term "the signatory States" shall mean those States the Governments of which shall have signed the Declaration recognizing and respecting the sovereignty, independence, neutrality and territorial integrity of the Kingdom of Cambodia.

Article 2

The introduction into Cambodia of all foreign military and para-military forces, fighting formations, foreign military personnel and foreign persons belonging to politico-military groups or pursuing a subversive purpose of any nature is prohibited.

Nevertheless, should the Cambodian Government deem it necessary, the French Government may as an exception leave in Cambodia, for a limited period of time, a precisely specified number of French military instructors for the training of the Cambodian armed forces.

The French and Cambodian Governments shall, through the Co-Chairmen, notify the States signatory to the Declaration of their agreement on the use of French military instructors by the Cambodian Government.

Article 3

The introduction into Cambodia of armaments, munitions and war material generally is prohibited.

Nevertheless, the Royal Government of Cambodia shall remain free to introduce such quantities of conventional armaments, munitions and material as it may itself acquire, or receive as gift, as necessary for the effective defence and security of the Kingdom.

Article 4

In conformity with the request of the Royal Government of Cambodia, the International Commission for Control, with the agreement and co-operation of the Royal Government of Cambodia, shall supervise and control the implementation of the provisions of the Declarations on the neutrality of Cambodia and of the provisions of this Protocol.

Article 5

For the exercise of its functions, the International Commission for Control, with the concurrence of the Cambodian Government, shall create appropriate fixed and mobile groups on which the three member States of the Commission shall be equally represented.

Article 6

Fixed posts shall be set up in sufficient numbers, particularly on the borders and in all places deemed fit by the International Commission for Control or by the Royal Government

Appendix

of Cambodia, in such a manner as to ensure the efficient functioning of the system of supervision and control.

Article 7

The representatives of the member States of the International Commission for Control shall come to an agreement regarding the settlement of the questions with which the Commission is competent to deal.

In cases in which the Commission fails to come to a unanimous agreement, it shall transmit a majority report and a minority report to the signatory States. The final decision shall be taken by the Co-Chairmen after consultation with those States.

Article 8

The International Commission for Control shall send to the two Co-Chairmen and to the other signatory States, every three months, a report on its activities. In cases of urgency, special reports shall be sent to them with all useful proposals for suitable steps to be taken.

Article 9

In the exercise of its specific functions as laid down in the preceding articles of this Protocol, the Commission shall conduct investigations (directly or by sending inspection teams) when there are grounds for considering that a violation of the Declarations of the Royal Government of Cambodia and of the signatory States on the neutrality of the Kingdom of Cambodia has occurred. These investigations shall be carried out at the request of the Royal Government of Cambodia or on the initiative of the International Commission for Control acting with the concurrence of the Royal Government of Cambodia.

The Commission shall submit, on these investigations,

reports on which its members shall agree and in which differences which may emerge between members of the Commission on particular questions may be expressed.

The conclusions and recommendations of the Commission resulting from these investigations shall be adopted by a majority.

Article 10

The costs of the operation of the Commission shall be borne by the States signatory to the Declaration in accordance with the provisions of this article.

(a) The Governments of Canada, India and Poland shall pay the personal salaries and allowances of their nationals who are members of their delegations to the Commission and its subsidiary organs.

(b) The primary responsibility for the provision of accommodation for the Commission and its subsidiary organs shall rest with the Royal Government of Cambodia, which shall also provide such other local services as may be appropriate. The Commission shall charge to the Fund referred to in subparagraph (c) below any local expenses not borne by the Royal Government of Cambodia.

(c) All other capital or running expenses incurred by the Commission in the exercise of its functions shall be met from a Fund to which all the signatory States shall contribute in the following proportions:

The Governments of the People's Republic of China, France, the Union of Soviet Socialist Republics, the United Kingdom and the United States of America shall contribute 17.6 per cent each.

The Governments of Burma, Cambodia, Laos, the Democratic Republic of Viet-Nam, the Republic of Viet-Nam and Thailand shall contribute 1.5 per cent each.

The Governments of Canada, India and Poland as members of the Commission shall contribute 1 per cent each.

Article 11

The Co-Chairmen shall at any time, if the Royal Government of Cambodia so requests, present a report with appropriate recommendations on the question of the termination of the Commission to the Governments of the signatory States for their consideration. Before making such a report, the Co-Chairmen shall hold consultations with the Royal Government of Cambodia and the Commission.

Article 12

This protocol shall enter into force ————.

It shall be deposited in the archives of the Governments of the Union of Soviet Socialist Republics and the United Kingdom, which shall furnish certified copies thereof to the other signatory States and to all other States of the world.

Draft Statement of Neutrality by the Royal Government of Cambodia

The Royal Government of Cambodia,

Being resolved to follow the path of peace and neutrality in conformity with the interests and aspirations of the Cambodian people, as well as the principles of the Geneva Agreements of 1954, in order to build a peaceful, neutral, independent and prosperous Cambodia,

Appendix

Solemnly declares that:

(1) It will resolutely apply the five principles of peaceful coexistence in foreign relations, and will develop friendly relations and establish diplomatic relations with all countries on the basis of equality and reciprocal respect for independence and sovereignty;

(2) It is the will of the Cambodian people to protect and ensure respect for the sovereignty, independence, neutrality and territorial integrity of Cambodia;

(3) It will not resort to the use or threat of force in any way which might impair the peace of other countries, and will not interfere in the internal affairs of other countries;

It is resolved to settle its international disputes, including those with countries which are not yet Members of the United Nations, by the peaceful means advocated in the Charter of the United Nations, in such a manner that international peace and security, and justice, are not endangered;

(4) It will not enter into any military alliance or into any agreement of a military nature which is inconsistent with the neutrality of the Kingdom of Cambodia, and will not allow the establishment of any foreign military base on Cambodian territory. It will not allow any country to use Cambodian territory for military purposes or for the purpose of interference in the internal affairs of other countries, nor recognize the protection of any alliance or military coalition;

(5) It will not allow any foreign interference in the internal affairs of the Kingdom of Cambodia in any form whatsoever;

(6) Subject to the provisions of article 2 of the Protocol, it will not allow the presence on its territory of any foreign troops or military personnel;

(7) It will accept direct and unconditional aid from all countries that wish to help the Kingdom of Cambodia to build up an independent and autonomous national economy on the basis of respect for the sovereignty of Cambodia;

(8) It will respect the treaties and agreements signed in conformity with the interests of the Cambodian people and the policy of peace and neutrality of the Kingdom, in particular the Geneva Agreements of 1954 and 1962.

This statement of neutrality by the Royal Government of Cambodia shall be promulgated constitutionally and shall have the force of law.

The Kingdom of Cambodia appeals to all States to recognize and respect the sovereignty, independence, neutrality and territorial integrity of Cambodia, to conform to these principles in all respects, to refrain from any action inconsistent with them and, should they be infringed, to take at the request of the Royal Government of Cambodia all necessary measures to ensure effective respect for them.

To this end, the Kingdom of Cambodia, in full enjoyment of its sovereignty, requests that an international commission be entrusted, under the terms to be defined in a protocol, with the supervision and control of the implementation of the provisions of the present statement.

Source: The texts of these documents were made available to the author by the Royal Embassy of Cambodia, Washington, D.C., and they are reprinted here with the permission of H.R.H. Prince Norodom Sihanouk, Chief of State of Cambodia.

APPENDIX B

Report of the Security Council Mission to the Kingdom of Cambodia and the Republic of Viet-Nam (Extract)

(b) *Discussions with the two Governments on the broader issues underlying their differences*

28. The Mission considered that the violations of the Cambodian frontier were the symptoms rather than the cause of the strained relations between the two countries; it accordingly examined a number of specific proposals designed to improve those relations.

29. The Mission's efforts can accordingly be classified in two categories: those aimed at improving the situation along the frontier and those designed to ease the tension between the two countries.

30. The Mission held frank and detailed discussions on both these issues with the Governments of the two countries. What follows reflects their respective positions as made known to the Mission.

IV. *Positions of the two Governments on the questions in dispute*

31. The Mission notes that the two Governments reaffirmed their desire to improve relations and took the view that the

resumption of political relations broken off on 26 August 1963 would be a significant contribution towards reducing tension between their two countries.

32. In addressing itself to this question, however, the Mission could not help being aware that, in addition to the ancient rivalries and suspicions between the two countries, there were fundamental differences between the policies each had elected to adopt. Cambodia has chosen a policy of neutrality. The Republic of Viet-Nam has made a different choice by unequivocally taking sides in the conflict which brought the great Powers face to face in that part of the world. Such choices are inherent in the principle of sovereignty and the Mission found that both Governments are firmly resolved to see that their choice is respected.

33. The Kingdom of Cambodia considers itself bound and covered by the Geneva Agreements of 1954, whose signatories took note of its Declaration of neutrality. At the same time the Government of Cambodia, while asking the Geneva Conference Powers to meet in order to recognize and guarantee Cambodia's neutrality and territorial integrity, is prepared, pending the convening of the conference, to accept its neighbours' assurances in the matter on a bilateral basis.

34. Conversely, the Republic of Viet-Nam takes a different view of those Agreements—of which it is not a signatory—and is indeed opposed to the idea of a new Geneva conference.

35. The Mission nevertheless found that, notwithstanding their divergent views on this fundamental issue, neither Government considers that these should constitute an obstacle to the resumption of normal peaceful relations between the two countries.

36. Thus the Government of the Republic of Viet-Nam has informed the Mission that it recognizes the neutrality of Cambodia and undertakes to respect it.

37. The Royal Government of Cambodia, in turn, has assured the Mission that it intends to refrain from any interference in the domestic affairs of the Republic of Viet-Nam and that it has no territorial claims against that country.

38. The Royal Government of Cambodia nevertheless feels obliged to point out that the Republic of Viet-Nam, in a note of 12 March 1960, laid claim to the islands lying off the coast of Cambodia opposite the town of Kep and under Cambodian administration.

39. The Royal Government of Cambodia informed the Mission that the withdrawal of this claim would make it possible for political relations between the two countries to be resumed. Should the Royal Government of Cambodia receive satisfaction on this point, it intimates its willingness to resume negotiations with the Government of the Republic of Viet-Nam on the other outstanding problems, including the delimitation and marking of the frontier.

40. The Mission broached the question of the off-shore islands with the leaders of the Republic of Viet-Nam on several occasions and is able to report that the Government of that country attaches no particular importance to the problem and does not intend to raise it. In addition, that Government showed itself quite favourably disposed towards an attempt to reach a satisfactory settlement of the question through bilateral negotiation, in so far as its goodwill on this point would make for a general settlement regarding the delimitation of the land frontier.

41. The Mission found that the Government of the Republic of Viet-Nam attaches considerable importance to the last-mentioned problem. It submitted to the Mission a large body of documentation purporting to prove not only that the Cambodian-Vietnamese land frontier is not clearly marked on the ground but also that it is not properly defined on the maps which were drawn by the Geographic Service of the former

French Indo-China and were used in the preparation of the maps published and currently used both by the Kingdom of Cambodia and by the Republic of Viet-Nam. The competent authorities of the Republic of Viet-Nam drew attention, in particular, to discrepancies of detail in regard to the frontier line in the 1/100,000 and 1/400,000 maps prepared by the above-mentioned Service. But it should be pointed out that the discrepancy between the two maps affects only an extremely small area.

42. The Government of the Republic of Viet-Nam proposes that the two countries should, by joint agreement, fix the line of their common frontier on the basis of a reference map chosen by both Parties and should then mark out this line on the ground. The Republic of Viet-Nam considers that the completion of this task will help considerably to prevent further frontier incidents.

43. The Royal Government of Cambodia does not attach the same importance to the question of delimiting and marking the frontier. In particular it argues that the absence of frontier marks had no direct bearing on the most recent incidents to which the Security Council resolution refers. It maintains that the frontier can be adequately identified by the ethnic type of the inhabitants, the kind of vegetation and the style of the dwellings. The Royal Government of Cambodia is nevertheless prepared to enter into negotiations with the Government of the Republic of Viet-Nam in order to settle the question of the frontier line, as soon as political relations have been resumed.

44. In view of the facts as stated by the two Parties, the Mission reached the conclusion that there is no territorial dispute between the two countries so far as the land frontier is concerned.

(c) *Question of international supervision of the frontier*

45. When requesting the Geneva Conference Powers to meet in order to recognize and guarantee the neturality and ter-

ritorial integrity of their country, the Cambodian Head of State and the Royal Government of Cambodia declared that with that end in view they would be ready to agree to general supervision of the frontier by the International Commission for Supervision and Control established by the Geneva Conference of 1954. It is the view of the responsible Cambodian authorities that the new conference should widen the powers of the International Commission so as to enable it to exercise the effective control which Cambodia desires.

46. While stressing this point the Royal Government of Cambodia is not unaware, however, that in the existing international situation it would hardly be feasible to convene the Geneva Conference, at any rate in the immediate future.

47. In view of this, and pending the convening of the Conference, H.R.H. Prince Norodom Sihanouk and the Royal Cambodian Government informed the Mission that as an earnest token of their good faith the Royal Government would agree to the dispatch of United Nations civilian observers if so decided by the Security Council. It should be understood however that such unarmed United Nations observers, whose nationalities would be subject to the approval of the Royal Government, would in no sense replace the International Commission for Supervision and Control, which would carry on its task as usual.

48. The idea of the Royal Government of Cambodia is that the United Nations observers would be organized in teams and would set up permanent fixed posts from which sensitive areas in Cambodian territory could be kept under effective supervision so as to establish Cambodia's good faith. In such circumstances, the Royal Government of Cambodia would not permit the observers to cross the boundaries of Cambodian territory, in order to avoid involving the United Nations in the domestic affairs of the Republic of Viet-Nam.

49. Cambodia has further declared that, in any event, it is not

in a position to share in financing the operation and considers that the cost should be borne "by the rich countries which say they are anxious that Cambodia should not be used as a base for the Viet-Cong." It is the Mission's understanding that the Royal Government of Cambodia attaches great importance to the settlement of this financial question and feels that it should be disposed of before any action whatsoever is taken with regard to the dispatch of observer teams.

50. The Mission's view is that the settlement of this question should be part of the implementation of the recommendation made below concerning the dispatch of a group of United Nations observers.

51. The Government of the Republic of Viet-Nam has put forward some other proposals for reducing the risk of further frontier incidents. It has proposed *inter alia* "the establishment of an international police force, or of a group of observers with sufficient personnel and resources to keep the frontier area under surveillance." Meanwhile, the Government of the Republic of Viet-Nam assured the Mission that it was prepared to accept measures of any kind which, if objectively and impartially applied, would help to improve the situation between the two countries.

V. *Conclusions*

52. The Mission believes that it has established the existence of important factors which could serve as a basis for a solution of the various problems at issue. Undoubtedly the two Governments have divergent views on a number of these problems, but it is clear that they are both animated by a spirit of goodwill and are anxious to reach concrete, even if limited, agreements.

53. The Mission found that the two Governments are aware of the need to make an effort to reduce the tension between their two countries. Hence, for example, the Government of

the Republic of Viet-Nam has assured the Mission that its armed forces will avoid approaching too close to the frontier in order to avert any possibility of frontier violation.

54. The situation in the frontier region nevertheless remains strained, and the Mission welcomes the fact that the two Governments have taken a positive attitude and have contemplated measures to reduce the risk of further incidents. Although there are substantial differences between the views expressed on either side, nevertheless there are still points which could be adopted as a basis for a solution acceptable to both Parties.

55. The two main problems to be solved are the resumption of political relations and the dispatch of international observers.

56. As to the first of these problems, the Mission considers that it would be unrealistic to ignore that fact that there are differences in political outlook between the two Governments. The obstacles to normal relations derived mainly from pride and mutual distrust—the outcome of age-old rivalries; the different historical circumstances in which the two States obtained their independence; and more recently, the divergent paths they have chosen in the matter of international politics.

57. Despite this, the two countries are aware of the geographical realities which make it necessary for them, as neighbours, to live on good terms. Indeed, inter-penetration exists at all levels of the two countries' national life. There is a Khmer minority living in the Republic of Viet-Nam, just as there is a Vietnamese minority in the Kingdom of Cambodia. The Mekong is not only the natural highway linking the two countries; it is also a fount from which could rise up great nuclei of prosperity essential for the well-being and progress of all of the region's inhabitants.

58. Moreover, as the Mission was able to note, both countries have declared that they have no claims with respect to the

common land frontier. Each State undertakes to respect the territorial integrity and the political system of the other. The Mission considers that the goodwill thus expressed on both sides constitutes a hopeful start toward the resumption of normal political relations between the two countries.

59. The Mission is compelled, however, to mention the problem of the offshore islands, which Cambodia raises as a prior condition for the resumption of relations with the Republic of Viet-Nam. The reaction of the latter on this subject is felt to be sufficiently conciliatory to justify the hope on the part of the Mission that this question will be satisfactorily disposed of during the first contacts established between the two Governments.

60. It should be noted that the resumption of political relations would be bound to lead to negotiations with a view to agreements on such matters as the delimiting and marking of the frontier.

61. While it is not in a position to say how far the lack of frontier marking may have played a part in the recent incidents, the Mission is of the view that anything that could be done to remedy the present inadequate marking would be most helpful in preventing frontier conflicts or regrettable incidents such as have taken place on Cambodian territory.

62. As regards the principle of international supervision in the frontier area, each of the Parties has made its views on this subject perfectly clear.

63. The Cambodian proposal was conceived in a spirit of evident goodwill, and the Mission believes that, taken as a whole, the proposal represents a real contribution to the problem. The Mission has therefore felt that it should recommend the Security Council to consider a formula that would embrace that proposal by establishing a United Nations observer group, its functions to be as defined in paragraphs 47 and 48 of this report.

64. The ways and means of applying such a formula would, however, have to be the subject of negotiations at a later date. The Mission did not feel called upon to initiate negotiations of this kind; it considered that the Council itself should have a thorough study made of all the points concerning the application of the formula.

65. As to the proposals regarding international supervision put forward by the Republic of Viet-Nam, the Mission considers that inasmuch as they go beyond what is acceptable to the Kingdom of Cambodia, they might not constitute a basis for an agreement between the two countries.

VI. *Recommendations*

66. In accordance with its terms of reference, which were to consider such measures as might prevent any recurrence of the incidents which have occurred on the Cambodian–Vietnamese frontier, within Cambodian territory, and having regard to what has been stated in this report, the Mission submits to the Security Council the following recommendations:

(i) That the Security Council should decide to establish and send to Cambodia a group of United Nation observers and should entrust the Secretary-General of the United Nations with the implementation of this decision in consultation with the members of the Security Council;

(ii) That the Security Council recommend the Governments of the Kingdom of Cambodia and the Republic of Viet-Nam to adopt whatever measures are necessary to bring about the resumption of the political relations broken off in August 1963;

(iii) That the Security Council should appoint a person of high international standing, approved by the two Parties, to arrange for a preliminary meeting between the two Governments for the purpose of re-establishing relations between the two countries and the resumption of talks on matters in dispute, particularly the delimitation and marking of the common frontier;

(iv) That the Security Council should take note of the assurances given to the Mission by the Government of the Republic of Viet-Nam that the Vietnamese armed forces have been issued definite instructions that every precaution is to be taken to avoid any risk of frontier violations;

(v) That the Security Council should take note of the statement by the Government of the Republic of Viet-Nam that it recognizes and undertakes to respect the neutrality and territorial integrity of the Kingdom of Cambodia.

Done at United Nations Headquarters, New York, on 27 July 1964.

> DEY OULD SIDI BABA,
> *Representative of Morocco,*
> *Chairman*
> MANUEL PIO CORREA,
> *Representative of Brazil*
> MOISE AKA,
> *Representative of the Ivory Coast*

Source: United Nations, Security Council, Doc. S/5832, July 27, 1964.

Bibliography

I. BOOKS AND MONOGRAPHS

Armstrong, John P. *Sihanouk Speaks*. New York: Walker and Co., 1964. A sympathetic account of Sihanouk's policies, based on the Prince's speeches and on extensive interviews.

Aymonier, Etienne F. *Le Cambodge*. 3 vols. Paris: E. Leroux, 1900–1904. A standard source on early Cambodian history.

Briggs, Lawrence Palmer. *The Ancient Khmer Empire*. Transactions of the American Philosophical Society, New Series, Vol. 41, Part 1. Philadelphia: The American Philosophical Society, 1951. The outstanding English-language history of ancient Cambodia. It covers the period up to the fifteenth century.

Burchett, Wilfred G. *Mekong Upstream*. Hanoi: Red River Publishing House, 1957. Anticolonial, anti-American, pro-Communist interpretation of Cambodia before and after independence.

Clubb, Oliver, E., Jr. *The United States and the Sino–Soviet Bloc in Southeast Asia*. Washington, D.C.: The Brookings Institution, 1962. The author, in addition to surveying the area, discusses the problems involved in establishing a neutral zone in Southeast Asia.

Coedès, Georges. *Les états hindouisés d'Indochine et d'Indonésie*. 2d ed. Paris: E. de Boccard, 1964. A classic study of Hindu and Buddhist expansion and influence in Southeast Asia, with great emphasis on the Khmer Empire.

———. *Pour mieux comprendre Angkor*. 2d ed. Paris: Adrien-

Maisonneuve, Librairie d'Amérique et d'Orient, 1948. A brief account of the early Cambodian kingdoms and the founding of Angkor.

Collective Defense in Southeast Asia, The Manila Treaty and Its Implications, A Report by a Chatham House Study Group. London: Oxford University Press, 1956. An early discussion of the problems which confront the Southeast Asia Treaty Organization.

Devillers, Philippe. "Cambodia," in Saul Rose, ed., *Politics in Southern Asia*. New York: St. Martin's Press, 1963. A well-informed French scholar's view of government and politics in Cambodia.

Eden, Anthony. *Memoirs of Anthony Eden: Full Circle*. Boston: Houghton Mifflin Co., 1960. Contains a firsthand account of the Geneva Conference on Indochina, 1954.

Fifield, Russell H. *Southeast Asia in United States Policy*. New York: Praeger, 1963. The author includes a discussion of Cambodia's relations with her neighbors.

―――. *The Diplomacy of Southeast Asia: 1945–1958*. New York: Harper & Bros., 1958. A study of the comparative foreign policy of nations in the area.

Groslier, Bernard P. *Angkor, hommes et pierres*. Paris: Arthaud, 1956. Outstanding introduction to the Angkorian period of Cambodian history.

―――. *The Art of Indochina, Including Thailand, Vietnam, Laos and Cambodia*. New York: Crown Publishers, 1962. An extensive discussion by a noted authority of the development of art and architecture.

―――, with the collaboration of C. R. Boxer. *Angkor et le Cambodge au XVIe siècle d'après les sources portugaises et espagnoles*. Annales du Musée Guimet. Bibliothèque d'Etudes—Tome LXIIIe. Paris: Presses Universitaires de France, 1958. A careful essay which casts a new perspective on Cambodian history. It contains a special section devoted to an analysis of the hydraulic system of Angkor Thom.

Bibliography

Hall, D. G. E. *A History of South-East Asia.* 2d ed. London: Macmillan Co., 1964. This outstanding study is a valuable introduction for the student who wishes to pursue the subject further. Several chapters trace the history of Cambodia from the early kingdoms to the present.

Herz, Martin. *A Short History of Cambodia from the Days of Angkor to the Present.* New York: Praeger, 1958. A brief review, mainly of modern political history, written from a marked pro-Western point of view.

Imbert, Jean. *Histoire des institutions khmères. Annales* de la Faculté de Droit de Phnom-Penh. Vol. II, 1961. A history of the development of public and private institutions, 802–1953.

Kahin, George McT. *The Asian-African Conference, Bandung, Indonesia, April 1955.* Ithaca, N.Y.: Cornell University Press, 1956. The best account of the Bandung Conference.

Lacouture, Jean, and Philippe Devillers. *La fin d'une guerre: Indochine 1954.* Paris: Editions du Seuil, 1960. This account of the Geneva Conference on Indochina, 1954, contains valuable information on the important role played by Cambodia in the conference's proceedings.

Leclère, Adhémar. *Histoire du Cambodge.* Paris: P. Guethner, 1914. One of several early histories, based on stone inscriptions, Chinese and Vietnamese annals, and European documents, written by French scholars.

Leifer, Michael. *Cambodia and Neutrality.* Working Paper No. 1. Canberra: Australian National University, Research School of Pacific Studies, Department of International Relations, 1962. A discussion of intra-area tensions and of international forces bearing on Cambodia.

Le Thanh Khoi. *Le Viet-Nam: Histoire et civilisation, le milieu et l'histoire.* Paris: Editions de Minuit, 1955. This extensive history contains a Vietnamese view of the relations between Cambodia and Vietnam.

Lévy, Roger. *L'Indochine et ses traités.* Paris: Centre d'Etudes de Politique Etrangère, 1947. Contains the texts of the Franco–Cambodian *modus vivendi* of 1946 and the Treaty of Washington of 1946.

Maspero, Georges. *L'Empire khmer.* Phnom Penh: Imprimerie du Protectorat, 1904.

Modelski, George. *International Conference on the Settlement of the Laotian Question, 1961–2.* Working Paper No. 2. Canberra: Australian National University, Research School of Pacific Studies, Department of International Relations, 1962. This analysis of the conference in Laos contains the texts of the several draft agreements (including Cambodia's) on Laos neutrality.

――――, ed. *SEATO: Six Studies.* Melbourne: F. W. Cheshire, 1962. An examination of SEATO in terms of its administrative organization, the roles of the Asian member and protocol states, the positions of India and China, and its economic role.

Moura, Jean. *Le royaume du Cambodge.* 2 vols. Paris: Leroux, 1883.

Nākhanāt, Prayat S., and Čhamrāt Dūangthisān. *The Khao Phra Viharn Case* (in Thai: Khwan Mūang Rūang Khao Phra Wihān). Bangkok: Sānsawan Press, 1962. A discussion, from a Thai point of view, of one of the major problems in Cambodian–Thai relations.

Norodom Sihanouk. *La monarchie cambodgienne et la croisade royale pour l'indépendance.* Phnom Penh: Imprimerie Rasmey, 1961. In this little book, which is used as a text in Cambodian secondary schools, Prince Sihanouk portrays the monarchy, from 802 to 1904, as the symbol of Cambodia's former greatness and of wise political conservatism. The second part is as account of Sihanouk's efforts to wrest Cambodia's independence from France.

Pannetier, A. *Notes cambodgiennes: Au coeur du pays Khmer.* Paris: Payot, 1921. An account of the protectorate administration and administrators, written by a doctor in the

French colonial service. Dr. Pannetier is often critical of his compatriots, especially concerning their pretense at giving Cambodians a voice in the government, and of the favored treatment accorded the Chinese community.

Preschez, Philippe. *Essai sur la démocratie du Cambodge.* Paris: Fondation Nationale des Sciences Politiques, Centre d'Etudes des Relations Internationales, 1961. A narrative of political events from 1945 to 1960 and an analysis of the return to authoritarianism.

Smith, Roger M. "Cambodia," in George McT. Kahin, ed., *Governments and Politics of Southeast Asia.* 2d ed. Ithaca, N.Y.: Cornell University Press, 1964. A review of Cambodia's history, its contemporary government and politics, and a discussion of several major problems now facing the country.

Steinberg, David J., *et al.,* eds. *Cambodia: Its People, Its Society, Its Culture.* New Haven: Human Relations Area Files Press, 1957. A generally useful handbook of information about Cambodia's history and contemporary politics, economics, and society.

Vadakarn, Luang Vichitr. *Thailand's Case.* Bangkok: Thai Commercial Press, 1941. A chauvinistic protest against Thailand's "loss" of territory in Cambodia and Laos.

Vella, Walter F. *Siam under Rama III.* Monograph of the Association for Asian Studies. Locust Valley, N.Y.: J. J. Augustin, 1957. Includes an extensive discussion of Cambodian–Siamese relations in the nineteenth century.

II. OFFICIAL PUBLICATIONS

Cambodia

Accords et conventions signés à l'issue de la conférence quadripartite de Paris (du 26 août au 29 décembre 1954). Phnom Penh: Imprimerie Khmère, 1955. Documents pertaining to the dissolution of the Federation of Indochina.

Bibliography

Address of H.R.H. Prince Norodom Sihanouk, Chief of State of Cambodia to the Asia Society, New York, September 26, 1961. New York: Permanent Mission of Cambodia to the United Nations, 1961. A discussion of Cambodia's domestic and foreign policy problems.

Agence Khmère de Presse. Phnom Penh: Ministère de l'Information, 1954 *et sqq.* The government daily news bulletin.

Aide-mémoire sur les relations Khmero-Thailandaises. Phnom Penh: Ministère des Affaires Etrangères, n.d. [1962?]. A discussion of relations with Thailand since 1961 with emphasis on the Preah Vihear case.

Cambodge. Charles Meyer, ed. Phnom Penh: Imprimerie du Ministère de l'Information, 1962. A compendium of modern Cambodia.

Cambodge d'Aujourd'hui. Phnom Penh: Ministère de l'Information, 1958 *et sqq.* An illustrated monthly review of political, economic, and cultural affairs. It appears occasionally in English as *Cambodia Today.*

Cambodia News. Washington, D.C.: Royal Embassy of Cambodia; frequency varies. A bulletin of information.

Cambodian Commentary: Review of Khmer Opinion. Phnom Penh: Ministère de l'Information, 1960 *et sqq.*; frequency varies. It recounts the principal domestic and foreign affairs of Cambodia.

Cochin China, Cambodian Territory. New York: Permanent Mission of Cambodia to the United Nations, n.d. [1958?]. This is the official argument, presented in the United Nations in 1958, concerning Cambodia's "inalienable rights" to territory now part of Vietnam. It formally avers that over 500,000 Cambodians living in Cochinchina are subject to persecution and forced assimilation by the government of South Vietnam.

Discours de S.A.R. le Prince Norodom Sihanouk, Chef de l'Etat à l'inauguration de la Faculté de Droit. Phnom Penh: Imprimerie du Ministère de l'Information, 1961. In this address, Prince Sihanouk presents his critique of the major powers' involvement in Laos.

Documents relatifs à la suspension des relations diplomatiques entre le Cambodge et la Thailande. Phnom Penh: Imprimerie du Ministère de l'Information, n.d. [1958?]. Official charges of Thai interference in Cambodia's internal affairs.

Dossier des agressions des forces Americano-Sud Vietnamiens à Chantrea le 19 mars 1964, soumis au Conseil de Sécurité de l'O.N.U. Phnom Penh: Ministère des Affaires Etrangères, 1964.

La mission aux Nations-Unies de S.A.R. le Prince Norodom Sihanouk, Chef de l'Etat du Cambodge. Phnom Penh: Imprimerie du Ministère de l'Information, December 26, 1960. Includes the text of Prince Sihanouk's address to the United Nations.

Les idées du discours-programme présenté par le Prince-Président devant l'Assemblée Nationale lors de l'investiture du 3ème gouvernement Sangkum, le 29-2-56. Phnom Penh: Imprimerie du Sangkum, 1956. This address includes a major foreign-policy statement.

Livre blanc sur la rupture des relations diplomatiques entre le Cambodge et la Thailande, le 23 octobre 1961. Phnom Penh: Imprimerie du Ministère de l'Information, n.d. [1962?]. An official review of Cambodia–Thai relations during 1959–1961 and an account of the crisis of 1961.

Livre jaune sur les revendications de l'indépendance du Cambodge. Vol. I, Paris: Imprimerie Centrale Commerciale, 1953; vol. II, Phnom Penh: Imprimerie du Palais Royal, 1954. A collection of important documents, with editorial comments, covering the period 1946–1953.

Ministère des Affaires Etrangères et des Conférences, *Accords, protocoles, conventions et échanges de lettres relatifs au transfert de toutes de compétences par le gouvernement de la république française au gouvernement royal du Cambodge.* Phnom Penh: Imprimerie Albert Portail, 1954.

Bibliography

Norodom Sihanouk. *Le Cambodge et ses relations avec ses voisins.* Phnom Penh: Imprimerie du Ministère de l'Information, 1962. This is Prince Sihanouk's analysis of Cambodia's international position after the international conference on Laos, 1961–1962.

———. *Rapport au peuple khmer au terme de mission en Amérique et aux Nations-Unies.* Phnom Penh: Imprimerie du Ministère de l'Information, 1961. Prince Sihanouk's personal commentary on his experiences in 1960 at the United Nations.

Petite anthologie de la presse thaie. Phnom Penh: Imprimerie du Ministère de l'Information, 1960.

Principaux discours et allocutions de S.A.R. le Prince Norodom Sihanouk en 1958, 1959, 1960. Phnom Penh: Imprimerie du Ministère de l'Information, n.d. [1959, 1960, 1961?]. These addresses contain much of Prince Sihanouk's thinking on many of Cambodia's foreign and domestic problems.

Sam Sary. *Conférence publique sur les accords de Genève et les élections générales au Cambodge, 23 août 1955.* Phnom Penh, 1955. One of Cambodia's delegates to the Geneva Conference on Indochina discusses the arguments which were used to assert his country's independence in international affairs.

———. *La grande figure de Norodom Sihanouk, telle qu'elle est dépeinte par les documents de valeur historique découverts dans les archives du palais royal.* Phnom Penh: Imprimerie du Palais Royal, 1955. Covers the period 1945–1955.

——— and Mau Say. *Bilan de l'œuvre de Norodom Sihanouk pendant le mandat royal de 1952 à 1955.* Phnom Penh: Imprimerie Portail, 1955. The documents of King Sihanouk's crusade for independence.

France

Gouvernement-Général de l'Indochine. Protectorat du Cam-

Bibliography

bodge. *Recueil des actes du gouvernement cambodgien.* Vol.
I. Saigon: Imprimerie Albert Portail, 1920. A collection of
documents relating to the establishment of the protectorate,
relations with Siam, administration, and reforms.

Haut-Commissariat de France en Indochine. *Bulletin officiel.*
Saigon, March 26, 1953, pp. 262–267. Text of the 1949
treaty with France by which Cambodia was granted a large
measure of internal autonomy.

Présidence du Conseil, Secrétariat Général du Gouvernement.
*Actes définissant les rapports des Etats associés du Viet Nam,
du Cambodge, et du Laos avec la France.* Notes et Etudes
Documentaires, no. 1,295. March 14, 1950. Paris, 1950.

Great Britain

*Documents Relating to the Discussion of Korea and Indo-
China at the Geneva Conference, April 27–June 15, 1954.*
Cmd. 9186. London: H.M. Stationery Office, 1954.

*Further Documents Relating to the Discussion of Indo-China
at the Geneva Conference, June 16–July 21, 1954.* Cmd.
9239. London: H.M. Stationery Office, 1954.

*Progress Report of the International Commission for Super-
vision and Control in Cambodia. . . . Cambodia No. 1
(1955) et sqq.* Cmd. 9458, 9534, 9579, 9671; Cmnd. 253, 526,
887. London: H.M. Stationery Office, 1955 *et sqq.* Reports
issued by the commission which the Geneva Conference on
Indochina established. The reports are concerned principally with Cambodia's fulfillment of the Geneva accord,
but they also contain much useful information on relations
with South Vietnam and on domestic political developments.

India

Ministry of Foreign Affairs. *Foreign Affairs Reports.* Vol I,
no. 3. New Delhi, March, 1955, p. 49. Text of the Nehru–
Sihanouk joint communiqué of March 18, 1955.

Bibliography

Indonesia

Asian–African Conference, Bandung, Indonesia, April 18–24, 1955, *Speeches and Communiqués*. Kementerian Peneragan [Ministry of Information], Republik Indonesia, 1955.

International Court of Justice

"Case Concerning the Temple of Preah Vihear (Cambodia v. Thailand), Merits, Judgement of 15 June 1962," *International Court of Justice Reports*. The Hague, 1962.

Philippines

"Address of H.R.H. Norodom Sihanouk before a Joint Session of Members of the Congress of the Philippines, February 3, 1956," *Official Text*. Manila: Department of Foreign Affairs, Division of International Information, 1956.

Southeast Asia Treaty Organization (SEATO)

Research Services Office. *Background Brief: Communism and Cambodia*. RSO/BB/25. Bangkok, December 31, 1959. A discussion of the Viet Minh in Cambodia.

Thailand

Ministry of Foreign Affairs. *Facts about the Relations between Thailand and Cambodia*. Bangkok: Prachandra Press, 1961. The official Thai account of the 1961 crisis.

Ministry of Foreign Affairs. *Facts about the Relations between Thailand and Cambodia*, III. Bangkok, March 1, 1963. Covers the period 1961–February, 1963.

Ministry of Foreign Affairs. *Foreign Affairs Bulletin*, I, no. 6, June–July 1962. This issue contains the decision of the International Court on the Preah Vihear case. It includes also the subsequent policy statements by the Thai government.

Ministry of Foreign Affairs. *Relations between Thailand and Cambodia.* Bangkok: Prachandra Press, 1959. Discussion of border problems and the severance of diplomatic relations in 1958.

United States

United States Congress. House of Representatives, Committee on Government Operations. *Hearings before a Sub-Committee of the Committee on Government Operations, Part I: Cambodian Port Highway.* 87th Congress, 1st Session, February 9–June 20, 1961. Washington, D.C.: Government Printing Office, 1961.

————. Senate, Committee on Appropriations, *Hearing, Report on United States Military Operations and Mutual Security Programs Overseas,* by [Senator] Dennis Chavez. 86th Congress, 2d Session. Washington, D.C.: Government Printing Office, 1960. Includes information on U.S. military aid to Cambodia.

————. Senate, Committee on Foreign Relations, *Viet Nam and Southeast Asia, Report of Senator Mike Mansfield, Senator J. Caleb Boggs, Senator Claiborne Pell, Senator Benjamin A. Smith to the Committee on Foreign Relations, United States Senate.* 88th Congress, 1st Session. Washington, D.C.: Government Printing Office, 1963. Cambodia is described in this report as "one of the most stable and progressive nations in Southeast Asia."

Department of State, Agency for International Development. *Aide économique américaine au Cambodge en 1962.* Phnom Penh. U.S. AID, 1962.

Department of State, Agency for International Development. *Termination Report, American Economic Aid Program in Cambodia.* Phnom Penh. U.S. AID, 1963.

Bibliography

Department of State, Agency for International Development. *U.S. Economic Assistance Program in Cambodia, 1963–1964.* Phnom Penh: U.S. AID, 1963.

Department of State, Agency for International Development, Statistics and Reports Division. *U.S. Foreign Assistance and Assistance from International Organizations: Obligations and Loan Authorizations, July 1, 1945–June 30, 1961.* Washington, D.C.: [Government Printing Office?], March 21, 1962. Includes official statistics for both American military and economic aid to Cambodia.

Department of State. Consulate-General, Hongkong. *Survey of Chinese Mainland Press, passim.* Contains a wealth of material on relations between Cambodia and China.

Department of State. "Economic Cooperation Agreement and Notes between the United States of America and Cambodia, September 8, 1951," *Treaties and Other International Acts Series 2343.* Washington, D.C.: Government Printing Office, 1952.

Department of State. International Cooperation Administration. *U.S. Economic Aid Program to Cambodia, 1955–1959.* Phnom Penh: United States Operations Mission to Cambodia, January 1960.

Department of State. "Military Assistance Agreement between the United States of America and Cambodia." Effected by exchange of notes, Phnom Penh, May 16, 1955. *Treaties and Other International Acts Series 3240.* Washington, D.C.: Government Printing Office, 1956.

Department of State. "U.S. Policy toward Cambodia" [Secretary Dulles to Foreign Minister Nong Kimny], *Department of State Bulletin,* XXXIV, no. 879, April 30, 1956, pp. 727–728.

Vietnam

Memorandum en réponse aux accusations formulés par le Gouvernement Royal du Cambodge contre le République du Vietnam devant le Conseil de Sécurité de l'O.N.U. Saigon: Ministère des Affaires Etrangères, 1964.

Secrétariat d'Etat aux Affaires Etrangères. "The Vietnamese of Khmer Origin," *Le Vietnam et ses relations internationales* (Saigon), III, nos. 1–4, December, 1958. The Vietnamese reply to Cambodia's claims and charges concerning Cochinchina.

III. ARTICLES

Briggs, Lawrence Palmer. "A Sketch of Cambodian History," *Far Eastern Quarterly*, VI, no. 4 (August, 1947), pp. 345–363.

————. "Aubaret and the Treaty of July 15, 1867 between France and Siam," *Far Eastern Quarterly*, VI, no. 2 (February, 1947), pp. 122–138. A discussion of the events leading up to the cession of Cambodia's northern territories to Siam.

————. "Siamese Attacks on Angkor before 1430," *Far Eastern Quarterly*, VIII, no. 1 (November, 1948), pp. 3–33.

————. "The Treaty of March 23, 1907 between France and Siam and the Return of Battambang and Angkor to Cambodia," *Far Eastern Quarterly*, V, no. 4. (August, 1946), pp. 439–454.

Christian, Pierre. "Son Ngoc Thanh," *Indochine Sud-est Asiatique* (October, 1952), pp. 48–49. A brief biographical sketch.

Dudman, Richard. "Asia Frontiers of Freedom," *St. Louis Post-Dispatch*, February 3, 4, 5, 6, 7, 8, 10, 11, 12, 13, 1963. Published also in *Congressional Quarterly*, March 4, 1963, pp. 3266–3280. Several of these articles discuss Cambodia's domestic and foreign policy problems.

Dubois, Robert. "Les origines de la neutralité cambodgienne," *Annales* de la Faculté de Droit et des Sciences Economiques de Phnom-Penh, IV (1962), 89–132.

Leifer, Michael. "Cambodia and Her Neighbors," *Pacific*

Affairs, XXXIV, no. 4 (Winter, 1961–1962), pp. 361–374. The historical background and current issues in Cambodia's disputes with Thailand and Vietnam.

———. "Cambodia and SEATO," *International Journal*, XVII (Spring, 1962), pp. 122–132.

Norodom Sihanouk. "Cambodia Neutral: The Dictate of Necessity," *Foreign Affairs*, XXXVI, no. 4 (July, 1958), pp. 582–586. The Cambodian Chief of State argues that if his country is to survive the vicissitudes of the cold war, it must remain neutral.

———. "Etude corrective de la constitution accordée par S.M. le Roi du Cambodge en 1947," *France-Asie* (Saigon), XI, no. 108 (May, 1955), pp. 656–663. An account of Sihanouk's modified constitutional reforms. In defending the need for strong central government, Sihanouk argues that democracy must be adjusted to Cambodia's conditions.

———. "Le communisme au Cambodge," *Réalités Cambodgiennes*, March 15 and 22, 1958. Prince Sihanouk writes of the dangers posed by Communism to his country's stability and independence.

———. "Nos amis . . . et les autres: I. Dans le camp occidental. II. Les neutralistes," *Réalités Cambodgiennes*, October 25 and November 8, 1963. A review of Cambodia's foreign relations. A third article, on "amitiés socialistes," was not published because of the *coup d'état* in Saigon.

———. "Un tragique malentendu," *Réalités Cambodgiennes*, October 4, 1963. A critique of Western policy toward Cambodia.

———. "Une politique de neutralité dans l'Asie troublée," *Le Monde Politique* (Paris), October, 1963, pp. 13–14. Prince Sihanouk discusses the reasons why Cambodia's interests would not be served by an alliance policy.

Simon, Jean-Pierre. "Cambodia: Pursuit of Crisis," *Asian Survey*, V, no. 1 (January, 1965), pp. 49–53. A good review of foreign policy developments during 1964.

Smith, Roger M. "Cambodia's Neutrality and the Laotian

Crisis," *Asian Survey,* I, no. 5 (July, 1961), pp. 17–24. An effort to relate the cold war in Laos to the problems of Cambodian security.

Thomson, R. Stanley. "Establishment of the French Protectorate over Cambodia," *Far Eastern Quarterly,* IV, no. 4 (August, 1945), pp. 313–340.

———. "Siam and France, 1863–1870," *Far Eastern Quarterly,* V, no. 1 (November, 1945), pp. 28–46. A discussion of Franco–Siamese relations, particularly with regard to control over Cambodia.

Warner, Denis. "The Prince on a Tightrope," *The Reporter,* XXII, no. 4 (February 18, 1960), pp. 33–34. The author argues that Cambodia is balanced precariously between the Communist and Western blocs.

———. "Unfinished Business, A Neutral Zone in Southeast Asia?" *The New Republic,* 149, no. 23 (December 7, 1963), pp. 17–20. A review of the problems of American foreign policy in Indochina. The author suggests that a neutral zone might save Indochina "from something well short of a Communist take-over."

IV. PERIODICALS

Annales de la Faculté de Droit de Phnom-Penh: Etudes Khmères et Asiatiques. Phnom Penh, 1960 *et sqq.;* issued once a year. Articles by members of the Faculty of Law, Phnom Penh, emphasize political economy, public administration, and law.

La Dépêche du Cambodge. Phnom Penh, 1958 *et sqq.;* daily except Sunday. The most important French-language daily newspaper in Phnom Penh.

Neak Cheat Niyum [The Nationalist]. Phnom Penh, 1959 *et sqq.;* weekly. Official organ of the Sangkum Reastr Niyum.

Réalités Cambodgiennes. Phnom Penh, 1956 *et sqq.;* weekly. The most important French-language newspaper in Phnom Penh. Semiofficial.

Index

Index

Index

Index

Index

Index

Index